RING OF DEATH

Famous Kerry Murders

ANTHONY GALVIN

MAINSTREAM
PUBLISHING

EDINBURGH AND LONDON

First published in Great Britain in 2013 by
MAINSTREAM PUBLISHING COMPANY
(EDINBURGH) LTD
7 Albany Street
Edinburgh EH1 3UG

ISBN 9781780575872

A catalogue record for this book is available
from the British Library

Printed in Great Britain by
CPI Group (UK) Ltd, Croydon, CR0 4YY

1 3 5 7 9 10 8 6 4 2

CONTENTS

INTRODUCTION

THE KINGDOM OF CRIME

KERRY IS THE wild side of Ireland, the primitive alter ego that contrasts with the civilisation and modernity of Dublin, Cork and Limerick. An isolated mountain enclave, the Kingdom has always been a place apart.

The Kingdom is an apt name. There is a sense of separation about the county, as if you are entering a different world. Physically, it is beautiful, with rugged mountains, spectacular beaches and deep sapphire lakes. Its position at the extreme south-west of Ireland – about as far removed from the capital as it is possible to get – contributes to the isolation.

Throughout much of the last century, it took most of a day to travel to the heart of the Kingdom. It was one of the last places to let go of the Irish language and switch to English. Some parts still haven't done so. The extreme tip of the county is 15 degrees of longitude – one time zone – removed from Greenwich. But in a sense, Kerry is a hundred years or more removed.

In his poem 'Ireland with Emily' John Betjeman describes the west of the country as an almost prehistoric landscape peopled by a prehistoric populace – the last of Europe's Stone

Age race. It is this Stone Age nature of the Kerry people – their rural isolation, strong connection to the land, deep conservatism and sense of independence and isolation – that gives a unique flavour to its murders. And there have been quite a few.

A murder gives an insight into the society that produced it. Limerick is dominated by gun crime and gangland killings. Dublin also has its share of killings related to the drugs trade. Northern Ireland produces many murders with a political twist. Kerry murders are a unique product of the Kerry landscape and mindset. In the first half of the last century, murders in Kerry were tied to the land and to petty disputes between neighbours. In recent years, the county – in particular the towns of Tralee and Killarney – has joined the twenty-first century. Drunkenness, drug use and organised crime have made their appearance.

In *Ring of Death* I will look at some of the most notorious killings in the Kingdom. I strove for variety in terms of location, motivation and time period. The cases stretch from the birth of the state right up to the present day.

One of the most controversial incidents in the entire criminal history of Ireland happened at the birth of the nation. During the bitter civil war that followed independence, violence became a way of life to some. People became used to daily horrors, and a certain coldness seeped into souls. When it was neighbour against neighbour, friend against friend, the memory of past associations kept a check on the violence. But in Kerry, things were different. Kerry was policed by a force of outsiders: Dubliners sent down to sort out the local anti-Treaty forces. It was an explosive combination that led to the worst atrocity of the civil war, when a number of unarmed prisoners were taken out late at night, strapped to a landmine and massacred at Ballyseedy, near Tralee. Hours later, the exercise was repeated at Countess Bridge, Killarney.

However, there was a survivor in each case, making a cover-up difficult. So when the forces of the state decided to carry out a third massacre of unarmed prisoners at Cahirciveen, they took no chances: they shot every prisoner in the leg before

8

blowing them up. No one was ever brought to book for the multiple murders that black week.

After the war, life returned to normal, but for a long time people were desensitised to violence. Some had used the war as an excuse for settling old scores, and when a farmer's wife in Killorglin was bludgeoned to death on Easter Sunday 1923 – in the dying days of the conflict – everyone immediately assumed it was a political murder. That was the culture of the time. But it wasn't: it was the result of a petty dispute. A servant had been fired for pilfering and had committed murder in revenge. Twenty years earlier, or twenty years later, it would not have happened. Such savagery was only possible in a county traumatised by war.

Sometimes the motive for murder can appear startlingly modern. People assume that serial killers and sex killers are a new phenomenon, but they are as old as murder itself. In 1931, a young man from Rathmore, on the Cork–Kerry border, became obsessed with a pretty neighbour. Yet she was engaged to another, and would not have looked at the shy and inadequate man in any case. One winter's evening he followed her home, dragged her into the fields, raped and killed her. Then he threw her body into a ditch and went home. The trial judge described him as Ireland's Jack the Ripper. He only killed once. But if he had not been caught, who knows?

It is very easy to look at crime from a distance and forget the pain suffered by the victims. There is the myth of the ordinary decent criminal who harms no one, a sort of Robin Hood figure. But the truth is that every crime has a victim, and when the crime is murder, the effects on the family left behind can be devastating. The killers are no heroes. Yet when Charlie Kerins shot a detective sergeant in the back in 1942, many made the champion footballer into a martyr for the republican cause. Kerins shot the detective in front of the man's home while his wife was inside preparing the children for school, and he had a housing estate in Tralee named after him as a consequence. His story is told here.

The most famous Kerry murder of them all went unsolved. In 1958, two farmers became embroiled in a dispute over a tiny stretch of boggy upland, worth almost nothing. But before the matter could come before a court, one of the men was brutally killed and his body thrown in a deep ditch. No one was ever caught, but the neighbours blamed the other man, who lived out his remaining few years isolated, shunned and boycotted. The case might have been forgotten, but an ambitious young playwright, John B. Keane, turned it into a classic. *The Field* tells the fictionalised story; on these pages, the true facts are recounted.

Kerry has a macho culture in which the footballers (who have won more All-Ireland finals than any other team) are idolised. In a society such as that, drink plays a big part. Drink is used both to drown sorrows and to celebrate great events. It is also used to kill an idle hour. When an elderly man went for a drink with his son in Castleisland in 1968, he did not expect to get into a row with a young man who had also taken too much to drink. But John Cronin wasn't going to lose to the younger man; he evened the odds by pulling a knife. In doing so, he killed a young man and destroyed his own life.

As the last century progressed, the petty greed and shallowness of much of modern culture began to pervade the Kingdom. In 1983, two young men needed money for drink, so they broke into a sweet shop belonging to an elderly pensioner and stole her takings, and when that was not enough, they beat her to death. Lil May O'Sullivan died for a little more than ten pounds – then her killers used every loophole in the law to try (unsuccessfully) to get away with murder.

Kerry, in common with many rural communities, has a deep conservatism at its heart. The people are friendly and supportive, but if you step out of line, morally, you are on your own. Rural Ireland was a difficult place for single mothers up until recently. Horrific events in Kerry in 1984 were responsible for much of that change. Two dead babies were found: one washed up on a beach, stabbed, and the other found in a ditch on a farm. A local woman was charged with double murder, but when it became obvious that the evidence did not stack up, she was released and a Tribunal of Inquiry was set up. The Kerry Babies Tribunal cast a very harsh light on the methods of the Gardaí, and on the treatment of women in Irish society. In many ways, those events created the society we have today.

The Kerry Babies case did show the county in a poor light, but people always knew Kerry was about more than narrow attitudes. It is a great place, and many people choose to make their lives there. One of those was an English farmer, Charles Brooke Pickard. However, he fell in with the wrong crowd and got involved in the drugs business. One spring morning in 1991, he was bundled into the back of a van on an isolated beach. He has not been seen since. His body is probably buried in a shallow grave in the mountains. Gardaí have their suspicions, but the case is likely to remain unsolved without some substantial new breakthrough.

Land was behind the dispute that cost Moss Moore his life in the murder that inspired *The Field*, but that wasn't the only murder in the county motivated by greed for ground. In the early '90s, two brothers who shared a farm fell out with one another. The younger brother owned the land, but the older one wanted to run the farm in a different way and to have his children involved. When the younger man – young is a relative term: he was a pensioner – refused to acquiesce, he was beaten to death and his body dumped down a well. His brother and his nephew were charged with murder.

Violent death is becoming more common, but most counties experience only a few each year. Ireland averages a little over one killing a week, with roughly a third being gang related. That means murder is still a rarity in the country. So Tralee, a medium-sized town in a rural county, was rocked to the core by three murders in ten months – and the murders were

11

particularly vicious. In one case, a young mother was stabbed to death by a schoolboy, just 15 years old. Only a few months later, another young mother was stabbed almost a hundred times. She had been about to make public an allegation of rape against a local man, and he had to cover it up. The final murder was that of a teenage schoolboy. He mixed with the wrong crowd, and ended up being beaten to death and dumped in a field on the outskirts of the town by a man he regarded as a friend. The man had a propensity for violence, and all Tralee was frightened of him. Three murders in less than a year and each one savage: it was becoming a violent place.

Thankfully that was an anomaly, and murder remains rare in the county. But there are always people who see crime as a quick way to their goals. A young Dingle fisherman became involved with a Dublin woman who was working in a bar in the county. He knew she had money put aside to go to Australia, but if he could get his hands on that money he could put together a stake and get involved in the lucrative Limerick drugs scene. He beat her to death and recruited a friend to help hide the body. It couldn't work, and Gerard Graham was caught within a day of the body being discovered. Murder only works if it is well thought out.

The final case concerns a troubled young man from Causeway in north Kerry, who felt a friend had slighted him. So he dressed in combat gear, got a pump-action shotgun, a hunting knife and a crossbow, and went to pay his respects. He shot his friend, and the man's father, in their isolated farmhouse, then signed himself into a psychiatric unit. It was a senseless and motiveless act that destroyed a family – and destroyed his own life as well.

The cases selected for this book cover most of the regions of Kerry, and most of the decades of the past hundred years. They are a record of greed, venality, pig-headedness and thuggery. They also showcase a society that was, at times, broken and intransigent.

Yet what struck me most in researching this was how rare murder is in Kerry. The Kingdom is a great county, populated by great people. I hope you enjoy this glimpse into one aspect of their lives.

1

MURDER BY LANDMINE

The Ballyseedy, Countess Bridge and Bahagh Massacres

THE HAGUE AND Geneva conventions are often among the first casualties in a civil war. The Irish Civil War was particularly vicious, pitching neighbour against neighbour, brother against brother and father against son. It dragged on for two years, and fighting was intense in Kerry. The constant violence had brutalised the population, but the events of March 1923 shocked even the most jaded.

On a bitterly cold night, nine IRA prisoners in Tralee were woken by their captors. They were used to that; each of them had been interrogated extensively over the past few days, two so vigorously that they were suffering from broken arms, and one so badly that he was unfit to be transferred to the prison camp in the Curragh. They were expecting the usual: to be marched out to the cold courtyard, tied to a pole against the stone wall and put through yet another mock execution. They were made to stand, and then rough hands went through their pockets, searching for cigarettes. Each man had his cigarettes taken from him before one was returned to each prisoner.

'That's the last smoke you'll ever have,' an army captain, Ned Breslin, said.

15

The nine prisoners were marched from their cells to a few transport trucks and made to climb into the back, where they were secured. They watched in horror as nine rough wooden coffins were thrown into one truck.

The trucks with the prisoners drove out of Ballymullen Barracks and took the road north out of Tralee towards Castleisland. About three miles out of Tralee, the trucks pulled into the side of the road and the men were made to get out. They were tied together at the waist, and then the soldiers bent down and tied each man's shoelaces to the laces of the man next to him on the chain. Their hands were still bound behind their backs. Secured like that, the line of prisoners slowly shuffled 200 metres to a turn. A small road led off to Farmer's Bridge, and the rifles of the soldiers poking into their backs made the prisoners take this turn. It was a clear night, and the moon revealed the faint ribbon of the road. They didn't have far to walk; they could see their destination almost immediately. A pile of rubble and brambles lay around a fallen log that was blocking the centre of the road completely.

The prisoners slowed instinctively, but harsh voices and cold metal gun barrels urged them on again. They shuffled forward, hope draining like the colour from their faces. They stopped by the rubble, but the soldiers made them march forward and around the obstruction, until the nine men formed a circle facing the pile of debris. The bindings on their hands were removed. Then the soldiers stepped back.

The prisoners were ordered to bend to the task of clearing the rubble. As they moved the smaller stones at the edge, they could hear their captors stepping carefully back, but laughing among themselves. One prisoner, Sam Fullerton, turned to peer into the darkness. At that moment, another of the prisoners – we do not know who – shifted the log at the centre of the roadblock. For a second, something metallic glinted in the moonlight, and he knew instantly that he would never get to have that final cigarette . . .

The events leading up to the Ballyseedy Massacre began a

few months earlier. They were rooted in the politics of the time, but they were equally rooted in petty jealousies and trivial disputes between small farmers: the minutiae of Kerry life. It all began with a quarrel between neighbours. Personal grievances, local rivalry and a desire for payback spilled over into the military arena, with death the inevitable result.

Castleisland is a small village in north Kerry, on the road between Tralee and Abbeyfeale, heading towards Limerick. Pat O'Connor farmed a plot of land at Glansaroon, Castleisland, and got involved in a row with two neighbours, Patrick Buckley and John Daly. Both were members of the IRA, the illegal organisation that was fighting against the state. The civil war was triggered by the Anglo-Irish Treaty, made with Britain in 1921, which gave the twenty-six southern counties freedom, but left six counties of Ulster (Northern Ireland) part of the United Kingdom.

The Free State accepted the Treaty and tried to get on with the business of independence. But those opposed to the Treaty wanted the fight to continue until the entire country was free. The IRA (Irish Republican Army) was the force of the anti-Treaty side, while the Irish Army and the newly formed Garda Síochána (civil police force) opposed them. Fighting was bitter throughout the country, but Kerry in particular was an IRA stronghold, and the county suffered greatly during the two-year-long civil war.

As the row grew between O'Connor and Buckley and Daly, the Free State troops carried out a number of raids on safe houses near Castleisland, although no arrests were made. Locally it was assumed the army had been tipped off by O'Connor, as part of his feud with the IRA men. Whether this is true or not, O'Connor was kidnapped by the IRA and held captive for three days. At a kangaroo court, he was fined £100 (a large sum in those days) as punishment for informing, a fine he refused to pay. So the IRA broke into the family home and stole a little over £36, then took ten cows to make up the balance.

Furious, O'Connor's son Paddy went to the military

headquarters in Castleisland and made a complaint. While there, he also enlisted in the Free State army. His local knowledge proved invaluable, and he had scores to settle. His information led to the arrests of several local activists, including his enemies Patrick Buckley and John Daly, who were taken into custody on 4 February 1923.

The IRA could not let that go. Their commanding officer Humphrey Murphy tried to bomb O'Connor, but failed, so he forged a letter to the troublesome soldier, telling him the location of an IRA arms dump at Bairinarig Wood, near Knocknagoshel. When O'Connor led a party of eight to investigate, they found a pile of loose stones. They began removing the stones to get at the bunker. As they moved one large boulder, a landmine concealed beneath it exploded. Five men, including O'Connor, were killed instantly. A sixth lost both legs.

The commanding officer of the Free State army in Kerry, Brigadier Paddy O'Daly, lost two close friends that morning. He reacted with fury. In a press statement after the explosion, the Kerry command announced that in future any obstacles found on roads or during searches would be removed by republican prisoners. Everyone assumed this was a safety measure; the IRA would not lay booby traps if they thought their own men would be killed by them. But within days, it became obvious that was not what the Kerry command meant. The message was far more sinister.

That night, 6–7 March, the Free State troops in Ballymullen Barracks in Tralee carefully selected nine prisoners for the first phase of their revenge mission. It was after midnight when the nine were woken up. Most were local men, including the two enemies of Pat O'Connor, the soldier the Knocknagoshel booby trap had killed. The nine were Pat Buckley of Scartaglin, John Daly of Castleisland, Pat Hartness of Listowel, Michael O'Connell of Castleisland, James Walsh of Tralee, George O'Shea, Tim Twomey and Stephen Fuller, all of Kilflynn, and John O'Connor of Liverpool. They were carefully chosen; the order had been given to select men who had no priests or other prominent men in their families, so that there would be no articulate relatives to lead the outcry afterwards. Buckley and Daly were included because of their original row with Pat O'Connor, which had had nothing to do with politics. None of the nine prisoners had been tried or was under sentence of death. The selection of prisoners was made by Colonel David Neligan and Captain Ned Breslin.

The nine prisoners were brought to the turn-off at Ballyseedy and marched down the road towards Farmer's Bridge, a local townland. No doubt they were expecting a bullet in the back and an official report stating that they had been shot while trying to escape. But then they saw the rubble on the road, and most of them must have realised, as they were placed in a circle around it, what was really about to happen. The soldiers cut the ropes binding their hands, but left the ropes around their waists, tying them into a circle. Their shoelaces were still tied together, making any attempt to escape impossible. Even if it had been possible, the prisoners knew that to run for it would mean a bullet in the back.

The night was bitterly cold and cloudless, with the moon casting a ghastly light over the scene. Hands trembling as much from the cold as the fear, the prisoners began to do as they were told. They moved some of the smaller bits of rubble around the fallen log at the centre. Experienced veterans, they knew what a fallen log meant on a country road: a landmine. What they did not know was that the Free State soldiers who had retreated to a safe distance had spent the afternoon constructing the mine and that a lorry had gone out ahead of their convoy to plant it. This was no IRA ambush they were clearing. This was deliberate murder.

Unable to do anything about their fate, the prisoners began to work methodically on removing the rubble from the road. At one point, Tim Twomey asked for a minute to pray. A soldier stepped forward and struck him with a rope-end. Then he stepped back again. 'You can pray as long as you like,' another jeered. Just as long as they kept working.

One of the prisoners muttered, 'Goodbye, lads.'

As Stephen Fuller turned to glare at his captors, someone moved the log. The tripwire was engaged and the night sky lit up in a brief blaze of light. The blast thundered across the fields, shaking windows of nearby houses. But no one came out to investigate; there was a war on, and they knew better.

As the noise died down, five bangs followed in quick succession, as the soldiers lobbed grenades into the melee, just to make sure of their dirty work. This was followed by gunshots. Torches on, they then marched forward and surveyed the carnage. There was a small crater on the road and the log had been flung clear. For a radius of several yards, body parts were strewn across the road and nearby ditches. They had had their revenge on Kerry No. 1 Brigade of the IRA.

Unknown to the soldiers, Stephen Fuller had been flung clear by the explosion, which had caught him in the back. He had been thrown a couple of dozen yards over the ditch, coming down in a field but close enough to the ditch that his body did not stand out in the moonlight. By a miracle he was still alive and conscious, though badly burnt. He listened as the Free State soldiers moved forward to examine their bloody work. He waited for the click of a hammer and the *coup de grâce* that would wipe out the only witness to the massacre. But the soldiers did not spot him. Slowly, he began to move up the ditch. He reached the river at the side of the road and slipped into it, the freezing water providing some relief for his burns. But it was a bitter night, and he could not remain long in the water.

He heard the moans of his dying comrades and listened in disbelief as the concussive booms of the hand grenades and the gunfire rang across the land. He went as far as he could in the river, but the cold forced him back into the field. Now was the moment of greatest risk, as he inched across Pender's Field, every second expecting to be spotted and shot. However, the soldiers did not believe anyone could have survived the explosion, so were less than vigilant.

Fuller got across the field. The further away he got from the carnage, the safer he felt. Eventually he was able to stand up and walk properly, always alert for the telltale sounds of a truck revving or a footstep on the road near the fields he was crossing. He walked for a mile and then found a house where he knew a sympathetic family lived. Gently he knocked on the door, careful not to create a disturbance. The door opened and welcoming arms helped him inside. He had arrived at the home of the Currans at Hanlon's Cross.

The following day, when it was safe, two volunteers came and removed Fuller to Daly's at Knockane, where he received medical treatment from a discreet local doctor. Over the coming weeks, he moved frequently, never remaining long enough in any place to compromise his cover. He moved from the Burkes to the Boyles, and finally was placed in a dugout at a farm owned by the Herlihys at Meenathee, Rathanny. This was nearly four miles (six kilometres) from the site of the massacre, and he remained there for seven months.

The authorities did not know initially that one man had survived the landmine and its aftermath. A lorry had gone back to Tralee to officially inform the authorities that nine prisoners had been accidentally blown up by an IRA landmine at Ballyseedy. Had no one escaped, the official version of events would have been accepted, probably without question.

The lorry with the nine coffins was dispatched to the site of the carnage, and as light began to dawn, the clean-up began. By now, the soldiers had heavily fortified themselves with alcohol to steel them for the grisly work. They began to drag body parts from the road, the ditches and surrounding trees. Quickly it became apparent that many of the bodies were mangled beyond recognition. There were not nine corpses to be boxed and removed. Instead, there was gore everywhere, with limbs and body parts strewn over a radius of several hundred yards. It would be difficult or impossible to decide which limb belonged with which, so the nine coffins were laid in a row on the road, filled in a haphazard manner and nailed shut. One body seemed to be missing, but the soldiers assumed it had been blown apart in the explosion. Once each coffin had a sufficient amount of material in it to give it a respectable weight, it was placed back in the lorry and the bodies were brought back to the barracks in Tralee. The plan was to sort out the bodies there and return them to their families.

Meanwhile, for weeks to come, the crows gathered at Ballyseedy Cross and feasted on the lumps of human flesh left high up in the bare winter trees.

Word had spread quickly that nine prisoners had died in the overnight 'accident'. Relatives crowded the barracks looking for news. The list of the dead was revealed, and the grieving relatives saw the row of coffins. Every nation has its own burial customs. In Ireland, we make a big deal of death. In rural areas in particular, it was common to 'wake' the dead. The corpse would be laid out in state on the kitchen table or in the front parlour, and all the neighbours, friends and relatives would gather to spend the evening reminiscing and drinking. Closed coffins would not do. And in any case, the bodies had to be identified so that each could go back to the right family.

A large crowd of grieving relatives gathered outside Ballymullen Barracks, eager to take their loved ones home for burial. Eventually the coffins were released, and the result was what can only be described as a frenzy. As the families opened the coffins for one final glimpse of a dead son or brother, the full horror of the carnage struck home. They were not looking at bodies, but at a hodgepodge of dismembered body parts. Relatives reacted with predictable fury, at one moment howling with inconsolable grief, the next hurling curses and abuse at the soldiers. It developed into a full-scale riot across the town.

The families took the bodies from the coffins the army had provided, and smashed the coffins to pieces outside the barracks gate. They then sent for new coffins and placed the bodies in them with proper respect. However, their anger overflowed, and the soldiers on sentry duty were pelted with stones and bits of wood by the angry mob outside.

By now, the authorities had realised that one man had escaped their vengeance. Initially they believed it was John O'Connor, but later they realised that they had made a mistake: Stephen Fuller was the man on the run. He remained on the run long after the civil war ended a month later. He knew that his story would give the lie to the official account of the Ballyseedy Massacre: the prisoners had been accidentally blown up by an IRA bomb at a booby-trapped roadblock. They did try that explanation for a while, before switching to an equally implausible story: the massacre had been carried out by soldiers acting independently of the command structure.

However, the circumstances were against the army from the start. Things looked bad after Ballyseedy, but by the end of that day no one was in any doubt what was happening. There was a second massacre. This time the victims were members of the IRA Brigade No. 2.

The second incident was eerily like the first. Members of the Free State army based in the Great Southern Hotel in Killarney, about fifteen miles from Tralee, selected five prisoners from their barracks and marched them to Countess Bridge, an isolated spot between Killarney and Kilcummin. The same cover story was used: the prisoners were to clear a roadblock, because it was too dangerous to expose the regular army to the possibility of a booby trap.

Just hours after the explosion at Ballyseedy, soldiers banged on the cell doors at Killarney Barracks, waking a number of prisoners. Five men were dragged from their beds, half-dressed. They were Stephen Buckley and Jeremiah O'Donoghue, both of Killarney, and Daniel O'Donoghue, Timothy Murphy and Tadhg Coffey, all from Kilcummin. Jeremiah O'Donoghue and Coffey had been sentenced to death for being in possession of arms. The other three prisoners were under no such sentence. All three had been badly beaten during their days of captivity.

The five bleary-eyed men were lined up before six officers and a number of soldiers. In single file, they were made to march out of the barracks and into the fields. They marched cross-country, heading north-west. They were travelling in the general direction of Kilcummin, a small village about five miles (eight kilometres) from Killarney. The Free State soldiers found the going easy. They were in full uniform and wearing proper boots. The prisoners were half-dressed and suffering from the bitter cold and biting wind. Many of them were in very poor condition. Timothy Murphy, who had been charged with no offence, was bent double from the injuries he had sustained after a number of beatings. His face was caked in dried blood, and he looked like an old man. Others were not much better.

After an hour, they came to a small bridge, Countess Bridge, not far from Kilcummin. The prisoners could see that the bridge was blocked. There was a pile of stones on the road and plenty of debris around it. They were ordered to move towards the blocked bridge. As they cautiously advanced, they noticed the soldiers withdrawing to a discreet distance and heard the sounds of bolts being drawn on rifles. If they had had any hope at the start of the march, it was gone now.

'Run, lads,' one of the prisoners shouted.

'My God, lads, this is a trap,' shouted Coffey.

Unlike those at Ballyseedy, the men had not been tied together. The five prisoners bolted for the barricade and leapt over it, trying to get to safety from the fusillade of gunfire they expected at any second. Yet the soldiers didn't fire; instead, they began throwing grenades. They hadn't bothered to mine the barricade. The grenades landed among the fleeing IRA prisoners, throwing them to the ground with massive injuries.

Coffey, who had been bending to see if the blockade was mined when they had made their run, was thrown to the ground by the first explosions. He looked around and could see Buckley, Murphy and Daniel O'Donoghue covered in blood and moaning. They were badly injured, but were trying to creep feebly along the ground. The grenades continued to fall, and now the soldiers were also firing into the group of prisoners. Coffey tried to stand, but his left knee gave under him. He could see that his close friend Jeremiah O'Donoghue was uninjured. Standing would be suicidal, so both men began to crawl away as fast as they could.

They managed to get around a bend in the road before being spotted by the soldiers. A burst of machine-gun fire rang out, and Coffey felt the bullets pass so close to him that his clothes were rent. O'Donoghue was less lucky. He took a direct hit and fell to the ground, dead. Coffey crawled on, desperate to put distance between himself and the soldiers. Life was coming back to his knee, and he risked standing. He began to run and jumped a high park gate, getting into wooded land. He ran until his heart was pounding and his eyes were watering with the exertion. When he thought he was out of range of the guns, he paused for a moment to regain his breath. He looked down. Clutched between his white fingers were his rosary beads. He muttered a quick prayer, and then ran again. He knew of one safe house in the district, that of Jack Moynihan, but he didn't know exactly where he was or where the Moynihan house was. By now, it was just chance whether he would manage to evade capture.

In the distance, Coffey could see a white house. Terrified, exhausted and hurt, he had to take a chance. He headed for the house. When he reached it, he waited a few minutes to allow his breathing to settle, then he smoothed his hair and tried to appear as normal as possible. He walked up to the window and tapped lightly, casually asking the girl who peeped out for directions to Moynihan's.

'This is Jack Moynihan's,' she replied. Coffey was safe.

Coming hours after the Ballyseedy Massacre, the incident at Countess Bridge was difficult to explain away, but the military authorities did their best. They insisted both incidents had been tragic accidents, caused by bombs planted by the IRA. They released a statement to the press, carried by the *Irish Times*:

The National Army Headquarters last Wednesday night issued the following official report: A party of troops proceeding from

Tralee to Killorglin last night came across a barricade of stones built on the roadway at Ballyseedy Bridge.

The troops returned to Tralee, and brought a number of prisoners to remove the obstruction.

While engaged in this work a trigger-mine (which was concealed in the structure) exploded, wounding Captain Edward Breslin, Lieutenant Joseph Murtagh, and Sergeant Ennis, and killing eight of the prisoners.

Sergeant Murtagh and Sergeant Ennis were seriously wounded.

On the Countess Bridge the troops found a barricade similar to that at Ballyseedy Bridge erected across the roadway.

While the obstruction was being removed a trigger-mine exploded, wounding two of the troops, and killing four irregular prisoners who had been engaged in removing the barricade.

The prisoners killed by the mine at Ballyseedy Bridge were: John Daly, Woodview, Castleisland; Patrick Hartnett, Listowel; Patrick Buckley, Scargtaglin; James Walsh, Lisodique, Tralee; Stephen Fuller, Lixnaw; George Shea, Lixnaw; T. Toomey, Lixnaw; T. O'Connor, Warf Terrace, Liverpool; and Michael O'Connell, Fahaduv, Castleisland.

The prisoners killed at Countess's Bridge were: Jeremiah O'Donoghue, New Street, Killarney; Tim Murphy, Kilbrean, Kilcummin; Stephen Buckley, Tierboul; Dan Donoghue, Lacka, Kilcummin.

The implication was quite clear: the anti-Treaty forces had barricaded the roads. The Free State army had done as they said they would: they got prisoners to clear the obstructions. Unfortunately, the prisoners had died in the attempt when concealed landmines exploded. The story was neat and it fitted the facts. Unfortunately, though, there was a problem. At Ballyseedy and at Countess Bridge, there had been survivors. Eventually the truth would out.

Tensions were running high in the days following the two massacres. On Friday, 9 March – just two days later – a group of prisoners were being escorted from Killorglin to Tralee. As they drove past Ballyseedy, an incident took place. There are conflicting accounts. The army reported that they came under fire and that one of the prisoners, James Taylor, from Glencar, was fatally wounded in the crossfire. That is the official version. Many people believed the alternative. Taylor was a staunch republican who had lost his brother in the War of Independence. It was widely believed that he had said something as the convoy was passing the site of the massacre just a few days earlier. The soldiers, hypersensitive because they knew they had stepped well beyond what was allowable even in a war, were on edge. They were also angry that they had lost friends and colleagues: war cuts both ways. Perhaps one of them reacted to a smart remark by pulling out a gun and shooting Taylor. Whatever the true version of events, death was becoming a constant background in the Kingdom. People were becoming inured to violence, and the atrocities were getting worse.

The army had taught IRA Brigades No. 1 and No. 2 a bloody lesson. Now it was time to hit the third brigade operating in the county, and when it came to targeting IRA Brigade No. 3, the army decided to refine its murder methods. This time there would be no survivors.

Twenty prisoners were being held near Cahirciveen. An old workhouse at Bahaghs, about three miles from the town, had been converted to a temporary prison. Many of the prisoners were members of the No. 3 Brigade. On 12 March, five days after the Ballyseedy and Countess Bridge massacres, members of the Dublin Guard – the official army of the new state – arrived at the workhouse. They arrived after midnight and announced that they were transferring a number of prisoners to Tralee. They were looking for specific men. A week earlier, a group of republican suspects had been surrounded at Gurrane Hill, near Cahirciveen, and during the operation two army men had been killed. However, the Gurrane prisoners had already been transferred.

The officer in charge of the Dublin Guard, Commandant J.J. Delaney, ordered the duty sergeant to pick five prisoners and hand them over, but the man refused. He said that only his commanding officer, Lieutenant McCarthy, could authorise a release of prisoners. But the officer was having none of that; he drew his revolver and pointed it at the terrified sergeant, telling him that he would shoot him unless he handed over the keys to the guardroom.

Delaney's men went in and picked five prisoners: Michael Courtney, Eugene Dwyer, John Sugrue, Daniel O'Shea and Willie Riordan. All five were from the Waterville area and were in custody for various republican activities. The men were told they had to be ready to go in half an hour. They began to pack their few belongings into parcels. According to some accounts, 20-year-old Daniel O'Shea asked if he should take his belongings. He was told by the officers that their belongings would follow in another lorry. It was an ominous sign of what was to come. One man, remembering the recent atrocities, suspected what was coming. 'We'll need no parcels, Dan,' said Michael Courtney. 'We're not going far.'

They left the barracks and drove a short distance through the night, but instead of heading towards Tralee, they travelled in the opposite direction, towards Valentia. They were told that they were being transferred to Tralee, but they were not too surprised when the lorry drew to a stop. There was a roadblock. The five men were ordered out of the lorry. However, there was one difference between what was about to happen and what had happened in the other two massacres: this time it would be done right. The five men were lined up close to the roadblock and tied together. Then the Dublin Guard drew their guns and shot the five prisoners in the legs. The screaming and pain-wracked men were then dragged across the roadblock. The officers stood back and the landmine was triggered.

The crack boomed through the darkness. When the air became still again, the officers were able to walk forward and check their handiwork. All five prisoners were dead. Brigade No. 3 had been taught their lesson.

Word quickly spread through the locality. When the Dublin

Guard had arrived at Cahirciveen, people feared the worst and they were waiting for some new horror. Two nurses went to the scene of the landmine. Nurse Sloan and Nurse O'Connor found clumps of earth and grass flung everywhere, and gaps in the walls bounding the road. There were cartridge cases lying about. One of the nurses found a chain of rosary beads. Michael Courtney was known to carry beads, and they were probably his. The beads were soaked in blood. Then the nurses came upon the shattered bodies, and they knew they could be of no use. They went back with their awful news to Cahirciveen.

Within hours, the father of one of the victims presented himself at the workhouse, looking for news of his son. He asked was there an O'Shea in the group of prisoners taken out the previous night. He was told that there was. When the officer described the prisoner, his father said, 'It was Dan, so, and you killed him.'

There were no witnesses to the third massacre in less than a week. But one man with a conscience was horrified by what had happened. Lieutenant McCarthy, the officer in charge of the workhouse at Bahaghs, was stunned when he heard that the five prisoners who had been removed from his custody had been murdered a short time later. He could not live with that preying on his mind, so he went public with what he knew. He accused the Dublin Guard of being a 'murder gang'. His allegation was published in the *Cork Examiner* on 10 March.

McCarthy also resigned his commission in the army. He said he was prepared to serve the state as a soldier and to fight against the anti-Treaty forces, but he was not prepared to be a party to murder. Even in war, there are limits.

McCarthy was a native of Kerry. The people who had been blown up were his people; they would have been friends and neighbours if the country had not been at war. Although the civil war pitted neighbours and friends against each other – sometimes even brother against brother – the number of casualties was relatively small, in comparison to the amount of action seen. One reason for this is that people tended to shoot high or low rather than have blood on their hands. In Kerry, though, the war became a lot more vicious than in other parts of the country. It has been speculated that the presence of the Dublin Guard, and so many officers from outside the county, was what made the difference. They had no ties to the towns and villages they were operating in, so they shot to kill. Gradually, a miasma of violence settled over the county, desensitising the population and creating an atmosphere in which atrocities became the norm.

As well as the testimony of Lieutenant McCarthy, there was other evidence of what really happened at Cahirciveen. The bodies of the dead were collected by grieving relatives for their wakes. Three of the corpses had been mangled beyond recognition, but two of the bodies had sustained less damage. Their relatives swore that they could see the bullet wounds in the legs of the two men. If the official version of events was true, there should have been no bullet wounds.

Locals erected a simple wooden cross at the site of the murders – for there is no other word for what happened. However, the army broke the cross and removed it.

The third massacre had happened five days after the first two, and the survivors' accounts of those atrocities had already begun to circulate; therefore the Army version of what happened was discredited from the beginning. It was the blackest month in Kerry history. Twenty-nine anti-Treaty men had been killed in the month. This was a staggering number, equivalent to a death toll that had mounted up over six months, earlier in the conflict. Of those 29, 17 had been deliberately blown up by landmines while they were unarmed and in custody. Another man had probably been shot for making remarks about the landmine massacres. In addition, ten Army men had been killed that month in the county.

There were calls for an inquiry into the massacres. Such flagrant breaches of the rules of war could not be ignored. A military court of inquiry was convened, but it exonerated all the officers involved in the three incidents. Not everyone was happy with that result. Labour Party leader Thomas Johnson raised the matter in the Dáil. But the National Army's Commander-in-Chief, General Richard Mulcahy, who was also a TD, said that he accepted the findings of the military court, which cleared his troops of all wrongdoing in any of the three massacres.

The families of some of the victims tried to sue the state for compensation, but with no luck. The official version of events – a spectacular cover-up – prevailed. But it was not accepted by everyone. In a memo to Home Affairs Minister Kevin O'Higgins, one of his officials expressed his concerns about events in Kerry and recommended a full criminal investigation into the Bahaghs killings. He had concerns about the military inquiry.

One of the concerns was that very few witnesses were interviewed, and all of those interviewed were National Army personnel. They were the ones who had perpetrated the atrocities, so of course their accounts of events were suspect at best. No one at the workhouse was questioned. The minutes of the official inquiry show that just three men were questioned. No one from the workhouse – prisoners or officers – had been summonsed. Moreover, the inquiry was chaired by Major General Delaney, the man who had ordered the use of prisoners for mine clearing just days before the first massacre.

Commandant J.J. Doyle, in charge of the Dublin Guard responsible for the third massacre, said, 'I told them [the prisoners] that mines were being laid and that some of our officers and men had been killed in this way, and that they would have to remove this barricade and take the chance of its containing a mine. The prisoners made no objection to removing the barricade. They appeared nervous. This was the only obstruction on the road. The prisoners were not maltreated.'

He added: 'It is a lie to say that the prisoners were shot.' According to his evidence, all five were killed instantly.

The finding of the inquiry was no great surprise: 'No blame is attached to any officer or soldier engaged in the operations in which these prisoners lost their lives.'

The military court went on to heap praise on the butchers, saying, 'The discipline maintained by the troops is worthy of the highest consideration.'

The earlier massacres were also investigated by military courts. Those inquiries produced similar results: the soldiers were not to blame and had behaved in an exemplary manner.

But there were dissenters. Inspector C. Reynolds, of Cahirciveen, backed the version of events told by survivors and the families of the victims. The father of Daniel O'Shea, just 20 when he was murdered by the Army, put in a compensation claim. The inspector wrote a letter in support of this claim, in which he said, 'This act was perpetrated by a number of men of the National Army known as the "Visiting Committee" and was not an official reprisal.'

Henry Friel, an official at the Department of Home Affairs, recommended that the Gardaí be instructed to carry out a full investigation, and if possible criminal charges should be laid against the soldiers involved in the massacres. Failing that, a full investigation could be carried out by the Department of Defence, but this time all the witnesses would have to be questioned. 'I find it difficult to impeach the value of a court of inquiry apparently accepted by the military authorities as satisfactory and yet on the facts of the case as presented to this ministry to date such a course appears to be a proper one,' Friel wrote in a memo to his Minister.

As there were compensation claims pending from the families of some of the victims, the matter could not be swept under the carpet, so it went to the cabinet for discussion. A note of the discussion stated: 'It was decided that prima facie evidence of complicity in an attack against the State on the part of an applicant for compensation or in respect of whom compensation is claimed is a bar to the claim.' In other words, the fact that the men murdered by the army were prisoners being held on charges of offences against the state meant that their families were not entitled to compensation, no matter how they met their deaths. The note concluded: 'The onus of preparing evidence in respect of any alleged excesses by the troops during the period of hostility rests upon the party who considers himself aggrieved.'

Just how an ordinary citizen was expected to convene his own inquiry and gather evidence against the forces of the state was never specified. Needless to say, none of the families had the resources to pursue the matter. After that decision by the cabinet, the matters of the massacres at Ballyseedy, Countess Bridge and Bahaghs were never officially mentioned again.

Renegade members of the army had got away with murdering seventeen unarmed and defenceless men over a five-day period.

2

EASTER MASSACRE

The murder of Margaret O'Sullivan by Hannah Flynn

KILLORGLIN IS SPECIAL. It is a small farmers' market town nestling in the foothills of the McGillicuddy Reeks. A little river wends its way past the town, and the main street runs sharply uphill away from the bridge and the river. The main street broadens out into a triangular town square, which is the scene, every year, of the oldest fair in Europe. The place oozes folk history.

The annual Puck Fair has been going on for centuries. Its origins are lost in the mists of antiquity, and no one knows for sure where the goat comes in, but every summer a hardy billy goat is captured on the nearby mountains, fattened up and brought to Killorglin in time for the start of what is still one of the greatest festivals in the country.

On 10 August every year, traders, buyers, sellers, chancers, cheaters, charmers and everyone in between make their way to the heart of Kerry for the Puck Fair. It is a three-day orgy of Irishness. Each of the three days is worth a month's trade to the pubs and shops of the town. The place is black with people, and the money they bring in has given Killorglin prosperity that similar towns lack. By the third day of the fair, it can take up to 30 minutes to make your way across the square, particularly if you are trying to cross during the crowning of the Puck, the king of the fair.

Ireland has a culture of hard drinking and craic, and all of that forms part of the fair. There is music in the bars and there are three-card men on the streets. Pubs stay open until the last man falls, and rows and ructions are common. Noses are bloodied and heads cracked. But it is all in good fun. Killorglin sees it all.

While men were floundering in the mud of Flanders during the First World War, Kerry farmers and merchants were gathering every summer at the Puck. When the civil war turned bitter, friends and enemies mingled at the Puck. The atrocities of the civil war touched the folk of Killorglin. They were not an insular people; they knew how cruel the world could be. If you draw a triangle between Tralee, Killarney and Cahirciveen, Killorglin falls right in the centre. In March 1923, the Ballyseedy, Countess Bridge and Bahagh massacres had taken place nearby. The stakes were high, and violence and death were the price of political progress.

As 1923 progressed, the people of Ireland – particularly along the western seaboard – became inured to horror and murder. Reports (false, as it turned out) came from Clare of a British major being buried on a beach with his head sticking out of the sand and left there to await the tide coming in. The Black and Tans had committed terrible deeds, burning and looting all before them, during the War of Independence. Now we were doing worse to ourselves during the civil war.

So when a farmer's wife was found hacked to death in her kitchen near Killorglin on Easter Sunday morning, it was a local sensation only. The rest of the country didn't bat an eyelid, probably putting it down to another political assassination.

There were plenty to choose from that weekend. In Tipperary, at the Glen of Aherlow, a captain of the Free State army and a militia leader were gunned down as they tried to protect a farmhouse that had come under fire from a group of anti-Treaty irregulars. Captain O'Dea and Jerry Kiely both lost their lives in that action. In Louth, the local army barracks came under heavy fire on Easter Saturday night, with many wounded, though no deaths. In Cork city, a power station was bombed. Anti-Treaty forces tried to blow up a bridge in Tullamore. There were clashes in Clare, Limerick, Monaghan and Waterford as well. The country was in turmoil. So was the Kingdom. On Good Friday, a railway linesman was kidnapped at Caragh.

The war came very close to Killorglin that weekend. Just three miles from the town, on the Glenbeigh Road, a body was found. Michael O'Shea was pro-Treaty, a volunteer on the side of the new state. He had been shot in the face and chest at point-blank range. It was an execution, and a particularly vicious one. The shot to the face is something forensic psychologists recognise as an attempt to completely destroy someone's identity. To shoot someone in the face rather than the back of the head – more traditional for executions – implies tremendous fury or hatred. A mocking message from the anti-Treaty forces had been hung around his neck, to reinforce the message.

When Margaret O'Sullivan's body was found that Sunday morning, with her face hacked beyond recognition, it was a forgivable mistake to assume she was just another victim of the troubled times. Her murder merited only a few lines in the papers, with the *Irish Times* dismissing it in one paragraph buried in the middle of a longer article about the crimes of the weekend: 'Mrs O'Sullivan, wife of a farmer at Beauford, County Kerry, was murdered on Sunday by a man who entered her house while her husband was at Mass and stole £29.' The article appeared on Wednesday, three days after the murder. The paragraph before related that a Mrs McGuinness of Carnscullens Post Office, County Sligo, had been shot dead and her son seriously wounded – the motive was obviously political. And the paragraph afterwards was about armed men derailing and wrecking the Enniskillen to Sligo train. Again, it was political.

But 40-year-old Margaret O'Sullivan was not a victim of political violence. Her murder was a purely domestic matter.

She died at the hands of someone she knew, over quite a minor grudge.

Easter is a special time in Ireland and has always been celebrated. Even in those impoverished times, long before it became a celebration of the birth of the Easter Bunny, it was marked as one of the most important religious celebrations on the ecclesiastical calendar. Like Christmas, all the stops were pulled out for the Easter Sunday dinner. A goose would be killed and roasted, and there would be exotic fruits such as oranges for afterwards. In the days before microwaves and processed food, the dinner was a major production. The woman of the house would slave over the stove for the whole morning to get everything ready on time.

So when Daniel O'Sullivan went to Mass that morning, his wife, Margaret, remained at home working. Usually the couple would have gone together, then separated at the door of the church, as the women went to one side and the men to the other. But Daniel went on his own that day. After the Mass, he hung around and chatted for a few minutes with friends and neighbours, then made his way home for dinner with his farmhand John Feehan.

Daniel O'Sullivan was a comfortable farmer. He had land in the townland of Cullinamore, between Beauford and Killorglin. Many Irish farmers struggled. The pattern was for a father to split the land between his sons, so farms got smaller and smaller, and the living more precarious. However, some rose above the poverty trap and held on to enough land to make a decent living. Daniel was one of those. He was able to marry, and hire a servant. He was also able to hire a farmhand to help out. The couple lived in a fine two-storey farmhouse with plenty of space, in contrast to many of the tiny cottages and hovels that littered the Kerry countryside. They had amassed a considerable fortune in savings, which they kept in share certificates. They were among the well-off in the community.

Sometimes success breeds resentment, and resentment grows like a canker in the system, corrupting thoughts and attitudes.

Those with less resent those who have managed to get ahead. Ireland is a great nation for begrudgers. Not everyone wished the O'Sullivans well.

One man who harboured a grudge was a local youth who did casual farm labour. Jeremiah Carey was one of life's losers, a young man going nowhere in a hurry. He was difficult to get on with and was considered troublesome. He had worked on Daniel O'Sullivan's farm for a while, but in the end Daniel had had to let him go.

Daniel wasn't alone in that. Several of the surrounding landowners had given Carey a chance, and they had all ended up doing the same. The young man could not hold on to work. In the days before social welfare, that kept him in a poverty trap and almost forced him to take advantage of every opportunity that presented itself, even if it involved breaking the law.

Jeremiah Carey was one man who did not wish the O'Sullivans well. Another was a former servant dismissed because she was useless around the house, and because she was suspected of pilfering.

No one has servants any more, but back then it was not uncommon for a strong farmer to have a lad to help out in the fields and a young girl to do the housework. Teenage girls with no prospects (and there were many of them) would go to hiring fairs, where they hoped to be taken in by a family. They worked for board and keep, and a small wage. Hours were long, and conditions could be poor, if the family chose to make them so. Others who lived locally would just work the days, going back to their own poor abodes in the evening.

Hannah Flynn knew all about domestic service. She had grown up near Killorglin, in a poor family. Her eldest brother had inherited the family farm, and her other siblings fled Kerry as soon as they were old enough. But it was not so easy for a woman to escape. Hannah's situation was made worse by the fact that she was neither bright nor well educated. Most people got only a few years of primary school, and Hannah finished unable to read at even a basic level or to write her own name. She was considered slow, and many thought she was feeble-minded.

In addition, she was big and plain, so marriage was not likely to prove a way out for her. Now approaching 30, she had spent more than half her life in and out of domestic service, and barely surviving. She lived alone in a miserable cabin about a mile outside Killorglin. She dressed in hand-me-downs and barely made enough to keep food on the table. Life was a constant struggle, with only the odd dance or fair to brighten an otherwise weary and depressing existence.

Hannah had worked for the O'Sullivans for a number of months. They had employed her in April 1922 and kept her on for a few months, but she had not worked out. She was stubborn and often slow to do what she was asked. She clashed with Daniel's wife. The couple also noticed that items seemed to disappear when she was around. The missing items were always small things, but they were convinced she was stealing from them.

Finally, in June, Daniel confronted her and told her she had to go. She was 'worthless in the house, and too much of a thief about the place', he said. Hannah, a wilful woman, did not take the news well. She lost her rag and abused Daniel, telling him that she would have his life for sacking her. Daniel thought nothing more of it; her words were the wild ravings of a hot-tempered woman. Occasionally Hannah would appear outside the house late at night, drunk, and would hurl obscenities at the occupants. She occasionally threw stones at the windows, but did no damage.

Once she confronted the household's other servant, farmhand John Feehan. He was wheeling a cart of turf to the house when she accosted him. She drove him off and took the cart, saying that it was for wages that were owed to her. She was a big woman, and Feehan let her take the cart.

As O'Sullivan and Feehan approached the house that Easter morning, it appeared quiet. But in those days before radio, this did not cause the men much alarm. Daniel pushed open the door and stepped into the kitchen – and immediately recoiled in horror. His wife, Margaret, was slumped on the floor, in a large pool of blood. There were splatters of blood everywhere. Great gouts of crimson were sprayed across the table, the chairs and the stove, where she had been working on the dinner before she was attacked. The blood seemed to be everywhere.

There was a hatchet on the ground near the body, with clumps of flesh and strands of hair clinging to it. Clearly this was the weapon used in the attack. But the most horrific aspect of the scene was his wife's face. It had been struck so many times it was no longer recognisable. The skull had been smashed and the face obliterated. There were also cuts and bruises on her body. The savagery of the attack was appalling. Daniel turned from the scene, ran outside and vomited in the yard.

It took him and Feehan a few minutes to compose themselves, but they quickly alerted neighbours to the tragedy. Someone rushed into the town to the Garda barracks and reported the murder. Neighbours began to gather. They were repulsed by the scene, and furious that one of their own should have come to such a savage end. It did not take long before the yard was crowded. There were angry men who wanted to go after the killer, curious people drawn to the gore and those anxious to comfort the husband. He was inside the kitchen with some neighbours when the Gardaí arrived.

Although they had got there within minutes, the crime scene was already well on the way to being compromised. It was before the days of forensic science, but even so Sergeant Pat O'Rourke knew that he needed to clear everyone away or vital evidence could be lost. He immediately came out to the yard and ordered everyone away, telling them that he would know where to find them if he needed them. Then he went back inside and began to examine the kitchen.

The hatchet was the obvious clue; it could not be overlooked. It was the murder weapon, and whoever had carried out the killing had left it behind. This could mean it was an opportunist crime rather than a planned assassination. If someone intended to kill that morning, they would have brought their own weapon and taken it away afterwards. The next clue was the savagery of the assault. A subsequent medical examination would reveal that Margaret O'Sullivan had been struck at least 18 times in the face and head by the axe. Her skull was completely shattered. One blow would probably have been enough to cause death; two would certainly have been fatal. Yet the attacker had continued smashing the weapon into the skull of the prone and lifeless victim.

The sergeant looked at the force of the blows and came to the conclusion that the attacker was a man, and a strong man at that. He must have been very angry with the victim, or hated her, because of the way he had destroyed her face. He turned to the grieving husband and asked did the family have any enemies, or was there any man that angry with them?

Daniel thought as best he could, but his brain was addled with grief, and he, like the sergeant, was probably trying to come up with the name of a man. Only one name came to mind. Jeremiah Carey was a young man who carried out casual labour on many of the nearby farms. He was difficult to get on with and had a reputation as a troublemaker, which is why none of the local farmers had kept him on for long. Daniel O'Sullivan was just one of the farmers who had given him his marching orders.

It seemed a weak motive, and the sergeant needed more to go on. He decided to search the house. Both Daniel and the farmhand John Feehan helped out. They quickly discovered that the house had been ransacked. Drawers had been turned out, cupboards opened and boxes strewn around the rooms. They quickly discovered that robbery was a real possibility as a motive: £500 in share certificates and securities had been stolen. That was a small fortune in 1923: enough for someone to relocate and start a new life, if they could convert the securities to cash. There was also £16 16 s. missing from a tin box.

When they came to the bedroom, they got a real surprise. Several items of clothing had been taken, but they were all women's clothing. The Gardaí began to consider the possibility that the killer had a female accomplice. They took a note of the items that were missing, and then continued their search of the house and yard.

The yard and surrounding fields were saturated with water. That Saturday it had rained heavily all day and night, and parts of the ground were a quagmire. It should have been excellent ground for spotting footprints, but the neighbours who had gathered around Daniel O'Sullivan had obliterated many useful clues.

The attacker, or attackers, could have fled by road, or they could have made their escape across the fields. Gardaí felt that if they had used the road, they might have been spotted by someone. The neighbours were questioned, but no one had been seen approaching or leaving the house. There were a large number of footprints around the back of the house and near the back door. But one set continued on through the yard and into a potato field, veering off in the direction of Killorglin. Sergeant O'Rourke thought they might belong to the killer. If they did, one shoe was clearly bigger than the other, which could be helpful in identifying the suspect.

Very quickly, a consensus grew that the killer had been the troublesome youth Jeremiah Carey. Proof of his involvement seemed to come when he attempted to flee. However, he was apprehended and brought to the barracks in Killorglin. Once in custody, the case was quickly wrapped up: Carey admitted his involvement and made a full confession. He told the Gardaí that he had come to the house that morning and found Margaret alone. He accosted her and demanded money, and when she refused to give it to him, he used an axe he found there to split her head open. He then made off with whatever money he could find. When asked how much he had got away with, he replied that he had found £29.

That's where the confession came unstuck. There had not

been £29 in the house, and Carey had not mentioned the missing shares. Reluctantly, the Gardaí released Carey and relaunched their murder investigation.

Witnesses were scarce, because the crime had taken place on a Sunday while everyone was at Mass. No one had been seen near the house. Finally, Gardaí managed to find two witnesses who had seen something. They were two brothers who worked as farm labourers on land about a mile outside Killorglin, on the road towards Beauford. William and Timothy O'Neill had not been at Mass that morning, and they remembered meeting a woman on the road, coming from the direction of Cullinamore and heading back towards Killorglin. The woman had been dressed very poorly, but she was wearing a very good-quality shawl, which did not go with the rest of her clothes. She had something hidden under the shawl and seemed to be in a big hurry. Her feet and tattered stockings were covered in mud, and she had a furtive air about her. One thing that struck them as peculiar was that she was wearing odd shoes: one seemed bigger than the other. Both boys recognised her: it was Hannah Flynn.

Hannah Flynn was brought in for questioning, but denied any involvement in the murder of her former mistress. She had a solid alibi for the time of the murder: she had been in Tralee looking for work. Tralee is about 18 miles from Killorglin and is a far bigger town. The chances of finding work would have been far higher. According to Hannah, she had set out for Tralee early on Saturday and met a prospective employer. She had set out on foot, and it had taken her several hours to get to the town. Once there, she realised the wages on offer were too small, so she declined the job. However, it was too late to come back to Killorglin. She spent the night in Tralee and set out for home at 7 a.m. on Easter Sunday morning. It took her seven hours to walk home, and she got back to Killorglin around 2 p.m., so she could not have committed the murder that morning.

However, Hannah did not know that she had been spotted

in the townland of Cullinamore on Easter Saturday evening around 10 p.m. She might have gone to Tralee, but she was back the night before Margaret O'Sullivan met her gruesome end. Her alibi was a lie.

Garda Inspector Ryan, based in nearby Killarney, formally arrested Hannah Flynn. At the subsequent remand hearing in Tralee, on 14 April, he told the court that she had made no comment when arrested. He described the horrific injuries suffered by Mrs O'Sullivan. Hannah Flynn sat passively through the proceedings and showed no signs of emotion. The *Irish Times* reported: 'The accused seemed indifferent to the proceedings, and asked no questions of the inspector.'

Hannah Flynn was held for nearly a year before her trial opened. The trial was held before the Dublin Commission on 27 February, and was presided over by Mr Justice Pim. Hannah Flynn never made any admissions about her involvement in the murder and never gave any explanation of what drove her to commit such savagery that morning. She didn't make a statement to the Gardaí, and she offered no explanation to the court. But even without that, there was no doubt about the outcome. The defence did try to claim that Hannah was too feeble-minded to be held accountable for her actions. The defence of insanity is always a difficult one to play, and high levels of proof are required. Ms Flynn certainly appeared pathetic to the court. She muttered her replies to questions and had to be asked repeatedly to speak up and speak clearly. Yet the judge did not accept that she was so feeble-minded as to be not accountable for her actions. The insanity defence failed.

Throughout the proceedings, Ms Flynn showed no emotion and no signs of remorse. After hearing the evidence, the jury retired. But they returned after just half an hour, unable to reach a verdict. Mr Justice Pim sent them back to deliberate some more. Within an hour, they trooped back to the court, and the foreman passed the verdict along to the judge. Hannah Flynn had been found guilty of murder.

The jury recommended that mercy be shown to her, on

account of her circumstances, and her clearly subnormal mental state. The judge noted their recommendation, but did not act on it. He donned the black cap – traditional in capital cases – and sentenced Ms Flynn to death. She was to be taken back to Mountjoy Prison and hanged.

Finally, the accused showed some sign of emotion. As she heard the death sentence pronounced, she broke down. Sobbing, she had to be assisted from the court.

The death sentence was rare in Ireland, even back then. The country did not have a hangman and used the services of the Pierrepoint family in the UK. The sentence was normally carried out within a few weeks of conviction.

However, on 6 March 1924, the Secretary to the Ministry of Home Affairs (now the Department of Justice) announced that mercy would be shown. In a statement, he said, 'In the case of Hannah Flynn, a prisoner in Mountjoy Prison under sentence of death, the Governor-General has been pleased, on the advice of the Executive Council, to commute the sentence to penal servitude for life.'

Hannah Flynn served more than a decade in Mountjoy. To her dying day, she never admitted her involvement in the horrific and senseless murder of Margaret O'Sullivan.

3

IRELAND'S JACK THE RIPPER

David O'Shea and the murder of Ellen O'Sullivan

RATHMORE IS A nowhere town in the middle of nowhere. Nestling along the Cork–Kerry border, between Millstreet and Killarney, it is a tiny hamlet, barely more than a thriving village. It is not too far from either Killarney or Millstreet, but it feels like a million miles from anywhere. Even today, it has a population of just 600.

Rathmore nestles in the heart of the Sliabh Luachra region. This mountainous upland is famous for its music and culture, and for producing more poets per square mile than any other corner of Ireland, including Aodhagán Ó Rathaille and Eoghan Rua Ó Súilleabháin, who were both born in the village.

A little over 80 years ago, Rathmore became famous for something else: it was the scene of a horrific murder, so brutal that the trial judge compared it to the work of Jack the Ripper. The victim was a young dairymaid of the village who was beaten to death, then dragged across the fields and dumped near a stream.

The post-mortem revealed that though she died '*virgo intacta*', she had been 'outraged' before her death. It was a trial that gripped the nation, and a huge crowd, mainly women, stood outside Mountjoy Prison on the day that the murderer was hanged.

Yet it all began rather innocuously. The victim had been missing for the best part of a week before anyone even began to search for her.

Ellen O'Sullivan had grown up on a farm at Knocknaloman, near Rathmore. She had four sisters and a brother, and she left school in her early teens, like most of the population at that time. She stayed in the district and got a job as a dairymaid in the local creamery. Over the coming decade, she rose to be chief dairymaid and butter maker. She continued to live at home, but spent occasional nights in her aunt's house in Rathmore town. Her mother had recently passed away, leaving her father a widower.

Ellen was an attractive young woman. She stood about 5 ft 5 in. and was slim but shapely ('well nourished and well developed', in the words of the autopsy), with dark brown hair. She cycled into work every day on a bicycle that was showing its age: it had a distinctive rattle when she rode it.

In her early 20s, she began seeing a young man from a few miles away. Jeremiah Cronin was a farmer, but he also had an interest in cars. Rather unusually for the time, he had a car of his own, and he also occasionally carried out repairs for others, to supplement the farm income.

The couple had been going out about two years. No announcement had been made, but in time they would become engaged, then marry. Arranged marriages were still common in rural Ireland, particularly in Kerry, with young girls regularly being matched with withered old bachelor farmers. But Ellen was having none of that: she would marry for love.

Sunday, 8 February 1931 was a busy day for the 25-year-old woman. She went to an early Mass with the family, and then she accompanied her father to two local funerals. After that, they went home for lunch. It was a dull wintery day, but around four o'clock Ellen decided to go out visiting. She took her bicycle and rode into the town to call on her cousin Kathleen

Moynihan, who lived at the far end. It was the last time her father, Denis, was to see her alive.

She arrived safely at her cousin's house and spent a good two hours there, finally leaving at 6.30 p.m. Strangely, she had not gone to the dance that day in the village, even though her boyfriend Jeremiah had gone there with two friends, Eugene Murphy and Timothy Kelleher, whom he had brought in his car. Ellen borrowed a book from her cousin: *The Gamblers* by William Le Queux. Le Queux, completely forgotten now, was the James Patterson of his era, churning out 150 thrillers and espionage novels of dubious quality. Kathleen went with her and they walked out into the village, Ellen wheeling her bicycle. Jeremiah Cronin was waiting at the bottom of the village; he had come out of the dance to meet his sweetheart. One of his friends, Timothy Kelleher, had driven Cronin's car out of the village to Shinagh Cross and was waiting for him there. The two girls joined Cronin and chatted for a few minutes, and then Kathleen went back home. Ellen and Jeremiah began to stroll at their leisure back towards her house. It was about 6.45 p.m., cold and dark, with the temperature not much above zero. But at least it wasn't raining.

The walk normally took half an hour. They could have gone faster, but it was a few minutes they could spend alone, so they took their time and savoured the stolen moments. Ellen wheeled her bicycle, while Jeremiah walked beside her. They made the trip regularly: perhaps once a fortnight over the two years of their courtship. Other people were out; they met several people along the way. One of the final people they passed was Timothy Hickey, a neighbour of Ellen's. They said hello as they passed.

Finally they stopped near Hickey's cottage, where they chatted for another 15 minutes. Then Cronin turned and walked back to Shinagh Cross, where Kelleher was waiting for him with the car. He hopped in and drove the seven miles home.

Meanwhile, Ellen turned down a dark country lane to walk the few hundred yards to her home. The only one to ever see her alive again was the man who stalked and killed her.

Ellen never got home that night – but, strangely, no one in the house raised the alarm when she did not appear. As her father later explained at the inquest, 'She used to stay with her aunt in Rathmore, and we thought she was staying there.'

Denis O'Sullivan was in Rathmore the following day and called in to Ellen's aunt, but they did not speak of Ellen. He assumed she was staying there and was out at work, so he passed no remark. There was no opportunity to ask for her at the creamery either, as he sent his milk to a different creamery.

The following day, Tuesday, he discussed Ellen with his other daughters, and they told him not to worry; she was staying in town with her aunt. The weather was too bad for any of them to walk into town to check on the girl. 'The day was so bad that no one could go until Wednesday, or until Thursday evening,' he said.

By then, they realised Ellen was missing. She had not been staying with relatives in town. No one had seen her since the previous Sunday. A niece of Denis's went to the creamery and found she had not been at work that week. She had never been absent for such a long period. This struck her father as peculiar, but as he said, 'The times are idle, and we did not take much trouble about it.'

At that point, when Ellen had already been missing for three days, no one seemed unduly worried. However, they notified the Gardaí on Thursday and began a search for her all the same. The first thing they found was her bicycle, lying against a ditch about 250 yards from Shinagh Cross. Now they were worried.

By Friday, the Gardaí were being helped by several volunteers from the town and parish, and were scouring the fields and lanes. The breakthrough came on Saturday, when John T. Murphy and Patrick Donovan, two of the searchers, spotted something under the furze bushes near the banks of the river. They were searching along the banks of the Owngar River, which forms the border between counties Cork and Kerry. They were on the Kerry side, about two miles from Rathmore town.

One of them saw something dark under some briars and bracken. Bending down, he realised it was human hair. He pulled the bushes aside, uncovered the body of Ellen and cried for help. A Garda was quickly on the scene and helped them pull the body out. Ellen had been lying on furze, and more furze had been thrown over her to conceal her. Although she had been there for nearly a week, the cold weather had prevented any substantial decomposition.

Sergeant Murphy was the first Garda on the scene. He discovered that the young woman had been seriously assaulted, and her clothing was in disarray. She was naked from the waist down, apart from a badly torn stocking on her left leg and a full stocking on her right one. Her overcoat was torn at the back and stained with mud. She was wearing a pullover, slip, corset and chemise, all stained and tattered.

A subsequent examination by Dr Collins of Rathmore showed a mark, apparently blood, on the left shoulder of the victim's pullover. There was a cut an inch and a half long on the girl's head. A soft swelling extended six inches from side to side over the head. It was caused by blood clotted under the skin, which was the cause of death. The swelling had probably been caused by a blow from a blunt object, such as a heavy stone. There was also a wound over her left eye and a slight bruise over her right eye. Another bruise extended from the centre of her cheek to her right ear. The doctor thought that this had been caused by two fingers violently gripping the girl's cheek. However, he saw no evidence of strangulation. Ellen O'Sullivan had been bludgeoned to death.

The doctor added, rather quaintly: 'The girl had been outraged immediately before death.' The outrage had been partial. She had been *virgo intacta* at the time of her murder. Her attacker had tried to rape her and beat her to death during the attempt. According to the medical evidence, he had then tried to rape her again, as she was unconscious or already dead. It was a truly horrific crime.

Superintendent John Galtly and Chief Superintendent Galligan were in charge of the murder, assisted by Inspector Mahony. They examined the scene and noticed that there were marks on the ground, and evidence of flattened grass and plants. It was apparent that something heavy had been dragged along the ground. It could only have been the body of the dead girl. They followed the trail, which led back to a fence dividing two fields. Along the trail they found discarded items of clothing.

They also found items on the Cork side of the river, including the girl's hat, handkerchief and belt. These had been left on some gravel in the corner of the field, which was just off the road leading to Ellen's home. More items were uncovered over the coming days, including a shoe on top of a hedge running by the main road to Shinagh Cross. The book she had borrowed from her cousin was torn in two. The title page and cover were found in the grass at the side of the road, while the body of the book was hidden in a nearby field.

It became obvious that there had been a ferocious struggle, before the body was dragged for over 200 yards on the Cork side of the river and then dropped over a small cliff into the river. There was five feet of water in the river at that point, but nearby was a shallow ford with a small island in the middle. Somehow the killer had dragged the body across the river, possibly using the island, then raised it and dragged it to the boggy area on the Kerry side, where it was eventually found. As Ellen weighed 10 st., whoever killed her had been strong and evidently knew his way around the isolated and desolate locality.

Some of Ellen's undergarments were missing, but most were recovered by Gardaí over the coming days. However, it took until 9 March to find her knickers. They were finally recovered under a fence on her father's farm, rolled up in a ball and stuffed into a hole in the grass. A car cushion with some stuffing attached was found nearby.

But the Gardaí did not wait that long to make an arrest. For the crime of murdering Ellen O'Sullivan, there could only be one suspect. Her boyfriend was arrested and charged with murder. Thirty-five-year-old Jeremiah Cronin, of Cloonbannin, was taken to Cork City Gaol and then brought before a sitting of Killarney Court. He was charged with murder.

Superintendent Galtly told the court that he had arrested Cronin on Saturday, 14 February, at Rathmore Garda Station. When charged, Cronin had said nothing. The superintendent said that the Gardaí were still pursuing a number of lines of inquiry and they attached importance to 'certain information' given to them by a farmer. Unknown to the court, this farmer was David O'Shea. He had a smallholding adjoining the O'Sullivans and was their nearest neighbour. He was not considered a suspect; the Gardaí were happy that they had the murderer in custody. Something about O'Shea's answers did not quite gel; however, he was able to give a satisfactory account of his movements on the night of the murder, so that was that.

At the request of the Gardaí, Mr Cronin was remanded in custody for a week, to allow them to continue to build their case. While Cronin was held in Cork, an inquest was swiftly convened. It was held on 18 February in Hassett's Hotel, just a few days after the body was discovered. On the same day, a large crowd gathered in Rathmore. People came on sidecars, in cars and on foot, crowding the village. Blinds were drawn in nearly every house, as everyone expected the funeral to take place that day. In that, they were disappointed; it was decided to hold the funeral the following day, after the inquest.

'This is a cruel and brutal murder, and it has profoundly shocked the people here and all over the country,' said the coroner, local doctor and senator Dr William O'Sullivan. 'It is a terrible blot on the fair fame of the south, and I am sorry to be here today to investigate it. It is a disgrace, and I hope that the perpetrator will be brought to justice, and that he will get fully what he merits, because if the full facts of the evidence could be disclosed to you here today you would be as profoundly shocked as I was when I heard it. I am sorry that I cannot read the pathologist's report for you. It would shock any civilised community, I may tell you.'

Denis O'Sullivan, the elderly father of the victim, appeared visibly upset during the proceedings. The coroner said to him, 'We are sorry for you, Mr O'Sullivan. It is a terrible thing that a man of your years should be deprived of your daughter in the full bloom of her life, and in such circumstances. We are very deeply grieved.'

Mr O'Sullivan told the inquest, 'On February the eighth she came along with me to attend two funerals, and then we returned home. She left the house some time in the evening. It would be about four, and that was the last I saw of her alive. She used to go somewhere every Sunday evening. She used to stay with her aunt in Rathmore, and we thought she was staying there.'

'Did you make any inquiries when she did not return home?' asked Superintendent Galtly.

'I was in Rathmore on the next day and was in her aunt's house, but we did not speak about Ellen. You see I thought she was there all the time. I think I spoke to my daughters about it and I think they said that she must be at her aunt's house. The day was so bad that no one could go until Wednesday, or until Thursday evening.'

'Then it was Thursday evening you heard of her being missing?'

'Yes, it was Thursday evening. One of my other daughters went into the village on Thursday evening, and found that the girl had not been attending to her business during the week. A niece of mine went up to the creamery, and she was not there at all.'

'Did that strike you as being peculiar?'

'The times are idle, and we did not take much trouble about it,' said the widower. After confirming identification, the inquest was adjourned.

Ellen O'Sullivan was laid to rest the following day in Millstreet Cemetery, after Mass at Ballynally Church. A large crowd attended. The Gardaí, not content to rest on their laurels, appealed for anyone with information to come forward and help them. They decided to interview all the men of the parish.

As the *Irish Times* reported, 'The guards and detectives today searched for further clues. They continue to take statements; but so far as is known no new clues, excepting those found yesterday, have come into their possession. They have cut down the hedge of furze where the girl was supposed to have been attacked first, and where her shoe was found.'

Although they had a man in custody, the Gardaí knew there were problems with their case. One neighbour had been strangely evasive about his movements and had not come forward when the Gardaí asked the men of the region to call into the barracks to account for their movements. He might not have heard the appeal, but it was broadcast at the Sunday Mass, and they knew his sister, who lived with him, had seen the notice. David O'Shea was becoming a person of interest.

The search of the surrounding fields was intensified. It emerged that Ellen O'Sullivan's dog, of which she was very fond, had also disappeared. But the Gardaí were inclined to believe this had nothing to do with the murder of the girl. It was just coincidence.

General Eoin O'Duffy, the chief commissioner of the Gardaí, was keeping a very close eye on the investigation, which was causing a bit of a national sensation. He scheduled a visit to Rathmore to rally the troops and speak to the investigating officers.

Finally, on Tuesday, 24 February, at a special sitting of the court in Mallow, the Gardaí acknowledged that they had arrested the wrong man. Jeremiah Cronin was discharged from custody. The application for release was made by Superintendent Galtly, who said that the investigation indicated that Jeremiah Cronin was not the guilty person. As Mr Cronin stepped down from the dock, he was applauded by the crowded court, and many of his friends shook hands with him.

Solicitor D.E. Ferguson from Kanturk, representing Mr Cronin, said that the victim was his intended wife. On the night of the murder, he walked her to her home. 'But hardly had he left her when a devil in human shape assassinated her, and subsequently, by his actions, set out to implicate Cronin, whose account of his movements, fortunately for him, had been verified in every detail,' said Ferguson.

'Cronin goes a free man today. But his life has been clouded and I think he deserves the sympathy of everyone. I have known his family and acted for them for years, and I have known him personally since his boyhood. He is a splendid type of young Irish farmer, with nothing against him, hard-working and industrious. The girl who was to be his wife now lies dead at the hand of the assassin, and Cronin was charged with her murder – a tragedy upon a tragedy.

'The assassin endeavoured to make a case that would damn Cronin. He brought her bicycle to a certain spot in order deliberately to implicate Cronin. There was however a divine providence over all, and the links in the chain that the devil endeavoured to forge against Cronin will be forged into a chain against himself that will ultimately bring him to expiate his crime on the scaffold.'

The solicitor also explained that he had not applied for bail for his innocent client, because Mr Cronin had instructed him to do nothing that would embarrass the Gardaí or interfere with their investigation: 'He told me that if he were to suffer jail for ten years, or for life, he would gladly do it to bring the murderer to justice.'

It was not long before Gardaí arrested a new suspect. On Thursday, 26 February, David O'Shea, described as a labourer, of Knocknaloman, Rathmore, was charged with murder at Millstreet Barracks and brought before the court.

The court heard from Superintendent P. O'Sullivan of Kanturk that he had visited O'Shea's house on 15 February, about two days after the body was discovered. O'Shea lived quite close to the victim. Superintendent O'Sullivan was not there to arrest the accused, only to interview him, as O'Shea was under no suspicion. The accused made a voluntary statement. He was represented by Killarney solicitor T. O'Shea, who immediately objected to that statement being entered into evidence. He said that when the statement was taken his client was not a free agent, as there were numerous Gardaí all over the town and surrounding countryside, and everyone was under suspicion; therefore it was wrong of the superintendent to say that O'Shea had not been under suspicion at the time the statement was taken. Neither had he been cautioned.

Mr Justice Gallagher, the judge, said that a witness only had to be cautioned if he said anything in the statement that was likely to incriminate himself.

Mr T. O'Shea replied, 'I hold that my client was not a free agent when he made that statement, and further, this man was treated in a frightfully cruel way by some of the officers who were dealing with this case. I take it that it was all done in the heat of their zeal.'

The judge disallowed the objection, and the statement was read to the court. O'Shea said he left his house around 5.30 p.m. on his own and went as far as Shinagh Cross. On the road, he met a number of people and greeted them. Among those he met were a tall man and a girl, who had a bicycle with her.

'The girl was nearest to me, and he nearest the ditch,' the statement went on. 'I would say he had his arm around the girl. I could not hear what they said.'

O'Shea reached Shinagh Cross about seven o'clock. He did not go to his father's house, though he had intended to. He stopped at Shinagh until about eight.

'I stood and walked in the vicinity of the cross. It would only take me five minutes to go to my father's house. I saw no motor car at the cross, nor did I see anyone about it. I did not see anyone. It would be 8 p.m. or up to it when I started for my home. I know the short cut across the river, and I did not go that way since summer, nor was I down there on February eight. I am positive that I met no one between Shinagh Cross and my own house on my return. It was a calm dry night. I am sure I met no men.

'The last time I saw Ellen O'Sullivan was on Sunday, 8 February, at 3 p.m., going home past my house in a horse and trap. She saw me also. I did not see her since. I was in Paddy Collins's cottage last Friday night, and Johnny Long drew up about the missing girl, but it was passed off at that.'

The statement added that O'Shea did not participate in the search for the missing girl, because no one asked him to.

Immediately there was controversy over the statement, and subsequent ones made by O'Shea, with his solicitor saying that one Garda had banged the table with his hand and threatened that O'Shea would hang, as a result of which he felt intimidated into accounting for his movements. The Gardaí also denied that the interrogation went on until 5 a.m. or that O'Shea had been drinking before he was questioned. However, all the statements made by O'Shea were admitted into evidence.

The trial opened at the Central Criminal Court in Dublin on 10 June, with O'Shea entering a not guilty plea.

Barrister Vincent Rice, prosecuting, said that Ellen O'Sullivan had been murdered within a quarter of a mile of the spot from where she parted with her fiancé and headed for home. 'She never reached home,' he said. 'She was murdered on the way. No alarm was raised, for she had a married sister living not far off, and it did not occur to her parents that anything had happened when she did not come home. After a long interval a search was made for her through the wild and desolate countryside, which was covered with furze and scrub. Two civilians who took part in the search noticed something under furze. It was the body of Ellen O'Sullivan. When you hear the evidence as to the condition of the girl's body you will come to the conclusion that she was murdered with most extraordinary ferocity. She was outraged.'

The cause of death was given as a cut on the left side of her head some inches above the ear, inflicted with a heavy blunt instrument.

The court heard that a number of items of clothing were recovered by investigators over the days following the discovery of the body. These included the items missing from Ellen – but they also included a black legging, which came from a man. The legging was worn on the lower leg, to keep the trousers clean and mud-free. Not everyone wore leggings, but the defendant, O'Shea, did. He had two sets of leggings: a brown set for weekdays and a good black set for Sundays. A number of witnesses had seen him earlier that day wearing the black leggings. Yet when Gardaí searched his house, they could not find those leggings. O'Shea and his sister both said that the legging found near the murder did not belong to him.

Another item found was a grey sock. It was downstream from the point where the body had been thrown into the water. When Gardaí searched the home of O'Shea, they found a sock in the prisoner's bedroom, stuffed into a milk tankard.

The court heard that the Gardaí decided to use a bit of subterfuge when they found the sock. They withdrew from the house, telling O'Shea that the interview was over. They left him, but unknown to him, one Garda remained behind and hid under a bed to see what would happen.

Garda John Keane, from Killarney, heard Kate O'Shea, the sister of the accused, saying, 'My God, where is the legging? Did they get it?'

David O'Shea replied, 'See if it is behind the box. Look, quick. It is here.'

Kate O'Shea then said, 'Rush, quick, take it away and burn it.'

The hidden Garda heard footsteps leaving the kitchen and going out to the yard. O'Shea returned a few minutes later and said, 'It is all right now.'

His sister answered, 'Wasn't it the luck of God they didn't take it away? We were ruined, and that was a nice guard that was looking for it. We were lucky the others didn't see it.'

Later, David O'Shea said, 'What did you do with the sock?'

Kate replied: 'I was looking for it all day and could not find it. My God, I must burn it if I find it.' She did not know that the Gardaí had the sock at that point. She went on, 'They must have some suspicion for you. Do you think they will come for you tonight? They might come for you in the middle of the night.'

Her brother answered, 'Let them. They will have to prove it. I gave a good account of myself in the statement I gave.'

The statement was the one in which O'Shea had outlined his movements on the night of the murder. He had walked to Shinagh Cross, where five roads meet. He had met a number of people along the way. He had remained there for a period and then had gone home. The problem was, he had only been spotted on the way towards Shinagh Cross. No one at all remembered actually seeing him there. Several people who passed the cross specifically remembered seeing no one there. And O'Shea, in his statement, failed to mention the car of Jeremiah Cronin, containing his friends Timothy Kelleher and Eugene Murphy. The car had been at Shinagh Cross for a period while the friends awaited the return of Mr Cronin, before they drove home.

Detective Tormey told the court that he was in David O'Shea's house on 18 February with another Garda. He noticed that O'Shea's hands bore marks of scratches, which were dried up. The accused said that the scratches occurred while he was cutting furze.

Kathleen (Kate) O'Shea, the sister of the defendant, said she lived with him and their mother on a smallholding close to the victim. She said that herself and her mother both went to bed around 8 p.m. on the night of the murder. Roughly half an hour later, she heard footsteps in the house; it was her brother returning.

She denied having the conversation that Garda Keane said he had heard while he was hidden under a bed in the house.

She was cross-examined on why her brother had not voluntarily gone forward to make a statement to the Gardaí. She said that she had seen a notice asking all the men of the district to go to the barracks, but she did not tell her brother about it, and he did not go.

'If you were perfectly innocent and he was perfectly innocent, so far as you know, why should he not go to the barracks?' asked Mr Justice Hanna, the trial judge.

'I don't know,' replied Ms O'Shea.

David O'Shea's solicitor, Mr Thomas O'Donnell, addressed the jury after the evidence had been heard. He made much of the confusion in some witness statements over the exact times people had spotted other people, including the victim and Mr O'Shea. 'It is easy to make confusion with regard to times even with people accustomed to having watches in their pockets. It is still easier in the case of people with the mentality of the prisoner in the dock,' he said. He continued, 'The state say that O'Shea met Cronin and Ellen O'Sullivan, whom he knew, and that then, by some extraordinary perversion of mind, and some unexplainable act of malice, he, the friend of the father, his co-worker and friend of the girl – who had opportunities of meeting her morning, noon and night – suddenly decided to follow her for the first time, and to murder her in the brutal fashion in which we know she was murdered.'

He asked the jury to disregard the evidence of Garda Keane, gathered from under the bed, which he described as contemptible and mean. 'It is the most extraordinary and unbelievable ever made in a court of law – on the face of it, unbelievable,' he said.

'Why would O'Shea do this murder? Murder, in the mind of any civilised Christian man, is the worst and the last form of brutality. It is only conceivable of man – if he is not drunk or insane – when some desperate and overpowering passion drives him to act as if he were insane. There must be some motive – anger, spite of long standing, desperate will or jealousy.

'Where was one of these passions – jealousy, anger or hatred – that should arouse the prisoner to do this dastardly deed to the girl with whom he had been friends and to the daughter of the man who was his best friend in the district? From beginning to end of the case there has not been one shadow of a motive for the prisoner's committing the crime,' he concluded.

Barrister Cecil Lavery summed up for the state. He said that it was obvious that the murder had been committed by some person living in the locality and familiar with it. The prisoner met that description. He said that it was a week before the alarm was raised, and this gave the murderer plenty of time to cover his tracks, by moving Ellen's bicycle towards Shinagh Cross and away from the scene of the murder. This drew the search in the wrong direction and lost precious days.

He pointed out that, though O'Shea denied wearing black leggings such as the one recovered near the murder scene, five witnesses had seen him wearing those leggings on the day of the murder.

When Mr Justice Hanna summed up before sending the jury out to deliberate, he made it clear what he thought of the crime. He compared it to the work of Jack the Ripper, and made mention of necrophilia and sexual perversion. 'This crime is known to criminologists as a lust murder,' the judge began. 'To those who have not studied crime, this crime seems not only appalling, but incomprehensible. But to the scientist it is known that a characteristic of crimes which are the result of sexual lust is their appalling, atrocious character. The association of cruelty or murder with lust is a sexual perversion called by scientists sadism. A lust murder is the result of abnormal sexual excitement, which has murder as its main or intended object, or uses the murder as an artificial stimulus.

'We have examples of this, not in the history of this country, but in England, in the Whitechapel murders of the eighties, committed by Jack the Ripper. The person who is seized with the impulse of murder seldom ceases short of the murder, but they have to go a step further to approach the horrible crime which was committed in this case.

'In the olden days – and not so long ago – people did not allow young girls to walk alone in lonely roads, but now they have claimed their emancipation, and they go alone in ignorance of what might lie in store for them,' said Mr Justice Hanna.

He then commented on the demeanour of the accused, saying,

'You have seen the manner in which O'Shea answered the questions in the box, sometimes taking half a minute to answer, sometimes not answering, possibly forgetting it. The man was in a peculiar position, and you cannot expect him to show the same glibness and alertness of mind as other people. You should take into account the fact that there was no inconsistency in his story.'

Commenting on the evidence gathered by Garda Keane, he said, 'It is sometimes said that the police do things that are not according to the rules of the game. Criminals have no rules of the game. In this case the Gardaí were quite entitled to put one or two Gardaí under the bed. It was unfortunate that they did not put two Gardaí there, because it would have provided corroboration for Garda Keane's evidence.'

The judge finished his summing up at 5.15 p.m. and sent the jury out to begin their deliberations. They returned to the court at 7.30 p.m. with a question. It was an interesting one: why had the prisoner not presented evidence as to his good character? 'Is there any definite reason why no evidence was given of the accused character by his parish priest, or any other responsible person?' asked the foreman.

Judge Hanna replied that it was the right of the accused to call witnesses to speak to his general reputation. It was not the job of the state to do this. The accused also had the right not to call character witnesses, and nothing could be read into it either way.

The jury retired again, this time for 45 minutes. They returned at 8.15 p.m. and handed their verdict to the judge. He read it. David O'Shea had been found guilty of murder. The jury did add a rider to the verdict, expressing their opinion that the crime had been unpremeditated and committed during a period of mental abnormality. They recommended that special consideration should be given to this.

When the verdict was announced, O'Shea collapsed in the dock. He had to be supported as the judge asked him whether he had anything to say. O'Shea looked up at the judge and said forcefully, 'I am not guilty, sir.'

Justice Hanna put on the traditional black cap and pronounced sentence of death. The date of the execution was set for 8 July. After a trial that had lasted four days, O'Shea had less than a month to live.

His defence team immediately swung into action. The judge had refused leave to appeal, so they went to the High Court to get that overthrown. The hearing on whether an appeal would be allowed lasted almost as long as the trial itself. The legal team argued for three days. They had a number of grounds for asking for an appeal. They said that the judge had misdirected the jury on the question of character witnesses. They also said that the comparison of the crime with the murders of Jack the Ripper had prejudiced the jury against O'Shea. But, in the end, leave to appeal was turned down. A new execution date was set, for Tuesday, 4 August.

Early that morning, David O'Shea was woken and a Mass was celebrated in his cell. Then he was given his final breakfast. By 7.30 a.m., a large crowd had gathered outside the stern doors of Mountjoy Prison. About 200 people – most of them women – waited in silence. At 8 a.m., the door creaked open and a warden came out. He pinned the notice on the door. The ultimate sentence of the law had been carried out. David O'Shea had been hanged by the neck until dead. The state had avenged the murder of Ellen O'Sullivan.

4

THE COP KILLER

Charlie Kerins and the murder of Detective Sergeant Denis O'Brien

ON THE MORNING of 9 September 1942, Detective Sergeant Denis (Dinny) O'Brien said goodbye to his wife, Annie, and left his house in Ballyboden, near Rathfarnham, Dublin. He walked out the front door, exchanged a few words with his father-in-law and then stepped into his car, pulling the door closed behind him. Then he switched on the engine and drove down the lane from his house to the gate and the main road.

They lived in a bungalow set on an acre of land off the main Rathfarnham to Ballyboden road. It was a secluded home, especially in a city, bounded by high walls and with a 100-yard-long driveway. At one point, the driveway turned sharply as it crossed a small stream. It was a perfect country retreat, yet part of the suburbs too, and he shared it with Annie and their two daughters.

Both girls had already left the house for school. They attended the nearby St Louis Convent. Just before he stepped into his small saloon car for the drive to Dublin Castle, Detective O'Brien had stopped for a brief chat with his father-in-law, Michael Cooney. They discussed preparing a bed for sowing onions.

Then the detective got into the car and drove down the driveway.

Detective O'Brien was almost a legend in the Special Branch. He was one of the men who targeted the IRA, and during the war years he was very busy. He had been involved in a few armed incidents in which IRA men lost their lives. Therefore he was a target for the organisation.

According to historian Tim Pat Coogan in *The IRA: A History*, 'An iron-gloved approach to the IRA was the order of the day, with vigorous raids and interrogations. As a result, relations between individual IRA men and the Special Branch became understandably strained. The IRA came to regard the Special Branch as a greater enemy than the British Crown.'

O'Brien was a sensible man; he knew the dangers. He was constantly vigilant, but he was not expecting an attack so near to home. He had just reached the bend in the driveway, where the drive passed over a small stream, when the first shot rang out. O'Brien could see he was being fired upon from the field that adjoined the avenue leading from his home. The windshield of his car was shattered by two rounds, as were the side windows, but both shots missed the detective. He slammed on the brakes and jumped out of the car, crouching low. He managed to get hold of his pistol. He ran down towards the gate, probably hoping to use the four-foot wall there as cover to return fire.

He kept moving down the avenue – and away from his house. He fired a number of shots into the field. But as he reached the gate, two or three men suddenly appeared on the main road, armed with Thompson machine guns. Nicknamed the tommy gun, the Thompson was an American sub-machine gun first produced in 1919. It fired a .45 round at between 600 and 1,500 rounds a minute. Nearly 300 of them had been brought to Ireland in 1921 by Harry Boland. They were used at the end of the War of Independence, and during the civil war. Despite their impressive statistics, tommy guns were not very accurate. They were only useful over distances of 50 m or less, and had proved of little use during the civil war.

But the men lying in wait for Detective O'Brien were far closer than 50 m; they were only feet away from him. He probably never even spotted them. They opened fire immediately. One was close to the gate, while the other was directly across the road and firing straight through the bars of the gate. As Dinny O'Brien prepared to return fire, a round from one of the Thompson guns caught him in the back of the head, killing him instantly. He fell to the ground in a pool of blood.

Back in the house, his wife, Annie, heard the two shots ring out, and she knew her husband was in trouble. Then she heard the rapid rattle of machine-gun fire. She ran from the house in time to see three men running towards Bolton Hall Lodge, nearby. Two of the men were dressed in trench coats and caps. 'The other coward – for you could not call them men – had no cap,' she later recalled.

She couldn't see her husband, so she began searching the avenue. She found him lying by the gate, dead, with his revolver by his hand. Screaming, she knelt down by his side. 'While kneeling by my husband's side two men came down the road on bicycles and flashed by me, followed closely by a third man. They were the three men I had seen earlier,' she said. One of the men had an object wrapped in sacking clipped to the side of his bicycle – presumably one of the machine guns. The men disappeared down the road, their bloody work done.

There are so many motivations for murder, and often that motivation only makes sense to the killer. We kill out of envy, out of greed, out of desire to keep our secrets or protect our loved ones. We kill to get out of relationships, or to get what we feel should be ours anyway. We kill in drunkenness or in anger. But always when we kill, we understand that we are doing wrong. However strong our motivation might be to us, some part of us realises that we are still killers and have stepped beyond the pale of civilised society.

One of the few exceptions is political murder. When we kill over politics, we can feel self-righteous over the slaughter and hold our heads up high, at least among those who share our views.

When a detective was gunned down in his own driveway, with his wife only a short distance away, it showed the IRA in very poor light and severely dented the organisation. It lost them a lot of public support. However, there was a sizable minority that backed the killers and regarded them as heroes. Two men were charged with the murder. Both were from Kerry. One was acquitted; one was hanged. The man who was eventually convicted of the murder of Detective Dinny O'Brien was widely lauded in his home county. An estate in Tralee is named after him, and his local football team changed their name in his honour. Cop killer Charlie Kerins is a hero to many.

To tell the story properly, we must start a generation earlier, at the foundation of the Irish Free State. During the First World War, a feeling grew among certain sections of the population that England's pain was Ireland's opportunity. While the old enemy was busy with a war in Europe, there was a chance to strike and gain our freedom. The Easter Rising was the result. What the rebels forgot was that Britain was on a war footing and inured to blood and hardship. The London government sent in gunboats and crushed the rebellion viciously and decisively.

The Easter Rising had no popular mandate, but once the leaders were executed, sympathy turned to support, and by 1919, the War of Independence had broken out. After the losses in the trenches, Britain did not have the stomach for a protracted guerrilla campaign, and in 1921 a settlement was reached, granting freedom to most of the country – apart from the six counties in the North. This started a bitter civil war that was particularly vicious in Kerry, perhaps as a result of the presence of Dublin soldiers in the county, who had no ties to the land and who did not hesitate to kill their fellow Irishmen, as we saw earlier in the Ballyseedy, Countess Bridge and Bahagh massacres.

When the pro-Treaty side won and the weapons were laid down, bitter resentments continued to fester under the surface. It was a fertile ground for dissent, and the IRA remained a factor in Irish politics for a further 80 years. Their importance (and the number of active volunteers they could call upon) waxed and waned over the years, but they never went away.

It was against this background that Charlie Kerins grew up in Kerry. He was born in Caherina, Tralee. His father, Tom, was a builder, but had a reputation in the town as a knowledgeable and thoughtful local historian. His mother, Joanna Griffin, was a native of nearby Blennerville. She died when Charlie was still young.

The boy was lively and bright. He went to the local Balloonagh Mercy Convent, then to the Christian Brothers on Edward Street, Tralee, where he completed his primary education. Most people back then finished school after primary, but at the age of 13 Charlie won a Kerry County Council scholarship, which allowed him to attend secondary school with his fees paid. He moved to the Christian Brothers School on The Green, and also attended the Jeffers Institute in Tralee. One of his tutors at the Institute was Fr Donal Herlihy. Herlihy was only a few years older than Kerins, but the young Cork priest had seen horrors. As a boy, he had been in a crowd of school children when the Black and Tans opened fire indiscriminately on them. He had been seriously injured. Perhaps his tale influenced the political thoughts of the maturing Kerins?

Charlie passed his Intermediate Certificate and then took his matriculation exam, which he also passed. This would have allowed him to move on to university, but the costs of that were prohibitive. Instead, the young man did a commercial course and then took up employment in Fennell's radio business in Tralee. Radio was new technology then. RTÉ (then known as 2RN) began broadcasting experimentally in 1925, and radio was both a novelty and the cutting edge of technology.

Kerins had good prospects. He was a young man with an education and a job, and he was also a dashing sports hero. At the age of 21 he had been a full-back with his local club, the O'Rahillys. His plucky play helped them secure the county football title in 1939. Kerry is football mad, and the players were treated like gods.

However, Kerins was steeped in republican values and was living in a county where the republican movement had deep roots. When the Second World War broke out in 1939, the IRA saw it as an opportunity to expand their operations and continue their war against the British. They began a recruitment drive, and in 1940, Kerins took the oath and was sworn in as a member. He had been hovering on the periphery of the movement since he was about 17.

The government were concerned about the increasing strength of the IRA and were anxious to quash the movement. Under the Emergency Powers Act, they began to move on the IRA, arresting and interning republicans at the Curragh. This forced IRA volunteers to go undercover. They stayed on the run and relied on sympathisers for food and sustenance. Charlie Kerins was one of those who found themselves on the run. Just 21, he had gone from football hero to wanted man.

While he was on the run, he was busy recruiting and strengthening the movement. The IRA had been disorganised before the war, but was in the throes of a reorganisation. It was particularly active in the border counties, in Dublin and in traditional areas, such as Kerry. As an example of how they were doing, Gardaí seized documents in September 1942 – shortly after the murder of Detective O'Brien – that showed the strength of the organisation in Kerry.

In Killarney, there were six rifles, four pistols, two Webley long rifles, one Lewis gun (light machine gun) and a Thompson machine gun. The town also had six hundred rounds and ten pounds of explosives. Nearby Listowel had twelve rifles, one Lewis gun, two Thompson guns, three pistols, six grenades, a Winchester rifle, a shotgun and over twenty pounds of explosives. However, there were fewer rounds available to the movement in that town. In Killorglin, there was a Thompson gun, a Colt Webley, three rifles and several hundred rounds, as well as thirty pounds of gelignite. Ardfert had a Thompson gun, four rifles and a Webley. Castlegregory had ten rifles, a Thompson gun, three pistols and a supply of grenades. In Cahirciveen, there were fourteen rifles, a Lewis gun and a Thompson gun, five revolvers and four shotguns, as well as forty grenades.

That was just Kerry. The state had reason to fear the IRA and the young men who were revitalising it.

And what of Kerins's victim, Dinny O'Brien? A native of Dublin, he had been born in 1899 and was 20 years older than Kerins. He had also seen a lot more action. He was one of the men who had created the new state, and was a genuine hero. O'Brien had fought in the Easter Rising. With his two brothers, Lawrence and Patrick, he took part in the action at Marrowbone Lane, off Cork Street. There was a distillery on the street that was used as a stronghold by more than 100 rebels under the command of Éamonn Ceannt and Cathal Brugha. The fighting was vicious, but the three brothers survived. Eamonn Ceannt was one of the leaders subsequently executed.

When the War of Independence broke out three years later, the brothers remained active in the IRA and did their bit for Irish freedom. But after the war they chose to reject the Treaty and joined the anti-Treaty IRA. Both Dinny and Patrick were part of the IRA force that seized the Four Courts in June 1922, the event that triggered the week-long Battle of Dublin and started the Civil War. Patrick died during the war, killed in action at Enniscorthy, but Dinny survived and remained a member of the IRA for another decade.

Eamon de Valera was one of the leaders of the anti-Treaty side, but after the war he became a legitimate politician, and by 1933 he was the leader of Fianna Fáil and prime minister of the new Irish Free State. That year he issued a call to IRA veterans to leave the organisation and join the Gardaí. This was a self-serving move on his part: he wanted men who were opposed to the Treaty, as he was himself, in official positions. Dinny O'Brien answered the call, leaving the IRA and joining the Gardaí that year.

When the Second World War broke out, O'Brien had risen

to the rank of Detective Sergeant at the Special Branch. The Special Branch was the section of the Gardaí devoted to combating threats against the state and fighting subversive groups. Headquartered at Dublin Castle, their job during the war was simple: to track down foreign spies and members of the IRA, who would then be interned at the Curragh Camp. The government feared that elements of the IRA were cooperating with Nazi Germany.

O'Brien was very good at his job and captured a number of IRA men. He was also involved in shoot-outs, and the organisation blamed him for killing two of their members, Charlie McGlade and Liam Rice. Both were 'shot while resisting arrest' in Dublin. It cannot be known for certain who fired the fatal shots, but Detective Sergeant O'Brien was present on both occasions, and the IRA held him responsible. He had become the man they most wanted to get rid of.

By the summer of 1942, Charlie Kerins was living around Dublin, moving from safe house to safe house. Sometimes he and his colleagues would use guest houses, while at other times sympathisers would put them up for a few days or weeks. It was important that they stayed a step ahead of the Special Branch, so they never remained long at any one spot. They travelled a lot by bicycle, as petrol was rationed, and they were generally armed. One landlord at a place where Kerins and some comrades stayed said that they never seemed to work, but were always off somewhere on bicycles. Barely into his 20s, Kerins had given up his career, his football and his prospects for his political beliefs, and he was rising through the ranks of the IRA.

However, the IRA was never going to be very effective with the Special Branch closing them down at every turn. The order went out: it was time to strike back. Charlie Kerins was part of the team assigned to the job. The others probably included Michael Quille and Archie Doyle, and one other. Several people were involved in the planning stages.

After the team assassinated Dinny O'Brien, they made off

on foot, running towards nearby Bolton Hall. They had hidden their bicycles in the ground of this mansion, and at least two of the team mounted their bicycles and made off. For some reason Kerins remained on foot, abandoning his bicycle.

As the men made their getaway, they were spotted by a member of the Special Branch. They were cycling past the Yellow House pub when he noticed them. However, he was not aware of the murder of his colleague at that point, and he was off-duty and on his way to the bog to cut turf, so he didn't stop the cyclists.

Another Garda also spotted the cyclists and gave chase, first on his own bicycle, then in a lorry he commandeered, but he lost them. However, he did identify one of them as Michael Quille, although he did not recognise the others.

The country reacted with horror, and a large reward was immediately offered for any information that might help catch the killers. Three government ministers called in to the O'Brien house on the day after the killing to offer their condolences. One of them was Seán Lemass, the Minister for Supplies. His private secretary was Larry O'Brien, the detective's younger brother and the man who identified the body after the shooting.

Taoiseach Eamon de Valera sent a telegram to Mrs O'Brien, and another to the detective's brother, Larry, saying, 'The dastardly murder of your brother, who served the Irish people so bravely and so devotedly throughout his life, has shocked every decent citizen, and filled every just mind with anger, and with a firm determination that those who are responsible will be brought to account.'

After that, the assassination team went into hiding. They found plenty of people willing to give them shelter, despite the widespread revulsion in the country at the murder of a policeman. Some remained in Dublin; others scattered to the four provinces.

The Gardaí did not have much to go on, just vague descriptions, but the IRA was a small band, so the range of suspects was narrow. Posters and wanted notices were circulated to Garda stations and post offices around the country. A number of men were sought in connection with the attack, including Kerins and Hugh McAteer, the Chief of Staff of the IRA. Kerins leaving the bicycle behind him during the getaway had been a crucial mistake; the forensics experts combed it for clues and found a fingerprint. The print proved Kerins had ridden on that bicycle at some point close to the shooting. It might have been a few days before or on the day, but the fingerprint linked him to the assassination. He was one of the men the Gardaí were particularly anxious to bring in. But he wasn't going to make it easy.

A reward was offered for information leading to the capture of the murder team. The state offered £5,000: the equivalent of over €100,000 in today's money. Yet there were no takers. The men on the run were careful only to associate with those whose loyalty they could depend upon.

In October, a month after the murder, the IRA chief Hugh McAteer was captured by the Royal Ulster Constabulary (the RUC, the Northern Irish police force) in Belfast. He was sentenced to 15 years in prison, eventually being released in 1950. That left a vacuum in the leadership. Charlie Kerins was promoted to Chief of Staff. He was now the overall leader of the IRA and the biggest thorn in the side of the Irish government. Perhaps his role in the death of Detective O'Brien was one of the factors leading to his promotion.

Kerins stayed on the run, moving around the country by bicycle, and occasionally using public transport. He used a variety of fake names, but was sometimes recognised. His interest in football was nearly his undoing. He attended a game in Galway disguised as a Christian Brother, but was recognised when he began to cheer for one of the sides. However, the official who recognised him was a fellow Kerry man, so he did not raise the alarm.

He also continued to be involved in criminal activities. Along with Jackie Griffiths and Archie Doyle (who was part of the murder team who took out Detective O'Brien), he planned a robbery on the Player Wills cigarette factory on the South Circular Road, Dublin. The three men arrived at the factory gates on bicycles. When the van with the cash for the wages arrived, they wrapped scarves around their faces and produced their guns. They didn't just steal the money; they stole the whole van, tossing their bicycles into the back and making off with £5,000. Then they disappeared back into the underworld.

One of the more prominent IRA sympathisers at the time was a Dublin doctor, Kathleen Farrell. Based on Upper Rathmines Road, she provided a safe house when it was needed. She also found other havens for the men on the run. At one point, she persuaded her sister to take in Kerins for a few weeks. Her sister's young daughter, Dervla Murphy, grew up to be a famous travel writer. She remembers Kerins appearing in their household. In her autobiography, *Wheels within Wheels*, she described seeing a tall, handsome young man climbing over their back wall and sneaking across the yard to their house. She was not alarmed, because he appeared 'so amiable and vulnerable'.

She said that he had a strong Kerry accent and called himself Pat Carney. He stayed with them for a number of weeks, before going to Dublin to stay with Dr Farrell. He was on red alert: the Special Branch was more vigorous than ever, and one of his colleagues had already been taken into custody.

One alleged member of the murder team, Michael Quille, was captured in October 1942 in Belfast and handed over to the Gardaí a week later. He went on trial for the murder of Detective O'Brien in January 1943. His case was heard before a military court rather than a jury. Like Kerins, he was a Kerry man, born in 1918 in Listowel. At the trial, Quille pleaded not guilty, but he refused to account for his movements on 9 September, the day of the murder.

Barrister G.D. Murnaghan said, 'If any combination of persons had a motive for putting Detective Sergeant O'Brien off this earth, it was the illegal organisation, the IRA.' He presented a picture of a highly organised conspiracy to kill the detective. 'Quille is not being presented to the court merely as an individual, but as one of a group of men who occupied a back room in 12 Grosvenor Square, Dublin, for some months prior to the shooting, and who vacated the house about 9 September [the day of the shooting]. Quille, then known as Michael Barrett, left the house with three other men on bicycles. On 16 September, when the Guards took over the house, they found five dust coats in the backroom [similar to the ones witnesses described the assassins as wearing], containing documents relating to military activities, and the use of Thompson guns. The house was a nest of members of the illegal organisation's activity.'

Annie O'Brien told the court that when she heard the opening gunfire, she thought someone was shooting pigeons:

But when I heard another revolver shot I knew something was wrong. I hesitated for a moment, and then I realised that someone was attacking my husband. As I ran down the avenue I heard three more revolver shots in quick succession. I knew there was a fight going on, and I kept running towards the gate. Then I heard a machine-gun going. I kept running. As I reached the bridge I glanced towards a little paddock on the left, and saw three men running away. They were running in the direction of a little lodge some distance away.

When I did not see my husband running after them I knew there was something wrong. I ran on towards the gate. I saw the car, with all its glass shattered, and my husband was not in it. I found him lying at the gate. His revolver was in his hand. When I came to him, his hand was just loosening its hold on the revolver. I knelt down beside him and I realised he was dead. I said an Act of Contrition into his ear.

Just as I had the prayer finished, two men passed by on bicycles; they were the same two men I had seen crossing the paddock previously. I shouted out: 'They are the two men who did it.'

A third man passed a minute later, and she saw his face in profile. She said that after Quille's arrest she had gone to the Bridewell Garda Station and identified him as the man who had cycled past moments after the murder of her husband.

A Special Branch Garda, who was not identified, told the court that he was off-duty and cycling out to the Dublin Mountains to cut turf when he heard the sound of gunfire. He thought it might be a military exercise. Then he saw two men flash by on bicycles. He identified one as Michael Quille.

Another Garda, also not identified, told the court that he was on a bicycle when two cyclists passed him. He noticed that one man had his hand in the coat of his pocket, which he found odd. After the men passed, he turned around and saw that the one with his hand in his pocket was staring back at the Garda. Immediately suspicious, he turned his bicycle around and gave chase. The men speeded up, and they had a head start. He thought they would get away, so he flagged down a lorry, to help him give chase. But while the lorry was turning, they made their getaway. He did not recognise the men.

A builder told the court that on the morning of the murder he had seen four bicycles parked near Bolton Hall Lodge. Later that morning, three of the bicycles were gone. The fourth one was the one that had a fingerprint, identified as that of Kerins, still on the run at that point.

Barrister Sean McBride appeared for the defence. Under cross-examination he threw doubt on the police identification of Quille as one of the killers. The Special Branch Garda who had spotted Quille cycling past him said that when he went to the identification parade at the Bridewell, after Quille's arrest, he had been shown a photo and given a description of the accused before the identity parade. This threw the evidence of identity into doubt, and the defence asked the court to throw out the case. However, the judge refused, saying there was a case for Quille to answer.

Sean McBride argued that there were two identifications of cyclists as Quille. Annie O'Brien said that two cyclists passed her gate, followed by a third, lone cyclist, whom she identified as Quille. The Garda, however, identified one of the pair of cyclists as Quille. Clearly they were both identifying different people as Quille, which had to throw doubt on the identification. 'The accused man is therefore in the unfortunate position of having to defend himself of being two different persons. This is the best proof of the unreliability of the identification in this case,' McBride said. He added that apart from the evidence of identification, there was no other evidence in the case. He said that Quille had been in Belfast on the day of the shooting.

After an eight-day trial, the military court took only a few minutes to find Quille not guilty. The president of the court said that they had to give him the benefit of whatever doubt there was in the case.

However, there were still other suspects to pursue, and the Gardaí were confident of their case against Kerins. They had a fingerprint. Now all they needed was the man. They continued their efforts against the IRA, and on 4 July 1943 they brought down another member. Jackie Griffith was cycling along Holles Street in Dublin when the Branch ambushed him and riddled him with bullets. They were now using the weapons of the enemy, and Griffith met his end under a hail of rounds from a Thompson machine gun.

Finally, in mid June 1944, almost two years after the murder, they had a tip-off. Kerins was back in Dublin and was being sheltered by Dr Farrell in Rathmines. In Dublin Castle, headquarters of the Special Branch, the arrest was planned carefully. There would be no mistakes.

In the small hours of the morning of 15 June, armed detectives surrounded the house. Machine guns were trained on all the exits. The men who were going in were issued with bulletproof vests. It was in the days before sneakers, so noise might be a problem. The assault team removed their hobnailed boots and crept across the garden in their stockinged feet. They came to a side door and forced the lock, and crept through the house without making a sound. It was 5 a.m. and the occupants were sound asleep. Kerins had taken precautions. There was a gun lying beside the bed. He never got a chance to use it. When he was woken up, there was a gun trained on his head and the handcuffs were slapped on his wrists before he could react. The primitive SWAT team, in their thick woollen socks, had done their job well.

With Kerins secured, the detectives searched the house. They were shocked to discover a complete arsenal. There was enough weaponry in the house to hold off an army. In Kerins's room alone, they found a Thompson machine gun, a Colt automatic, a .25 automatic, bomb springs, hand grenades and detonators, as well as over a thousand rounds of ammunition.

The Thompson gun was in a rough sack in a cupboard beside Kerins's bed. The magazine was loaded and the gun was ready to fire. There were over 500 loose rounds in the sack. Within easy reach of the bed was the Colt automatic. It was in a shoulder holster and fully loaded. There was a bullet in the breech and the safety catch was off. The gun was ready for immediate use. The detectives had been right to remove their hobnailed boots!

In a chest of drawers near the bed, detectives found a clerical collar, similar to those worn by Christian Brothers. It was the gear that Kerins had worn when he was spotted at the football game in Galway. They also found a black gabardine clerical coat and hat. It explained how the man had evaded them so often.

The trial of Charlie Kerins opened on Monday, 2 October, in Collins Barracks, Dublin. Like Quille, Kerins was facing a military court. These courts had been set up to deal with IRA and other subversives, and there was no jury to intimidate or to influence with republican rhetoric.

Quille had fought the charge and won. Kerins adopted a different strategy; he refused to recognise the court. This meant that he took no part in the proceedings and offered no defence. It was a high-risk strategy, but the court had to proceed with its work whether he acknowledged it or not. The trial opened and a plea of not guilty was entered on behalf of Kerins. Even if he did not participate, the state had to go through the formalities and prove its case.

Early in the trial, some maps and photographs of the murder scene were produced by barrister R. McLoughlin, representing the state. Kerins, unrepresented, was asked if he would like to see the documents. 'I am not interested in them,' he said. He added that if the state wished to try him, there were legitimate courts they could have used, rather than a military tribunal. 'If the authorities wish to give me the semblance of a fair trial there are law courts in the country,' he told the president of the tribunal.

The president replied, 'You are entitled to counsel, and this court will delegate counsel for your defence.'

Kerins said, 'I consider it an insult to my intelligence to be expected to recognise this as a court of justice, or the men here as supreme judges.' That was emphatic. Kerins would not be playing this legal game.

The parade of witnesses began. Dr J. McGrath, the State Pathologist, testified that Detective O'Brien had been killed instantly from a round that hit him in the back of the head, about two and a half inches above his collar. The bullet had penetrated the skull, sliced through the brain and made an oblique exit wound through the scalp, slightly to the right. 'He must have been shot from behind,' said the doctor.

Several witnesses described men in trench coats cycling away after the attack. Annie O'Brien, widow of the dead detective, described hearing gunfire and running out. She could not see her husband, but she could see three men running towards Bolton Hall Lodge.

'Two of them were dressed in trench coats and caps. The other coward – for you could not call them men – had no cap,' she told the court.

The evidence from the first trial – of the identification of Michael Quille at the murder scene – was repeated.

A ballistics expert from the Garda Technical Bureau said that there were nine bullet holes in the gate pillar of Detective O'Brien's house. From the positions of the bullet holes, he concluded that two Thompson guns were used in the ambush. One was fired from across the road from the gate. It had left the bullet holes, and one bullet was recovered buried deep in an elm tree in the driveway. A .45 Colt automatic was recovered from the scene, from which one bullet had been fired, with seven still in the magazine. This was probably the gun used in the initial ambush that shattered the windscreen of Detective O'Brien's car and forced him out into the open.

The expert was able to tell the court that the Thompson gun recovered from 50 Upper Rathmines Road was not the one used to murder the detective.

Another Garda technical expert told the military court that he had removed three fingerprints from the bicycle abandoned at Bolton Hall Lodge on the day of the murder. They belonged to IRA activist Liam Burke, one of the suspects, and to Charlie Kerins. This tied Kerins to the murder scene.

Evidence was produced that proved that Kerins was a member of the IRA and high up in the organisation. At the time, the IRA was an illegal organisation and membership alone would have been enough to put Kerins behind bars. At the end of the state case, barrister G.D. Murnaghan, for the state, said that Kerins was a member of the IRA and 'one of the higher-ups'. This in itself was sufficient to establish a motive for the murder. 'As regards means, Kerins undoubtedly had at that time a bicycle, by means of which the assailants got to the scene of the murder,' he said. 'He had access – if not actual possession – of arms and ammunition; witness the amount he actually had in his possession when arrested. As regards opportunity, Kerins left the house where he was living before eight o'clock, giving him ample time to reach Ballyboden at ten o'clock.'

One of the members of the tribunal said that Kerins had not challenged any of the evidence heard so far. Kerins replied that this was due to the fact that he did not recognise the court.

Murnaghan said that the evidence before the court was that

Michael Quille had been at the scene of the murder and was part of the murder team. The court had heard evidence that Kerins was an associate of Quille, and his fingerprints were found on a bicycle at the scene. Even though no one identified him at the scene, there was enough indirect evidence to put him there.

At that point, a member of the judging panel pointed out that Quille had been acquitted of the murder. 'Does not the acquittal by a military court put Quille out of it?' he asked.

'No,' replied Mr Murnaghan. 'This court has to determine on the evidence before it without any reference to evidence taken by another court. The evidence before the court at the moment, if accepted, establishes that Quille was at the scene of this occurrence.'

The barrister then made a slightly controversial point: 'The finding of the not guilty verdict in the case of Michael Quille does not of itself mean that Quille was not there, and while it does not mean that he was there, it might well be that there are facts before this court that were not before the court which acquitted Quille, and which, if they had been before the court, would have caused the court to find Quille guilty.'

He said that Kerins's associations, the fact that he was using a number of aliases and the fact that his fingerprint was found on the bicycle at the scene should be taken into account by the judges. He continued, 'When he was arrested Kerins said that he could not account for his movements on September 8, 9, 10 and 11, 1942. At that time he was deputy Chief of Staff of the IRA, and if the court accepts that the murder was carried out by the IRA, it is a very easy step to ask the court to hold that Kerins should be able to give a better account of himself than that.'

When the barrister stood down after his summation of the case, Kerins asked him if he could read out the regulations concerning circumstantial evidence in criminal trials.

Mr Murnaghan read from a legal textbook: 'A jury may convict on purely circumstantial evidence . . .'

Kerins interrupted: 'Jury! That is just the word I want to hear. That means a jury of twelve unprejudiced men.'

The president of the tribunal stopped Kerins and said he would have plenty of time to put his case to the court. However, when the case resumed the following day, Kerins again refused to participate. The president said:

Although charged with murder, the most serious offence known to the law, the accused man, Charles Kerins, refused to plead when this case opened, and he made no attempt to refute the evidence for the prosecution by cross-examination or otherwise. An offer to assign counsel for his defence was also refused by him.

The case for the prosecution is now closed, and there is no doubt that the late Detective Sergeant Denis O'Brien was foully murdered near his home on the morning of 9 September 1942, by assassins armed with Thompson guns and other weapons. Evidence was given on behalf of the state which would seem to implicate the accused man with this terrible crime, particularly the finding of a fingerprint, which corresponds to that of his right ring finger, on a bicycle found abandoned near the scene of the shooting.

The court considers it right to inform you at this stage that a prima facie case has been established against you. In order to give you an opportunity to consider your position, and, if you so desire, to obtain legal advice and assistance, to enable you to answer the case made against you, the court has decided to adjourn until Monday morning.

Kerins had the weekend to consider whether to change his mind, recognise the military tribunal and fight the charge. When the court resumed on Monday, the president asked Kerins whether he had had a change of heart.

'You could have adjourned for six months as far as I am concerned, as my attitude towards the court will always be the same,' Kerins replied.

The court then adjourned to consider its verdict, returning in the afternoon. The president delivered the verdict: the state had proven their case. Kerins was guilty of the murder of Detective Dinny O'Brien. Kerins was then asked whether he had anything to say as to why sentence of death should not be passed upon him.

'All I can say is that, if the Free State authorities are satisfied that I got a fair trial here, I hope their consciences are clear on the point. If this is an example of de Valera's justice, freedom and democracy, then I would like to know what dictatorship and militarism are. That is about all I have to say,' he said.

Kerins was sentenced to hang on 31 October. He had just three more weeks to live.

Kerins was asked if he wished to appeal the verdict or the sentence. He said that he had no application to make. However, others were not so passive. The day after the sentence, Sean McBride, a prominent barrister, journalist and budding politician, moved to appeal the verdict. McBride shared the political views of Kerins and had himself been Chief of Staff of the IRA before the outbreak of the war.

He had a number of grounds for seeking an appeal. He said that the court had relied on methods of identification (in relation to Michael Quille) that had been rejected by an earlier court. The court had subsequently proceeded as if Kerins had murdered Detective O'Brien in association with Michael Quille, despite the fact that Quille had previously been found not guilty of the crime. He said that there was no real evidence against Kerins. These grounds for appeal were rejected; the sentence stood. However, the execution date was pushed back to 1 December.

Although there was tremendous sympathy for the family of the murdered detective, the fact that the murder was politically motivated muddied the waters. Many people supported moves to commute the death sentence. However, it was a time of war, and the government had emergency powers that allowed them to control the media. Mentions of meetings in support of Kerins were removed from papers by the official censors. Support for

Kerins could be interpreted as support for the IRA, so the government stamped down on it vigorously. When Kerry County Council tried to organise a meeting at the Mansion House in Dublin, a number of men were arrested for putting up posters. Armed Special Branch detectives roamed the city tearing down the posters that did go up. This did not stop more than 5,000 people showing up at the public meeting on Monday, 27 November.

A number of politicians tried to use their influence to push for clemency. Among those who raised the matter in the Dáil were Michael Donnellan of East Galway, a member of the Farmers' Party, and Oliver J. Flanagan, then an independent, but later a prominent member of Fine Gael. Kerry deputies also sprang to the cause, including Dan Spring, father of Dick Spring, a future Tánaiste, and Patrick Finucane. Yet the Ceann Comhairle ruled them all out of order.

On the day before the execution, three deputies – Finucane and Spring from Kerry, and James Larkin – were suspended from the Dáil for trying to force a debate on the trial. A government spokesperson said that the deputies could debate the matter the following afternoon: after the execution!

Albert Pierrepoint, the UK executioner, took the boat from Holyhead to carry out the execution. It being controversial, he was brought to Mountjoy under tight security. The night before the execution there was a candlelight vigil outside the gates of the prison, and another at the GPO on O'Connell Street. The crowd intoned the rosary while baton-wielding Gardaí looked on.

Kerins attended Mass every morning on the last week of his life. He was in good cheer when he made his way to the gallows. Dr Kathleen Farrell, in whose house he was arrested, wrote to her niece Dervla Murphy: 'There is no need to tell you that Charlie Kerins met his death with the greatest possible courage and bravery. I was allowed to visit him on Wednesday and Thursday last and he gave me courage, too. He was so proud and happy to die for Ireland that one could not feel depressed – sad, indeed heartbroken – but not depressed.'

Poet Austin Clarke eulogised Kerins in his poem 'The Last Republicans', describing how a paltry five pounds to hangman Pierrepoint was enough to see the last republican buried in quicklime. It was the start of a process to turn a cop killer and armed robber into a martyr and republican hero. Back in Kerins's native Tralee, the local football club, the O'Rahillys, changed their name to the Kerins O'Rahillys in his honour. Later, Tralee Urban District Council named a new housing estate Kerins Park.

In sharp contrast, Dinny O'Brien was a genuine Irish hero. He fought in the Easter Rising, the War of Independence and the civil war. He then tried to put the civil war behind him by working diligently in the service of the state. He was shot from behind in a cowardly ambush. He died for Ireland, but he is remembered in no street name or housing estate. No GAA club commemorated him. He died for his country, and was forgotten.

5

. . . .

THE FIELD

The murder of Moss Moore by Dan Foley

THE TWO MOST famous murders to take place in Kerry are both fictional, but both were based on horrific real events. The first happened in the late eighteenth century, the second in the 1950s.

The first murder was the killing of the Colleen Bawn (Gaelic for 'blonde girl'), which was based on a real murder that took place in 1819. In the fictional account she is a young beauty who is murdered because she catches the eye of a man above her station. Hardress Cregan, a minor member of the gentry, has fallen on hard times, so his choice of paramour is of vital interest to the rest of his family. His mother wants him to marry Anne Chute, who has money. It will secure the family name and support both their lifestyles. Cregan is agreeable – but there is one problem. Unknown to his mother, he has married a local beauty in secret. He is besotted with Eily O'Connor, and the only way he could seduce her was to tie the knot. Now he has a problem. He has had his way, and now he wants rid of Eily so that he can marry money. Cregan's servant, the hunchbacked Danny Mann, gets the idea that his master has settled on murder as the best solution.

That was the story of the murder when it was turned into

a play called *The Colleen Bawn*, a melodrama, by Dion Boucicault. However, the wily playwright decided on a happy ending: it made for better box office. Danny Mann is discovered, Eily is saved and everyone lives happily ever after. *The Colleen Bawn* is a perennial favourite and is regularly revived.

The story was also turned into an opera, *The Lily of Killarney*, which was very popular during Victorian times, although it fell out of popularity in the twentieth century. Both the play and the opera were based on the book *The Collegians* by Limerick journalist Gerald Griffin. In the book, Griffin stuck more closely to the facts: Eily O'Connor is not saved at the last minute. This is because Griffin was a journalist, and he covered the original trial.

The novel is a fictionalised account of the true story of the Colleen Bawn, and the first surprise for many is that it did not happen in Kerry. Ellen Hanley was a 15-year-old girl from around Rathkeale, in Limerick. A local aristocrat, John Scanlan, became besotted with the teen and secretly married her, but he quickly realised that the unpolished peasant would not be accepted into his family. So he decided on divorce, Irish style. He persuaded his servant, Stephen Sullivan, to kill her.

On 14 July 1819, Sullivan took Ellen out on a boat from Kilrush onto the Shannon Estuary. Once they were on the water, he used a musket to kill her. He stripped the girl's body and then tossed her overboard into the dark and swift flowing waters. He assumed that she would sink to the bottom or be swept out to sea.

But six weeks later, the body washed ashore at Moneypoint, about four miles from Kilrush. Both Scanlan and Sullivan immediately fled. Scanlan was the first to be caught. He went on trial, and he had a great Kerry man, Daniel O'Connell, in his corner. But even the oratorical skills of the Liberator were of no avail; Scanlan was convicted and hanged at Gallows Green, on the banks of the Shannon, in Clare. Shortly after Sullivan was caught, and he too was hanged, looking across the estuary to the distant Kerry hills. The only thing the real

Colleen Bawn had to do with Kerry was the view from the gallows.

The second-most-famous Kerry murder was the killing of a farmer in a dispute over a piece of land. The story is told in a famous play, *The Field*, by Kerry playwright John B. Keane. The play is based on a real case, which happened close to where he lived, in Listowel. This time the murder happened in the heart of Kerry. It was a case that gripped the nation, and in the end it all boiled down to the love of land that seems to be rooted in the souls of Irish people.

There is something elemental in the relationship between Irish people and the land. It is as if the clay is in our blood. We are tied to the land in a way few other European races are. It is part of our culture and our way of thinking. When we sang of freedom, we sang of four green fields. Perhaps it is down to our history. A predominantly Catholic country, we lost our land to the English Protestants. It took a succession of land acts, each one hard fought for, to allow us to own the farms we worked. Even when we moved to the cities, we did our best to own our dwellings rather than rent them like many in Europe are happy to do.

It gets even the most modern of us. When I bought my first house, a cottage with a half-acre of land, I fell into the trap. There was a section of my garden close to a neighbour's field, and for decades a thin strand of barbed wire, two feet out from my wall and enclosing nothing but ditch and scrub, had kept the cattle from eating the previous owner's beautiful rose bushes. The day I moved in, the owner of the field snipped the wire. My roses were destroyed by the munching cattle in a day. She was making a point: I had no claim to even the shadow of her ditch. A few years later, I moved. My neighbour owned all the land around me, and she wanted my little field. But I remembered the roses and refused all her offers. I could be as petty as she.

From such silly disputes can spring vicious feuds between friends and neighbours. People have gone to court over tiny parcels of land barely big enough to hold the legal briefs.

Neighbours have fallen out, and the bitterness has lasted decades.

John B. Keane understood well that aspect of the Irish psyche, and it formed the background to his most celebrated play, *The Field*, first performed in 1965. The Listowel playwright set the action in north Kerry, among the poor hill farmers. 'The Bull' McCabe is a typical alpha male who insists on getting his own way all the time. He is renting land, and when it comes on the market, he tries to bully the auctioneer into letting him buy it. However, the auctioneer insists on the public sale going ahead. Bull has no worries; none of his neighbours will dare bid against him. But then a stranger arrives, a Galway man who has been in England for years. He wants to come home and he wants to buy the land. He is an outsider; he is not intimidated by Bull. So Bull decides to deal with things in his own way. He kills the stranger. Yet everyone knows he has gone a step too far, and he finds himself shunned and ostracised by his own community.

It was a powerful story, later adapted brilliantly for the screen. Veteran hell-raiser Richard Harris played the Bull, and for his towering performance he was nominated for an Oscar.

The real Bull did not kill a stranger; he killed a friend and neighbour. He was never charged, but lived out his remaining years a lonely and boycotted man. His family say the isolation broke him. And he didn't kill his neighbour over a field. The dispute was over a stretch of land so narrow it would barely have contained the two men who fought so long over it.

The story is rooted in the land of north Kerry. North Kerry could be a different county from the more popular and touristy south Kerry. The areas around Killarney, Killorglin, Sneem and Waterville are dominated by the Reeks, the vast mountains that tower over the landscape. North Kerry is hilly as well, but the hills are smaller, boggy affairs. The land is poor, and there is a feeling of isolation on the desolate, windswept uplands. John B. Keane described them as too small to be mountains but too big to be hills, and it is hard to argue with this imprecise but accurate description.

Reamore is a townland – barely a crossroads on two narrow country lanes – in the district of Lyreacrompane, in the Stack's Mountains of north Kerry. It is in the middle of the hilly land that fills in the triangle from Abbeyfeale in south Limerick, to Castleisland, to Listowel. It is wet and boggy, the land is poor and production is low. No one gets rich on those smallholdings.

But the area is rich in culture and music, song and story. The people are close and speak lyrically in lilting accents that lend a charm to everything they say. As a young man, Keane spent his summers around Lyreacrompane and absorbed the language and the stories. Lyreacrompane was, and still is, a tiny village on the side of the mountain. It services a wide hinterland of dispersed townlands, with Reamore about five miles down the road. The way of life remains firmly rooted in the past.

Keane described the area lovingly: 'I fell immediately in love with this strange and wonderful countryside, with the character, colour and language of its people, and with its numerous dancing streams. The unbounded freedom of the hills and glens amount to sheer paradise. The Stack's Mountains have a magic all of their own where the green pastures and meadows merge into boglands. The dominating colour is brown but ever and always it is a brown that is warm and comforting.'

But even paradise has a dark side. The young boy enjoying his summer holidays might not have seen it, but under the surface there were tensions – and the land was at the root of many.

Maurice Moore, known to everyone as Moss, was born in 1912. The hilly land between north Kerry and south Limerick was a hotbed of activity during the War of Independence and the civil war, and he grew up in exciting times. But things settled with the birth of the new state. He reached maturity and eventually inherited the small farm he had grown up on. It could support him, but only if he had no great expectations out of life. Times were tough, and it was quite common for men to leave it late to marry. In the winter of 1958, Moss

Moore had reached the comparatively young age of 46 and had shown no signs of wanting to find a wife. He was a small bachelor farmer, struggling to make a living in a community of small farmers.

Neighbours liked Moss because he was a friendly man with a sense of fun. When he was younger – up to the age of about 40 – he loved to go to the local dances and was always out and about whenever there was something on, even though he didn't actually enjoy dancing. He would go along, listen to the music, chat to his friends and remain resolutely in his seat.

He was very fond of children, and whenever he was in the village he would fill his pockets with sweets at the local shop, so that he would have something to give the kids of the district.

Moss lived in a tiny three-room house, but he did have a slate roof, which stood out from the thatch roofs of some of his more impoverished neighbours. His farm was small. He managed to keep four cows, two pigs, a pony and some fowl. He sold the milk from the cows to the local creamery, dropping it off every morning. It was a chance to catch up with the neighbours and have a chat. All the neighbours used to help each other out; it was essential for survival. There was just enough in the land to make ends meet. Living so isolated from town and its attractions, there wasn't much to spend money on, even if he'd had it.

The rural electrification scheme was a decade old and making good headway by 1965: 80 per cent of the houses in the countryside were connected to the network. But in the late '50s in the Stack's Mountains, electricity was still a long way away. A battery-operated radio was as close as they came to technology. Television was a distant dream. However, the people did not lack for entertainment. At night, when the work was done, they would gather in houses to play cards, dance, listen to music or tell stories. Moss was a card player. He loved a night in at a neighbour's, playing 45.

Of late, though, he had been trying to avoid one of his neighbours.

Dan Foley was 12 years older than Moss, but despite the age difference, the younger man had reason to fear Foley. Foley was a forceful man and used to getting his own way. He was also bigger and stronger than Moss. Farming is a physical job, and despite being nearly 60, Foley was as tough as a man half his years. Physically, the two men could not have contrasted more. Moss was a small, thin man with a narrow face. He weighed barely 10 st. People said he looked timid, but he could be feisty when the occasion arose.

The two men had been friends for years. They farmed adjoining land in the hills, and they were near neighbours. They met daily at the creamery and often at night in various houses as they played cards or socialised. They lived only a hundred yards apart and were said by neighbours to be very fond of each other. They often worked together. Today, they would be cutting turf together for Foley; tomorrow, for Moss.

Foley lived with his wife and her brother, in contrast to Moss, who was a bachelor. He just had the two dogs for company.

A sod ditch separated both farms, and they removed it in the late '50s. The plan was to eventually put up a new wall, but they did not get around to it. There was a lot of commonage on the higher ground, and animals could roam freely. That was fine for sheep, but farmers liked to keep their cattle close at hand. They had to be milked nightly. Dan Foley became concerned that his cattle were wandering further and further from the house, up onto the bog. He decided he would put a fence down along the boundary to keep his cattle in.

This was not the wall the two men had agreed to build. Foley was acting alone. He went out and put up the simple fence – wooden stakes and wire – and was well pleased. However, he had encroached on Moss's land, and the younger man was not happy. He moved the fence, Foley moved it back and the tension began to mount.

The piece of land the two men were arguing over was the narrow strip along which the fence ran. Along the total length of the boundary, it would not have been half an acre, but it was enough to sour the relationship between two friends.

Finally Moss took a court action against his neighbour to have the fence moved back a few feet. Ireland is one of the most litigious countries in the world, and such land disputes often come before the court. The hearing was set for December 1958. Now there was genuine bad blood between the neighbours. People urged both men to settle, but they were having none of it.

One neighbour, Paul Reidy, remembers the time. When interviewed for a documentary on the background to the famous play (*Fuil agus Duch*, 2007), he said, 'They were arguing over a boundary in the worst bit of land in Ireland. Moss had to win it. I urged them to settle. I said to Foley, it will cost ye money. Foley said there will only be one man around for that case.'

Foley began trying to intimidate Moss. Moss told neighbours that he was being watched at night. When he went out to play cards, he began taking a stick with him, and he carried a torch, though he knew his way around in the dark from years of walking the paths.

Eventually he went to a place with a phone and contacted the Gardaí in Listowel. He said that Dan Foley was disturbing him and asked a Garda to come out to have a word with the man. Garda Pat Kavanagh said that he would drive out in a few days, but it was a busy time, and he could not arrange it. Events overtook him.

As the winter of 1958 drew down on them, Moss was avoiding his bigger neighbour. Privately, he expressed his fears to one or two of his friends, but he didn't give up on his nightly card games. He wasn't that worried. He had his stick.

On the night of Thursday, 6 November 1958, Moss Moore got ready to go out as usual. He dressed against the weather, pulled on his cap and got a stout stick. The stick wasn't for his protection. Everyone carried a stick in those days. It was useful for walking over the rough ground in the dark, for driving a cow back into a field or for knocking branches out of your way. He also took a small battery-powered torch for the way home. There were no lights, and it would be pitch black.

It was only a few minutes to the house of Mrs Julia Collins, about a quarter of a mile away. Moss arrived with the others, and they all sat around the kitchen table, playing cards by the light of the kerosene lamp and swapping yarns. Moss was a good player, but he wasn't lucky that night. He won no games, and at the close he had lost two shillings and sixpence. It didn't bother him. There would be other nights, and at the end of the day, breaking even was all anyone cared about.

The card game broke up around 10.15 p.m., and people headed home. Moss joined a neighbour, Timothy Sugrue, and they walked as far as Reamore Cross together. It was only a distance of 150 yards and took them two or three minutes. The night was dark, though dry. There was a cold north-westerly airstream over the country, with lots of clouds, but only a few scattered showers. It was cold, even for November.

At the cross, the two men paused for another minute or two, but it was too dark and cold a night to linger and chat. Sugrue told people afterwards that Moss said, 'He'll [meaning Foley] be up there waiting for me. But I'll be fine. I have my stick.' As Sugrue turned away, his friend and neighbour called out as usual, 'Good night. We'll meet again tomorrow night.' They were the last words that anyone would hear him speak.

Somewhere between Reamore Cross and Moss's home, Dan Foley stepped out of the darkness in front of him. The beam of the torch caught the big man and Moss stopped in his tracks. The confrontation must have taken place near the house rather than the cross, because Timothy Sugrue heard nothing, although the wind could have carried away the noises of the scuffle.

Moss, a feisty man, fought back against his attacker. He broke his stick in the course of the struggle. It is likely that the bigger man wrenched the torch from his hands and struck Moss a number of times in the face. His nose and jaw were badly broken. Finally Foley's hands were on his throat, and he was strangled to death.

Foley dragged the body across the yard and down into a deep ditch with a stream at the bottom. He pulled it right up against an overhang and concealed it with rushes. He worked in the dark, but he worked efficiently. It would be many days before the body was recovered. Then he went home and acted as if nothing out of the ordinary had taken place.

The following morning, Moss Moore did not show up at the creamery as usual. It was the first sign that anything might be wrong, but no one was particularly worried. He had mentioned the day before that one of his dogs had knocked over a bucket of milk, spilling it, so maybe he had nothing that day. It was no cause for concern.

That night Moss did not show up for his regular card game, and that did cause some concern. The following morning, Saturday, one neighbour met Dan Foley's wife. He asked her was there any news of Moss Moore, as he had not been seen for a few days. She said that he might have gone to Tipperary looking for work. This seemed unlikely, as his cattle were out on the field untended and he had asked no one to look after them.

A few neighbours called to his house. There was no answer to their knocking, so they entered the three-room bungalow. They were surprised to find there was no evidence that Moss had slept in the house the previous night. In fact, it looked as if it was a few days since the farmer had been home. And it was two days since anyone had seen him . . .

The neighbours immediately travelled to Listowel to report the disappearance of Moss Moore to the Gardaí. Listowel is the nearest large town, about 15 miles away. Rather unusually, they did not report that Moss was missing; they reported that he had been murdered. Right from the beginning, no one in the small, close-knit community was in any doubt as to what had happened – and they had a fairly good idea who had made it happen.

'You are looking for a corpse – and it will be hard to find,' one man apparently said.

The Gardaí arrived on Saturday afternoon and searched the small house and the surrounding farmyard, but they found nothing. By the end of the day, Moss had not returned, but no one really expected him to. They knew they were looking for a body. The Gardaí were less sure; it took them a few days to fully commit to the search.

By the middle of the following week, a large number of people were involved in the hunt. A team of Gardaí were joined by friends and neighbours of the missing man. Everyone lent a hand. Dan Foley was among the searchers. It can't have been easy for him. Already he could hear the tongues wagging. Neighbours were beginning to avoid him. The greetings had become a lot more frosty.

That week, a message was daubed on the gable wall of the local creamery, calling for a boycott of Foley. Moss was officially missing. No one knew for certain that he had been murdered, but the community had decided, and they were nailing their colours to the mast.

The search appeared to be very thorough. It began close to Moss's farm, but gradually the radius of the hunt was broadened. The daily searches over the wild boggy land eventually stretched for miles, stopping each night as darkness fell. The weather turned very wet, and the searchers had to deal with poor visibility and driving rain. Someone reported seeing donkey tracks higher up the mountains, so the search was broadened to include the uplands. The assumption was that Moss Moore's body had been put across a donkey and brought up to the bogs and dropped in a bog hole. If that was the case, he might never be found.

Days went by with no developments. Saturday, 15 November marked a full week since Moss had been reported missing. The day began misty on the hills, with a fog that gradually lifted as the air warmed up. The weather had changed for the better, and they had the first dry period in a week. There was a soft south-westerly breeze, and just occasional showers. It was a good day for searching. Teams were combing the outlying areas, but the search had come back to Moss's home and the path he had taken the last night he had been seen alive.

Gardaí donned rubber boots and began searching a stream in a deep ravine just yards from Mr Moore's home. A little after three that afternoon – only two hours from when they would call it a day until Sunday – Sergeant Michael Costello, based in Tralee, was poking in the stream with a stick as he walked. He hit something soft. Bending down to retrieve it, he found that he had found Moss Moore's flat cap. It was the first clue to be found in a week of fruitless searching. The discovery energised the searchers, and they redoubled their efforts.

A few minutes later, at 3.10 p.m., Chief Superintendent Pat Cronin, who had been leading the search teams, found the body of the missing man. Moss Moore was lying in a two-foot-wide stream overgrown with rushes. The stream lay in a deep but narrow ravine only 35 yards from the missing man's home. His cap had been found only 45 yards away from the body.

During the remainder of the afternoon, the searchers found a broken stick. This was the stick that Moss had taken with him when he walked home after the Thursday-night card game. There was no sign of his torch. That was not recovered for weeks. It was eventually found buried in a turnip field. Moreover, so many people had trampled over the area near where the body was discovered in the preceding week that no useful clues could be found.

Although neighbours wanted to remove Moss from the ditch immediately, the Gardaí knew this was a murder inquiry and that the scene had to be preserved. A small team of Gardaí spent the night outside guarding the body, while the State Pathologist, Dr Maurice Hickey, made his way down from Dublin. That night, an impromptu wake was held in Moss's little house. A photograph was placed on the table in place of the corpse, and many of the neighbours visited. This wake destroyed any chance of useful forensic evidence being uncovered in the house.

Dr Hickey arrived at the remote community on Sunday, where he was joined by Chief Superintendent George Lawlor, Detective Inspector Wall and officers from the Garda Technical Bureau in Dublin. About 60 people watched as Dr Hickey carried out a quick examination of the body in the stream. Mr Moore had been wedged under the bank. His legs lay upstream, and his trousers and long johns were rolled up above the knees, leaving the shins bare. This was probably caused by the flowing water in the stream.

When Dr Hickey completed his examination, Gardaí used hay knives to cut away the rushes and free the body. A team of eager hands helped the Gardaí pull it from the stream. A white sheet was thrown over the corpse, which was removed to Tralee County Hospital for the autopsy.

As this was going on, neighbours speculated and the rumours flew. The area around the house had been searched thoroughly; why had they not found the body a week earlier? Many put a sinister spin on this: whoever had killed Moss had hidden the body, then moved it to the ravine near his home, where it was discovered. However, the autopsy disproved this theory: Moss had been dumped in the ravine before rigor mortis had begun to set in. That was obvious from the way his limbs had subsequently frozen into place. Whoever had killed him had dragged him to the ravine and pushed him in, covering him with vegetation to cover his body. The reason he had not been discovered was that he was in a dark ditch covered in foliage.

Back in the '50s, justice proceeded at a quicker rate than it does today. An inquest was called for the Monday after the body was discovered. It was held in Tralee, before Kerry County Coroner Dr Denis Sheehan.

State Pathologist Dr Hickey said that when he arrived in Reamore, he found Moss Moore lying in a stream, obscured by rushes. The body was removed to Tralee Hospital, where he performed an autopsy.

The body was fully clothed. Rigor mortis had passed, and the body was beginning to decompose, but the decomposition was not sufficient to prevent a thorough examination. The bridge of Mr Moore's nose and the right side of his jaw, as well as portions of his voice box, were fractured. Extensive bleeding had occurred around the nose and the break in his jaw. This bleeding indicated that the fractures had been made while Mr Moore was still alive, rather than after his death. They had not been caused by his body being dumped into the deep ditch.

The nose was very badly broken, the fracture to the bridge extending back into the skull. However, the brain was uninjured: apart from some congestion of the blood vessels on the surface, it was normal. Mr Moore had not been beaten to death, though he had taken a fair hammering.

The lungs were congested, but the air tubes leading to them were not filled with froth. Therefore he had not drowned. His organs were healthy.

'I retained certain organs, including the voice box, and some of the neck tissues for further examination,' Dr Hickey said. 'Pending the result of that examination, which will require about a week, I am reluctant to express any definite opinion as to the cause of death.'

The coroner then adjourned the inquest. This is standard: when someone is murdered, the inquest is normally adjourned until all legal proceedings in connection with the death are concluded. But after completing his examination of the samples, Dr Hickey confirmed that Mr Moore had been strangled.

Gardaí interviewed everyone they could in the district. They got the same answer from everyone: Mr Moore was terrified of Dan Foley, and he was locked in a legal battle with the bigger, stronger man. They asked Foley to come into Listowel in the car with them so that he could be interviewed, but he refused. A few days later, he had a change of heart, and he rode his bicycle into Listowel and spoke to the investigation officers. He denied any involvement in the killing, claiming he was completely innocent. This was the story he stuck with to the day he died. He had marks on his face that were about a week old and beginning to heal. When Gardaí asked him about these marks, he said he had got them from the horns of a bull.

As the weeks dragged on and Foley remained in his home, denying any involvement in the murder, the community became more and more frustrated. It did not take long before the boycott of the farmer was general. His neighbours, his former friends: all now shunned him. The campaign against Foley became quite public. No one tried to hide their feelings about him. Before Moss Moore was found, there had been messages painted on the wall of the creamery. Similar incidents continued to happen. In the second week of January 1959, a poster was hung at the cross near Moss's home, threatening Dan Foley. The Gardaí removed it.

Foley was stopped from using the local shop. Old neighbours ignored him, and many people in the district refused to speak to him. He couldn't sell his cattle or buy in fodder. He was forced to run the farm on his own. Not only did he have no help; there were also constant hindrances thrown in his way. Life would have been very difficult for him.

Yet many were not content with that. On one occasion, a couple of months after the killing, shots were fired into Dan Foley's home, forcing him and his wife to dive for cover. No one was injured, but the strength of feeling in the local community was abundantly clear.

'The sentence passed on Dan Foley by the local people was far worse than any sentence that could have been passed by any court. Dan was a tough man, but he suffered a lot. He paid a heavy price for all this trouble,' said one man in *Fuil agus Duch*.

But not everyone agreed that he was guilty of the murder. There were some – a tiny minority – who accepted his word that he was innocent. Padraig Kennelly was a press photographer in Kerry at the time. He said, 'I believe Foley was innocent. He was an independent-minded Kerry man. He did not mind the Gardaí trailing him. He laughed, and told me: "Let them go into court and swear their perjury." He did not see any reason to defend himself. He was never charged with the crime.'

Dan Foley's nephew John also believes his uncle was innocent, framed by others who wanted to do in Moss Moore. The big problem with this theory is that Moss Moore was a well-liked man with no enemies, and he was a poor man with nothing to steal, so no one but Dan Foley had any reason to wish him ill.

As the weeks turned to months, the anger of the community turned towards the Gardaí. They had certainly not distinguished themselves in the investigation. It had taken them a week to find the body, even though it was only yards from the victim's home.

In March, the Garda authorities bowed to public pressure by appointing senior officers to help with three murder investigations that seemed to have stalled. A deputy commissioner and two assistant commissioners were appointed to oversee the three investigations. One officer went to Carlow to lead the investigation into the year-old murder of James Fitzpatrick, who had been found battered to death in his farmyard, near Tullow. The second officer took over the investigation of the murder of 65-year-old William Hannon, who was killed in his lock-up sweet shop in Wexford.

The most senior officer was Deputy Commissioner Thomas Woods. He was sent to Kerry to try to make progress on the strangulation of Moss Moore. Eventually a file was prepared and sent to the Director of Public Prosecutions, but the DPP decided that there was not enough evidence to secure a conviction against Dan Foley.

As spring turned to summer, Dan Foley continued to farm his land. But there was one difference now: he could not rely on neighbours to help out. Running a small farm, especially in the days before modern machinery, was a labour-intensive business. At the busy times of the year, everyone would muck in to get the job done. But Foley had no neighbours to help him. A proud man, he carried on regardless. However, his family believe that the strain was too much for him in the end.

Four years after the murder of Moss Moore, Dan Foley dropped dead close to his home, just yards from where Moss had been murdered. He had lived out his final years a lonely and avoided man. The case of the murder of Moss Moore is still an open one, but once Foley was buried, so was the file. Most people were happy that the killer was now facing a higher court.

The case would have faded into obscurity if the young man who holidayed in the Stack's Mountains every summer had not taken an interest. Around the time of Foley's death, John B. Keane began working on *The Field*. Then in his 30s, he had his own pub in nearby Listowel and had achieved success with his plays *Sive* and *Sharon's Grave*. He took the murder as a starting point and wrote a masterpiece about one man's obsession with the land. Being a local, he had to change many of the details. Dan Foley became 'The Bull' McCabe, while Moss Moore, the victim, was replaced with an outsider who wanted to buy land the Bull had his eye on.

In the first production, at the Olympia in Dublin in 1965, award-winning actor Ray McAnally played the Bull. The play was an immediate success. In 1990, Jim Sheridan made a film of the play, starring Limerick actor Richard Harris as The Bull. The film was a huge commercial success, ensuring that Moss Moore will always be remembered and that Dan Foley will live on in infamy.

The film revived bad memories for Dan Foley's family. His nephew John Foley broke years of silence to insist his uncle was an innocent man. Speaking in a TG4 documentary on the case, he insisted his uncle was framed: 'There is no question that Dan Foley was framed. There were those who used the situation for their own gain, and two innocent people suffered as a consequence. My uncle died on the roadway just up from the house when he was about 64. The pressure that was placed on him with the boycott, and all the effort he had to go through in his daily life, put him under continuous strain. He was doing things all on his own, whereas he might have had the help of some neighbours before. The whole thing climaxed on him and brought about his death.'

The final word should go to John B. Keane, the man who brought the story to the world, speaking in *Fuil agus Dúch*: 'Both men were honest and decent men. It is unfortunate that one provoked the other into the ultimate revenge.'

6

THE BRAWL AT THE SILVER DOLLAR

The murder of Cornelius Crowley by John Cronin

GODS MAKE THEIR own importance, Patrick Kavanagh reminded us, and often it is from small local rows that great epics are created. But the opposite is also true: morons define themselves, and life-changing events can be sordid and trivial.

Murder is one such event. A murder leaves everything changed for ever. A person is dead, taken from their family, often leaving a partner alone and children without a parent. Yet the perpetrator also has his life changed. He can face up to two decades in prison, tearing his own family apart.

In Ireland, drink is often at the bottom of it. That was certainly the case in Castleisland on 30 September 1968. Both the victim and the perpetrator were drunk. If either had been sober, the events of that evening would never have happened, and two families would not have been destroyed.

It had been a beautiful autumn day with a bright sun shining out of an almost cloudless sky: real Indian summer conditions. The afternoon had been warm and close, with the heat occasionally relieved by a soft breeze. Castleisland is a small town in north Kerry, roughly equidistant from Abbeyfeale, in south Limerick, and Tralee. It is on the main road from Limerick to Kerry, and benefits from a passing trade. There are few industries in the town, apart from a huge printing press on the outskirts. Back in the late 1960s there was nothing; Castleisland services the local farming community, and without agriculture, the town would have had no purpose.

Cornelius Crowley, 25, was a young farmer who lived with his uncle at Knockrour West, Scartaglin, about six miles from Castleisland. That morning, Crowley came into town with his tractor and trailer. The trailer was full of produce, which he hoped to sell before heading back to his uncle's house. That Monday was a market day, and the town was packed. There was also a funeral, which swelled the crowd. Then as now, the main street of Castleisland is wide. A relic of the old days of English rule, the main street was so wide you could have played a full game of football across it. There were normally a few cars scattered up and down both sides, and an occasional tractor, but there was no shortage of parking. That Monday was different, but he managed to find a place to set up his stall, because he got there early.

Mr Crowley arrived in town around 10 a.m. He parked the tractor and trailer, and then went about his business for the day. After a couple of hours, he took a break for his dinner in one of the local bars and had a few pints and a few half-whiskeys to wash it down. He continued to have the odd beer and the occasional shot through the afternoon. He was not drunk, but he was certainly well lubricated.

Around 6.30 p.m., there was nothing more to be done for the day. Mr Crowley joined two friends – Denis Dunlea and Patrick Kearns – and they went into Hickey's pub, a popular bar called The Silver Dollar, on the main street. They ordered their pints and settled in for a chat.

A lorry driver, John Riordan, spotted the men walking into the pub. He knew Crowley and wanted his help to get a car started, so he followed the three men inside and joined them. The car was not urgent. He could see that Crowley was drunk. He had obviously had a few over the course of the day.

There were several other people present that evening, including a father and son from Castleisland. John Cronin was from Desmond Avenue in the town and was aged 60. Desmond Avenue is a row of small council houses a minute away from the main street. Cronin was with his son Patrick. He had been in Tralee that afternoon, where his wife lived, but when they got back to Castleisland they went to Hickey's, where they stayed until after nine. It was four hours of hard drinking. They had at least four or five pints of stout and some shots.

Patrick Cronin said that he and his father arrived at the pub at 4.45 p.m. At around 6.30 p.m., Mickey McGlynn came over and joined them, talking to Cronin's father. It was not a friendly conversation, and after a few minutes John Cronin called over Mr Hickey and asked him to remove Mr McGlynn. Mr Hickey took McGlynn by the shoulder and led him to the top of the bar, and peace descended once more. But after a while, McGlynn came over again. Once more, Mr Hickey intervened and took the man back to the counter.

At that point, Cornelius Crowley came over and said to John Cronin, 'Don't be pushing an old man.'

John Riordan watched it all from the bar. He heard Cronin reply, 'No man will make me hold my mouth in this bar.'

On hearing this reply, Crowley reached forward and grabbed Cronin by the lapels of his coat.

'He hopped him off the ground,' said Patrick Cronin, who tried to pull Crowley off his father. 'I got a clout from John Riordan,' he added.

The fight was broken up. Patrick Cronin said that both himself and his father were quite drunk by that stage. They had each consumed nine or ten pints during the day. He tried to persuade his father to come home, but his father refused, saying that he would remain in the bar for a while. So Patrick Cronin got up and left, going home alone.

As he consumed more and more drink, John Cronin became

noisy and aggressive. He was causing a bit of a disturbance in the small premises. Around 7.45 p.m. someone called for a song. People turned to Patrick Hickey, the proprietor. He was known for his voice and often provided a tune when asked. He obliged on this occasion, standing to entertain his patrons. Someone called for order. But as he tried to sing, Cronin kept talking over him. Then he got into a row with Mickey McGlynn again. Both men began shouting at one another and a loud argument broke out. Several people turned to quiet the two men so that they could hear the song. One of the men who shushed them was Cornelius Crowley.

'He kept up this incessant talking,' said Mr Hickey. Cronin would not keep quiet. He seemed to take offence with the people who were trying to quieten him, and he singled out Mr Crowley, perhaps because of the earlier scuffle. Words were exchanged, and Cronin was clearly the aggressor.

After his song, Mr Hickey went out to change a barrel, but he overheard the exchange between Cronin and Crowley. He heard the word 'fight' mentioned, and he didn't want that in his premises. 'I told them: "There will be no fighting here. If you want to fight, you can fight outside,"' he said at the subsequent trial.

The two men went out the door onto the street, and a scuffle broke out. It was a scrappy affair, and within a minute both men stumbled back through the door and into the bar. Cronin fell to the ground, landing on his back. Crowley jumped onto him and tried to get on top of him. The older man struggled to keep him off, using his fists and his feet.

A barmaid, 17-year-old Margaret Reidy, said that she heard words between Crowley and Cronin, and the next thing she knew, Crowley had Cronin knocked to the ground.

Very quickly other patrons stepped in and separated the two men. As they were separated, she heard Cronin growl at the younger man, 'I am a man of 60, and I will kill you.' Mr Crowley did not reply. Mr Hickey, the proprietor, made a snap decision. He threw Cronin out of the pub. He had to throw someone out, and he felt that Cronin was the man who had started the trouble. As he was being removed, Cronin struggled and protested. He shouted that he should not be the one who was removed. While he was being pushed out onto the street, Cronin turned back to the bar, and said, 'I'll get you before the night is out.'

Crowley replied, 'You can get me now.'

Mr Crowley thought nothing more of it and sat back with his friends. Margaret Reidy remembered serving Crowley about four pints that evening. She had served four or five drinks – beers and halves of whiskey – to Cronin. She said that either man might also have been served by Mr Hickey, so might have consumed more than that. Crowley's companions finished their drinks, and at around 8.30 p.m. they got up and left Hickey's to go to another pub. There were four of them: Mr Crowley, Mr Dunlea, Mr Kearns and Sean Riordan, who had joined them in the pub.

Shortly after they left the pub, Cronin came back. He began banging on the door and shouting that he wanted to kill someone. 'Let him out or me in,' he roared.

As Crowley was gone, Cronin was let back into the pub. He had a drink he had left unfinished when he was thrown out, and he said he would finish it in spite of everyone. He sat down with the drink. But when he finished it, he was refused another. The publican obviously felt he had had enough for the night. Cronin sat there fuming, but he wasn't causing any trouble so he was left alone.

Creamery manager Sean Lyons was drinking nearby, and he said that he heard Cronin say, 'I'll finish my drink in spite of you, Hickey.' Hickey told him to finish up and get out. Cronin's son Patrick was still there at that stage, urging his father to go home. Cronin got up to leave, but returned to the bar again. His son did not return.

Meanwhile, Mr Crowley, who had gone to another pub, had realised he had left a parcel of meat behind him in The Silver Dollar. Sean Riordan agreed to go back with him. Both men entered The Silver Dollar around 9 p.m. They found the missing parcel, then sat down for a few minutes. All seemed quiet and peaceful. No words were exchanged, though Cronin must have seen both men entering the small premises. He was sitting on his own at the bar.

Local man Timothy O'Sullivan had come into the pub minutes before, and he remembered seeing Crowley come in with Riordan. He saw Cronin at the other end of the bar looking over at them. He heard Cronin mutter, 'I am afraid of no man.'

Crowley and Riordan ordered a drink and settled down for a few minutes – but Crowley did not finish his drink. The door of the pub opened and a young woman outside beckoned for him. He got up and followed her outside. As Crowley left the pub, Cronin slipped off his stool, also leaving his drink unfinished, and followed him outside. He was spotted by several people, including barmaid Margaret Reidy and Timothy O'Sullivan.

'Everything happened in a flash,' said O'Sullivan.

It may have been quick, but there were several witnesses. Many parts of their stories were similar, but there were some discrepancies. Most people thought that Crowley came out of the pub first and that Cronin followed him. Some thought it was the other way around. Almost everyone agreed that the first blow was struck by Cronin.

What nobody knew was that the elderly Cronin, just five years short of his pension, was carrying a knife. It was a penknife that he used for cutting his tobacco. He rushed out and with a roar attacked Mr Crowley. The fight should have been one-sided. Crowley was the younger and stronger man, and that is how it looked to a number of the witnesses, at least at the start. The fight lasted around five minutes, with a lot of shoving and pushing.

Sean Riordan remained inside, drinking his pint. He did not realise what was happening outside. Finally he stood and went to the door. He saw Crowley and Cronin standing near the Crown Hotel, wrestling. It did not look too serious, and he did not want to get involved. He went back into the pub.

At one point, Crowley managed to knock Cronin to the ground, and he was bent over the older man, punching him. Cronin was lying on his back striking upwards, trying to fend off the blows. He was trying to grab Crowley's coat, in order to get a grip on him and gain an advantage.

But then one of the witnesses, a man who was sitting in a parked car nearby, saw that Cronin had his hand on a knife. Timothy O'Connor, a farm labourer, had been sitting in the car with Eugene Clifford and Tom Clifford when he saw Crowley come out of Hickey's, followed by another man. O'Connor and his companions watched the fight unfold until they saw Crowley bending, grabbing the prone man by the coat and kicking him in the face.

O'Connor saw Cronin raise his hand, striking Crowley three times. He saw Cronin holding something shiny. Although O'Connor could not tell its size or shape, it looked like it could be a knife. After Cronin had raised his hand holding the shiny object, Crowley let go of him and staggered backwards, into the door of the pub.

O'Connor saw Cronin pick himself up from the ground, and put something into his coat pocket. He did not know if it was a knife.

Eugene Clifford said that he had seen the start of the fight and that Cronin had thrown the first punch. Then Crowley had knocked him to the ground and started kicking him in the head, while Cronin struggled to get up. The struggle lasted four or five minutes. His account differs from the others; he said that Crowley stood back and let Cronin get up, after which Cronin had struck him on the back of the head.

Tom Clifford gave the fullest account of the fight. He told the trial that he had seen two men come out of the pub. The first, Cronin, had a fighting attitude. He attacked Crowley, throwing a punch at the younger man. However, Crowley fought back, throwing a punch that staggered Cronin, and he followed up with a second punch, which dropped the older man to the ground. Crowley then stepped forward and kicked him twice in the head. But he didn't pursue his advantage, and stepped back. Cronin got to his feet and came at Crowley. He lunged towards his chest. After this strike, Crowley seemed to jump back, and he stretched out both his arms, while his body bent forward. He turned and staggered back into Hickey's bar.

One of the witnesses was a niece of Cronin. Bridie Moynihan said that she saw Cronin being kicked in the head by the younger man. 'The fellow on top of him got up and stood for a full minute before running into Hickey's bar,' she said.

Patrick Hickey said that he had gone to the door with one of his patrons when he heard the sounds of a scuffle outside. He could see Cronin on the ground on his back, striking up at Crowley. Crowley was bent over the older man and was striking him. 'Just about that time, Crowley started running towards my door,' he said. 'He came through the door, passed me, turned round and opened his coat. I saw blood all over the front of his shirt.'

Sean Riordan was stunned to see his friend stagger into the pub with 'blood coming out of his shirt'. He stumbled into someone's arms and then fell to the floor.

Timothy O'Sullivan said, 'I saw Crowley backing into the door with his shirt all blood. He got some kind of weakness and fell into my hands. I saw a long kind of a wound underneath his heart. Every time Crowley gave a sigh, we could see blood pumping out.'

Sean Lyons said, 'I saw blood dripping onto the ground. Crowley put his hand inside his shirt and said, "My heart . . . It's all over."'

Mr Lyons immediately rushed past Hickey to the street. He saw Cronin approach the door of the pub, his hands moving about in an agitated manner. He was shouting and roaring, saying, 'Come out, or I'll get in.'

Riordan ran to the door and looked outside. He saw John Cronin turn from the pub and go down a lane, then come back up again and walk around a bit of the town. He still appeared agitated.

Inside the bar, frantic efforts were being made to save Crowley. A doctor was sent for immediately. Dr Donal Geaney found Crowley semi-conscious when he arrived at the bar. He had a few injuries, but the most serious was a deep stab wound, one to one and a half inches long, in his chest. Realising that this was a life-threatening injury, the doctor bundled Crowley into his car and drove as fast as he could to the County Hospital in Tralee. It was a distance of a little over 12 miles, but the roads were poor and winding. The trip took almost half an hour.

Surgeon Colm Galvin was on duty when the doctor rushed Crowley into the hospital at 9.55 p.m. He could see a stab wound to the left side of the chest. The knife had penetrated through the chest wall, the covering of the heart itself. He decided to open Crowley's chest to try to stop the bleeding – but before he could do so, Crowley's heart stopped pumping. The surgeon immediately commenced cardiac massage, but to no avail. Crowley was gone.

The surgeon pronounced him dead at 10 p.m. Death was due to shock and haemorrhage, the result of a stab wound to the chest. He thought that the wound could have been made by an upward thrust of a knife. It was now a murder investigation.

The Gardaí were on the scene immediately and conducted a number of interviews with witnesses. There were enough of them. It didn't take Sherlock Holmes to figure out who was responsible. The street outside the pub was blocked off, with Gardaí on duty to preserve the scene. They also began a minute search of the area, to try and find the murder weapon. They found a bloodstained knife in a garden. One man, Michael Drumm, identified the knife as one he had seen in Cronin's possession a week before the murder.

Garda James London told the court that he was walking through Castleisland on the night of the murder, searching for Mr Cronin. He bumped into the man on his way home. Cronin immediately said, 'Are you looking for me? I was going down to you, but on the way I fell into the river and I am all wet.' Later, as the Garda was bringing him to the station, Cronin said, 'I am a man of 60, but I got the better of him.'

Cronin was searched. He had a bar of plug tobacco but nothing else on him. Garda London asked Cronin if he had lost his knife, but he said he had left it at home. The Garda was of the opinion that Cronin had taken drink, but was not drunk.

As they walked to the station, Cronin said, 'I was cursed to come home. I always stay in Tralee to see the missus, but Paddy brought me home to see the lads. I'm not dead yet.' A few minutes later, he said, 'He was a tall blondy fellow, and he fought with me. He knocked me to the ground, but he would not do it if I was younger.'

John Cronin was taken in for questioning as soon as they arrived at the station. Detective Sergeant Sean O'Connell told the trial that he had a rambling conversation with the chief suspect hours after the murder. Cronin told him that he had gone to The Silver Dollar that night, and had got into a row with the owner, Mr Hickey. After that, a 'blondy fellow' had started picking on him, and they had got into a fight in the bar. 'I got the best of the blondy fellow,' he said.

After that, he said, he had left the pub. But the man had followed him and attacked him. When the sergeant informed Cronin that Cornelius Crowley had died of stab wounds, the man replied, 'If he got stuck, I did not stick him.' He said that a number of times, and added, 'How could I stick him? I have no knife.'

He added that the 'blondy fellow' didn't have a knife either, and the fight broke up when people pulled the two men apart.

After the fight on the street outside the pub, Cronin said that he had ambled off and gone to the river, where he fell in. That sobered him a bit, and he waded across the river to the other side, and went home. 'You might commit me, but I did not do it,' he said.

When shown the knife the Garda had recovered from a garden, Cronin denied that it was his.

Later, his son Patrick visited him in the station, to give him some fresh clothes to change into after the fall into the river. Cronin was overheard saying, 'They are saying that I stabbed him, but I did nothing to him.'

A second Garda, John O'Connell, interviewed Cronin, who told him he had taken 14 or 15 pints that night. In his statement, Cronin said that he had been in Hickey's bar having a few drinks when Mickey McGlynn approached him. Mr Hickey pulled McGlynn away. He said that there was a 'blondy fellow' (Crowley) who was pushing McGlynn on him and his son all night. As he had had trouble with McGlynn's son in the past, he was not happy with the situation.

At one stage, the 'blondy' man had hit him. When he left the pub, the 'blondy fellow' followed him and knocked him to the ground. Some of the bystanders pulled the man off him, and Cronin went off. He went down to the river to urinate, and fell in. He waded across the river and headed towards home. He was found shortly after by the Garda.

Cronin was charged with murder. The case came to trial in February 1969, in the Central Criminal Court in Dublin.

Assistant State Pathologist Dr Raymond O'Neill told the court that he had performed an autopsy on Cornelius Crowley. He found six stab wounds. The fatal wound was in the cavity of the heart. There was a second wound to the chest, three on the hip and one on the thumb. Dr O'Neill said that it was unlikely that Crowley could have remained on his feet for more than a minute after receiving the fatal stab to the heart. He said he had been shown a penknife on which there were stains. The stains proved to be human blood, type O. The victim had blood type O. Beyond that, he could not confirm that the blood on the knife was that of Crowley.

The court heard from many witnesses, who gave conflicting

accounts of the final few minutes of Crowley's life. The case lasted four days, at the end of which Mr Justice Butler said that he was not happy that all the witnesses had been completely frank with the court. He complained of their selective memories, saying, 'A number of witnesses obviously know a lot more and were in a position to tell more than they stated in court.'

Although he did not go into specifics, he was probably referring to the fact that only one witness, Timothy O'Connor, mentioned seeing a knife, despite the fight taking place on a clear, light evening in front of a large number of people.

Mr Cronin did not testify on his own behalf. His barrister, P.J. Lindsay, told the jury that Cronin was not testifying on his advice. 'He is not obliged to give evidence, and the state's case falls far short of the proof necessary for a conviction,' he said. He argued that the deceased, Cornelius Crowley, was a big, stocky man who had picked on the much smaller and older Cronin in the pub, and had knocked him down. Later, he had come up behind Cronin on the street, and knocked him again. 'I would like to know who the aggressor was in those cases,' he said. 'Mr Crowley had a considerable amount of drink, was very irate and had the intention of attacking an old man.'

Lindsay said that his client denied owning the knife that killed Crowley, but even if it was his knife, possession of a pocketknife was not illegal. The jury would also have to consider the question of provocation, and of self-defence.

But the judge, Mr Justice Butler, said that the case did not meet the criteria for self-defence. 'The methods and the means used in self-defence must be in proportion to the force of the attack. If a person is attacked by fists or even a truncheon, he is not entitled to shoot a gun or take up a knife against the other person,' he said. The only question the jury had to consider was whether there was provocation involved. If there was, the jury had the option of reducing the murder charge to manslaughter. 'The evidence points to Cronin hitting Crowley first, and looking for a fight,' he said.

The jury took an hour and a half to return a verdict of guilty of murder against Cronin. They recommended mercy, due to his age. Judge Butler sentenced him to life in prison. A drunken fair day had proved very costly. Cronin would hit pension age behind bars, and all for something as trivial as a few drunken words in a bar.

7

SOUR END FOR SWEET SHOP OWNER

Patrick Walsh, Patrick Walsh and the murder of Lil May O'Sullivan

SOME THINGS NEVER change. The elderly and those who live alone are always vulnerable. In recent years, we have grown used to attacks on rural farmers, and gangs who prey on the elderly. Often when a person lives alone, the rumours grow of their great wealth, hidden under mattresses or in drawers. They seem like easy targets to the unscrupulous. But this is nothing new; those attacks were going on a generation ago.

On a summer night in Listowel in 1983, two young men – one not yet out of his teens – decided they could make a quick few quid by doing over a small sweet shop. It was a soft target, because the proprietor was an elderly woman who lived alone. When they did not find enough money to satisfy themselves, they savagely beat the old woman to death. They later tried to squirm out of the prosecution by blaming the Gardaí for extracting confessions from them. It was a strategy that almost succeeded, with one of the defendants coming close to getting away with murder.

Elizabeth Mary O'Sullivan was an institution in Listowel.

Known as Lil May, she had a small sweet shop on William Street, which she lived above. The shop was no gold mine, but she managed to do enough business to pay the bills and live a modest life. The 79 year old was known as a friendly and accommodating woman who was always nice to the children who were her customers. You could knock on her door late at night and she would open up and serve you. She was from a different era and operated to a different set of standards.

She had never married, but she did not live alone. Her widowed cousin, Margaret Snow, was staying with her, sharing the small living quarters above the shop. On the night of 1 July, Maureen McMahon, a friend of the sweet shop owner, was with her in the kitchen behind the shop. They chatted as Lil May counted the takings for the day and then put them away. At around 11.30 p.m., Maureen McMahon got up and left, leaving Ms O'Sullivan alone.

Around this time, Michael Hayes was passing the sweet shop. The lights were on, and he could hear voices. He thought they were children. It is possible that he heard Ms McMahon before she left. It is equally possible he heard, and misinterpreted, something more sinister . . .

The following morning, 2 July, Margaret Snow came downstairs and entered the kitchen. The sight that met her was horrifying. The place was a shambles. Drawers had been turned out, cupboards opened and items scattered all around the place. Furniture was overturned, and there were signs of a violent struggle having taken place in the kitchen and adjoining scullery. But the worst horror of all was the body of Lil May sprawled on the floor, with her head caved in. Nearby was a broken pot, which was covered in gore and human hair. It was a scene out of a nightmare.

The Gardaí were immediately called, and the house was sealed off as a murder investigation swung into action. It was not difficult to figure out what had happened. The premises had been broken into and ransacked for money. Ms O'Sullivan had been beaten badly, probably in an effort to force her to cough up more. Then she had been bludgeoned to death with a kitchen pot. It was a horrific, savage and senseless assault on an elderly and frail woman.

She had suffered several injuries to her face and head, including a severe gash on her head. Forensic tests showed that she had been struck with the broken pot. The medical evidence suggested that she had been hit with the pot initially, but when the pot broke, she was struck with the handle. The fatal blows had been delivered by the handle.

While the body was removed for the State Pathologist to begin the autopsy and while experts from the Garda Technical Bureau photographed and analysed the crime scene, the local Gardaí did their job. They went door to door, carrying out interviews and looking for potential witnesses. Real detective work is nothing like it is in television programmes, and progress is often slow. It is like putting together a jigsaw. You get all the pieces, and slowly and painstakingly you put them together until the picture emerges. Interviews are a vital part of the process, but the job of taking witness statements is time-consuming, especially as many of the people interviewed will have seen nothing and will have nothing to contribute to the investigation. To streamline the process, Gardaí use questionnaires. Everyone in the area is asked to fill them out. They ask the basic questions: where were you, what did you see, what time was that? Once the questionnaires are in, the Gardaí can quickly analyse them and see who was nearby at the relevant times and who needs to be interviewed in greater depth.

After carrying out the interviews, two suspects did emerge. Both were young men and, coincidentally, they shared a name. Both were also from the same part of town, O'Connell Avenue in Listowel. Patrick Walsh, 19, was known as Pa Ned, while Patrick Walsh, 22, was known as Baker. They were from the travelling community. Within three days of the discovery of the body, both men had been arrested and charged with murder. An efficient investigation and a quick result: it looked like an open-and-shut case.

However, it was when it came to trial that the whole sordid business got interesting, as an attempt was made by the defence to turn the spotlight on the Gardaí in order to get the two Walshes off the hook.

The trial opened in the Central Criminal Court in Dublin at the end of June 1984, almost a year after the brutal murder. Prosecuting barrister Anthony Kennedy opened by telling the jury that Ms O'Sullivan's injuries included brain damage and a broken skull. He said that the state would attempt to prove that the two men had ransacked Ms O'Sullivan's home and then beaten her to death: 'The attack was gruesome, sordid and merciless. The way she was done in was pretty gruesome. She was badly beaten up, and finally bludgeoned to death.'

Kennedy said that when Gardaí distributed questionnaires around the town, discrepancies were spotted in some of the answers. Patrick 'Baker' Walsh said that he was at home at 11.20 p.m., which put him out of the frame. Patrick 'Pa Ned' Walsh had been home even earlier, by 10.35 p.m. Yet several witnesses had seen them out and about long after this. 'It is plain that both of them were lying,' he said.

(For the sake of simplicity we will refer to both men from now on as Baker Walsh and Pa Ned Walsh.)

One man, Maurice Kelliher, saw both of them shortly after eleven in Joe Broderick's pub. Then a barmaid in Grogan's bar, Mrs Jetta Grogan, said that she had seen both accused in her premises at 11.10 p.m. They asked her for a plastic bag or a box, but she said she had neither, and the men left. The last sighting of the two, out and about in Listowel when they had told Gardaí they were home, was at 12.20 a.m. Those sightings put them firmly back in the frame for murder.

When the Gardaí checked out their statements, the inconsistencies were obvious. Baker Walsh's brother Dominick said that he got home at 12.30 a.m. and Baker was already home. There was some change on the table, and Baker said that he did not know if Lil May was dead or not. Before they went to bed, Baker had told him not to say anything.

Edward Walsh, brother of Pa Ned, made a statement to Gardaí in which he said that his brother told him to say that he was at home by 11 p.m. if the Gardaí asked him. But in court, on the opening day of the trial, he said that this statement was untrue and had only been made because the Gardaí had beaten and threatened him, and told him that he would be charged with being an accessory to murder.

This set the tone for the remainder of the trial.

On the second day, one of the two accused, Baker Walsh, attempted to have the statements he made to Garda thrown out. He alleged that he had made the statements under intense duress. It was a key moment in the trial. In the statements, he admitted his involvement in the murder. If the statements were thrown out, he would start the trial with a fresh slate.

Instead of considering the case, the jury were asked to decide on the question of duress: had the statement been as a result of threats? It was almost like a trial within a trial.

Baker Walsh claimed that he had been beaten and threatened. Referring to a statement taken by Detective Sergeant Tim Callaghan and Detective Garda Con Sullivan at Tralee Gardaí Station, he said he made the statement because 'I feared for my life.' He went on to allege that he had been beaten, punched and shoved against a wall by the Gardaí during his interrogation. He had been made to strip to his underwear and bounced off a table, before one of the Gardaí squeezed his testicles. His arms and legs had been twisted. At one point, a poker was shoved into his mouth. He was terrified when he finally made the statement, he told the jury: 'I just said anything that came into my head. I was sore all over from the beating.'

Such an ordeal should have left marks, but Dr Patrick English told the court that he had examined Baker Walsh on the night of 5 July, a few days after the murder and during the interrogation. He found no fresh injuries on Walsh that would support his claims that he had been beaten in custody.

The defence produced their own medical witness, who said that he had examined Walsh two days after Dr English, and

Walsh had complained of an injury to his right elbow. He seemed to have a full range of movement in the arm, but claimed it was tender and sore.

Detective Sergeant Callaghan and Detective Garda Sullivan both testified that the statement they had taken had been given voluntarily by Walsh and that there were no threats of violence towards or mistreatment of the prisoner.

After hearing each side, the jury decided that the statements were not made as a result of threats and should be allowed. Mr Justice Kevin Lynch agreed. It was a blow to the defence, but it did not change their approach to the trial.

The following day, the jury of nine men and three women were asked to make a similar decision about the statement made to Gardaí by the other accused, Pa Ned Baker. He, too, claimed that the statement had been beaten out of him. His barrister, Patrick McEntee, said, 'My client will say that he was told that if he didn't make a statement he would be killed in the station, his body taken outside, and nobody would care because he was a tinker.'

'That is not true,' replied Detective Garda John Grant, who was one of the officers who had interviewed Walsh. The Garda went on to say that he had not seen anyone hitting or mistreating Walsh, and that he had not hit him or mistreated him himself. He added that the accused had not been denied access to a solicitor.

The barrister accused the detective of being part of a team that were interviewing Walsh in relays, to keep the pressure on him. He said that some of the officers had used intimidation and violence during the interviews and had 'frightened the life' out of Walsh. Garda Grant denied this.

The next man to give evidence was a member of the Garda Technical Bureau, the forensics experts from Dublin. Detective Sergeant Patrick Lynagh was an interrogation expert drafted in to help out on big cases. He had interviewed Walsh along with Detective Garda Tom Byrne. He said that Walsh told him he knew the victim, Ms O'Sullivan, because he used to buy sweets in her shop. When he got older, he used to deliver briquettes to the shop. They broke the interview for a while, and resumed it in the afternoon. This time Walsh told him that the only thing he knew about the murder was what he had read in the paper: that the victim had been found 'in a pool of blood'. He made no admission of his involvement to the detective.

When cross-examined on the interrogation, Detective Sergeant Lynagh denied that he had screamed in Walsh's ear: 'We know you did it, we have people who saw you.' He also denied striking the prisoner in the genitals. This was backed up by the other interrogator, Detective Garda Byrne. He told the jury that he had seen no one pull Walsh's hair, slap his face or strike his genitals during the questioning.

The next witness proved emotional and harrowing. The mother of one of the accused spoke about her visit to her son during the interrogation. It did not make easy listening. Mary Walsh, Pa Ned's mother, said that she had gone to Tralee Garda Station on the night of 5 July. She had arrived there around 8 p.m., accompanied by her son Edward. They entered the station and asked to speak to Pa Ned, but the Gardaí told them to come back in an hour.

When she came back to the station at 9 p.m., she was led upstairs to a room by a plainclothes Garda. She was kept in the room. 'I was very frightened. One of them was pounding on the table and called me a fucking whore and a cunt and a prostitute. I was very upset,' the woman said. As this was going on, she could hear the sound of her son Edward shouting and roaring in one of the rooms downstairs. She asked for a drink of water, but was refused. She asked again, saying that she was diabetic. It was only then that she was given the water. Eventually a Garda produced a form and asked her to sign it. Being unable to read or write, she did not know what was on the form. She did not want to sign it. However, the Garda told her that if she did not, she would be charged as an accessory to the murder. Reluctantly she put an X on the paper.

It was midnight before she was allowed to see her son. She

was allowed a short conversation with him. 'He told me he had been kicked around, and that he was ailing in the stomach. He said that he had been kicked in the private parts. I got very frightened when I saw his condition,' she said.

But, as in the case of Baker Walsh, the state provided medical evidence that Pa Ned Walsh had not been abused while in custody. Dr English was called back to give evidence. He said that he had been present on the evening of 5 July at the Garda station in Tralee. He had examined Baker Walsh, whom he found had not been injured, but he didn't have time to examine the other man. So the following morning he returned and saw Pa Ned Walsh.

Dr English found a number of small abrasions on Walsh's left wrist and knuckle, and a scar on his abdomen. But all of these injuries were eight to ten days old, and he found nothing fresh that might have been caused while the accused was in custody. Walsh refused to remove his trousers, and the doctor respected this, so there was no evidence one way or the other about his claim to have had his testicles struck.

'While I was examining him, Detective Fitzpatrick asked him if he had any complaints,' the doctor said. 'He said that he couldn't sleep in the cell because there was a smell of piss, the blankets were dirty and he was cold.'

As the trial within the trial entered its third day, Pa Ned Walsh himself gave evidence. The 19 year old – who was only 18 at the time of the murder – said that when he was questioned by Detective Sergeant Lynagh and Detective Garda Byrne, he gave an honest account of his movements on the night. However, the two detectives made it clear to him that they did not believe him. According to Walsh, one of the detectives shouted in his ear, while the other slapped him in the face and pulled his hair.

Finally one of the detectives wrote out a statement and handed it to Walsh to read over. He was not able to read, so he just pretended to go over it. But he refused to sign it. Then the two detectives left, and another two took over the interrogation. They kept shouting at him, but he wouldn't budge: he did not sign the paper. Finally his solicitor arrived, and he got a break. He never mentioned the physical intimidation to the solicitor.

Walsh told the jury that the next interrogator was Detective Garda John Grant. Grant made him drop to the floor and do press-ups. He said that he was held on the floor for up to an hour, and then made to stand on his tiptoes for a further period. During this time, he was struck in the groin a number of times. He continued to be questioned in relays, with two detectives in rotation all day. One of the detectives said to him that if he didn't sign the statement, 'the beating will really start'.

'One of them said to me if you don't sign the statement we will kill you, throw your body on the road, and nobody will care because you are a tinker,' he said.

During the day-long ordeal, he met his co-accused, Baker Walsh, twice. Baker told him to sign the statement or the Gardaí would continue to beat him (Baker). From this, Pa Ned inferred that his co-accused was being given similar treatment to himself.

Pa Ned Walsh told the jury that one of the interrogators, Detective McCarthy, told him that if he signed the statement, he would be done for manslaughter rather than murder: 'In the end I signed it, because I was fed up being bullied and to get my brother and mother out of the Garda station. Nothing in the statement was said by me.'

Pa Ned Walsh's solicitor Robert Pierce said that he had visited Walsh in the Garda station. He made no complaints about his treatment, but when the solicitor returned later, Walsh looked very tired. He had bloodshot eyes, and he seemed to be very disorientated.

After presenting the evidence to the jury, both the state and the defence took one last chance to put their case. Barrister McEntee told the jury that the trial within the trial was not a 'disciplinary inquiry' into the conduct of the Gardaí, saying, 'You have to assess Mr Walsh from the evidence before you. It is clear that he is a youth of limited education and cultural resources. If there is any possibility that any of the statements at issue came about because Mr Walsh chose to do what was the lesser of two evils, those statements are not admissible in law.'

McEntee said that even if the jury did not believe that blows had been struck during the questioning, it was still open to them to find that the interrogation method was designed to sap Walsh of his will and so secure a confession.

Barrister Anthony Kennedy, for the state, described the allegations of Walsh as 'wild'. 'There has been a wild allegation that the accused was subjected to relentless interrogation throughout the day, and to non-stop barracking and physical abuse. This was not the case. The accused was allowed two visits from his solicitor, and the Gardaí did not put a time limit on those visits. Medical evidence has shown that he suffered no physical injury,' he said.

Now it was up to the jury. They had a simple choice. If they accepted that the statements made by Pa Ned Walsh had been made under duress, they could not be admitted as evidence. That would be a severe blow to the state, but they might still get the prosecution over the line. On the other hand, the jury could allow the statements into evidence. That would almost guarantee Walsh's conviction. Both sides awaited the outcome nervously. The state may have felt a touch of optimism; in the first trial within a trial, the jury had ruled that Baker Walsh's statements to the Gardaí could be used in the trial. Would they decide the same way this time?

In the end, neither side won. The jury were unable to decide whether to admit the statements or not. It left the judge in a difficult position. He had no choice: he had to release Pa Ned Walsh. The trial had collapsed. A new date would have to be set and a new jury sworn in.

But that still left Baker Walsh. He had lost his trial within a trial. Now the real trial could begin. The first proper witness was Detective Sergeant Tim Callaghan. He told the court that he had shown Baker Walsh the bloodstained pot they had recovered from Lil May O'Sullivan's kitchen. Detective Sergeant O'Callaghan said that Baker Walsh told him that he recognised the pot: he had seen it in Lil May's kitchen and had struck her a number of times with the handle of the pot. He then made a statement, which the sergeant read to the court.

Baker had met Pa Ned Walsh around 7 p.m. on 1 July, and the two men had gone on a pub crawl to several bars around Listowel. Around ten minutes before closing time – which was 11.30 p.m. back then – Pa Ned had said to him, 'Come on, drink up and we will knock off Lil May's tonight.' The two men went to the shop and pushed their way inside. Pa Ned locked the door behind them. Then he shouted, 'We are robbing the place. We want money.'

Lil May O'Sullivan, despite being nearly eighty, confronted the two men and told them to get out. But Pa Ned pulled her into the scullery and knocked her to the floor. He then beat her with his fists.

Detective Sergeant O'Callaghan continued to read Baker Walsh's statement to the court: 'She was on the floor and Patrick [Pa Ned] was hitting her, and I went over and started hitting her with my fist into the face. Patrick was shouting: "We will have to do her in. She knows us." He got up and got a big pot off the range and he struck Lil May a couple of times in the head with the pot.'

The handle of the pot broke off during the beating, and Pa Ned Walsh hit Lil May on the head and face with the handle a couple of times, then passed the handle over to Baker Walsh.

'I hit her a few times in the head and face with it,' the statement went on.

The two men then went to Baker's house, where they halved the money they had stolen. Pa Ned went home.

Dr English was called back to the box for the third time. This time, his evidence was damning. He said that when he was introduced to Baker Walsh in the Garda station on the evening of 5 July, he heard Sergeant Fitzpatrick, one of the interrogators, say: 'Pat, have you any complaints to make? Are you happy with your treatment so far? Do you feel better now you've said what you did?'

The doctor heard Baker reply, ''Twas a bad thing I done.'

The sergeant had replied, 'It was, but at least you are man enough to admit it.'

Baker Walsh was admitting nothing when it came to his turn to give evidence. He told the jury that he had been drinking on the night of the murder and was on his way home when he decided to go into the sweet shop for a packet of chocolate biscuits. While he was inside, Pa Ned Walsh had come rushing in, banging in the door. He shouted that he was robbing the place; then he jumped over the counter and chased Lil May O'Sullivan into the kitchen at the back. The woman was screaming as he chased her.

Baker said that when he followed them into the kitchen, Lil May was on the floor. Pa Ned said that she had fallen. He helped Pa Ned pick her up. Then he picked up the money that was lying on the table. Pa Ned had told him to do that. 'I went and got the money and ran,' Walsh told the jury. 'I did it because he shouted at me to do it. When I left the shop I didn't know she was dead.'

When cross-examined, he said he did not know how the frail old woman had suffered so many injuries. He denied that he and Pa Ned had beaten her in an attempt to force her to find more money for them.

The final witness was Dr Liam Daly of the Central Mental Hospital in Dundrum. He said that he had examined Walsh and found that he suffered from a disordered personality. He had experienced considerable neurotic conflict in his childhood and would likely react in panic when placed in a stressful situation.

After the drama of the two trials within the trial, the trial itself was quick. It lasted just two days, in contrast to the six that had preceded it. The jury took an hour and 20 minutes to find Baker Walsh guilty of murder. Mr Justice Lynch imposed the mandatory life sentence.

His co-accused, Pa Ned Walsh, was not off the hook either. Later in the year, at the end of October, his second trial opened in the Central Criminal Court in Dublin. His defence team had reason to be quietly optimistic. They had to convince the jury to disallow the statements made by Pa Ned Walsh while in custody, and they were home free. Alternatively, if they could divide the jury, like in the first trial, the proceedings would collapse. It was unlikely that the state would order a third trial on the same charges (though later, in the case of the death of farmer Paddy Daly, there were three trials for both men accused of the murder – see Chapter 10). Their man could walk. The third possibility was the one they did not like to contemplate: the jury would allow the statements, and Pa Ned would join Baker behind bars.

The prosecution barrister began quite forcibly, painting a picture of the murder that the jury were unlikely to forget: 'Ms O'Sullivan was bludgeoned to death with an iron kitchen pot at her home. It was a merciless attack on a defenceless old lady. Her head was bashed in a savage and horrific way. She could put up little resistance. She was hit so hard her skull was broken and her head was bashed in.'

Pathologist Dr Kieran Cuddihy piled coals on the fire, saying that the elderly spinster had been struck many times. Her injuries included depressed fractures of the skull, multiple lacerations and deep cuts, bruising to her nose and lips, and a fractured bone in her throat. She had died of cardiac failure as a result of head and brain injuries.

However, Dr Maureen Smyth, a forensic scientist, said that she had examined the clothing of Pa Ned Walsh, as well as that of Baker Walsh, already convicted, and had found nothing to connect them with the crime.

After the preliminaries were over, the real battle could commence. It was time to ask the jury whether the controversial interview statements would be allowed into evidence. Detective Sergeant Patrick Lynagh was the first to give evidence. He denied a defence suggestion that he had punched Pa Ned Walsh in the stomach and kicked him in the genitals during the interview.

Detective Sergeant Lynagh said that he had informed Pa Ned that his fingerprints had been found at the scene. The accused replied, 'They could be in the shop. I was there on Wednesday. No way are they in the kitchen or any other part of the house.'

Baker Walsh, who had already been convicted of murder, was called to give evidence. But he told the court that he had an appeal coming up (it would prove to be unsuccessful) and he declined to answer any question. 'I have been informed that I need not answer any questions that would incriminate me,' he said.

A series of Gardaí were called to the witness box. One by one they denied all suggestions that they had used violence and intimidation to secure the confessions from both Walshes. They also denied an allegation from Pa Ned Walsh that he had been prevented from using the toilet during an entire day of questioning.

Barrister Patrick McEntee, representing Walsh, as he had in the first trial, questioned the adequacy of the room made available for Walsh to consult with his solicitor, Robert Pierce. The day room of the Garda station had been used, and McEntee wondered why the billiard room was not given to the solicitor. He was told that the billiard room had been converted into a canteen and had been closed for security reasons. McEntee thundered, 'Was it that my client might pilfer chocolate bars?'

Sergeant Jeremiah Cronin answered that there were two windows in the canteen through which Walsh might have made his escape.

Mr McEntee replied, 'What? Mr Pierce might have lowered him down in a basket?'

It got a laugh from the jury, but Sergeant Cronin got the last word in the exchange: 'No need for that. The canteen is on the ground floor.'

It was not going well for the defence.

Mr McEntee also clashed with Dr English, who was giving evidence again of examining Walsh and finding no signs of fresh injuries. He questioned why Dr English examined Baker

Walsh on the night of 5 July, but came back the following morning to examine Pa Ned Walsh. By that time, signs of hair-pulling and slapping would have faded away.

'I saw no sign of assault or injury on the first man, and I assumed that I would find none on the second either,' replied the doctor. After more questioning from Mr McEntee, the doctor said that he had not spelled it out to Walsh that the medical examination was for his own good, as he assumed the prisoner would understand that a doctor was there for his good without being told. McEntee sneered, 'You might have had difficulty in convincing inmates of German concentration camps of that.' It was a remark that did not go down well with the jury.

Solicitor Robert Pierce was the next to give evidence in the trial within a trial. What he said was controversial and explosive. He told the jury that he had warned his client, Pa Ned Walsh, about a particular Garda at the Tralee station. 'I told him not to make a statement and I told him they [the Gardaí] were trying to get a statement from him. I particularly warned him several times about a particular Garda,' said Mr Pierce.

He said that he had seen Walsh twice on 5 July, the day he was questioned. On the second occasion, Walsh seemed tired and his physical condition had deteriorated badly. However, he did not make any complaint about being assaulted by the Garda.

After hearing several days of evidence, the judge told the jury that the Gardaí were entitled to keep up their questioning of a suspect, even over quite a long period of time. It was their duty to persevere to the utmost in their questioning, so long as they did not infringe on the rights of the person being questioned and so long as no improper means were used. The Gardaí were not entitled to shout, intimidate or degrade a suspect. A statement was not invalid because questioning went on for a long time, or because the accused was tired at the end of the day. But the jury would have to decide whether Walsh's story of not being allowed to go to the toilet during day-long questioning was credible.

The jury retired to consider whether to allow the statements at issue into evidence. The first jury had failed to reach a decision, forcing the retrial. Would the second jury do the same? They came close. But in the end they decided to allow three statements into evidence. Two were rejected, as the jury felt they were 'not made freely and voluntarily' and should not be considered.

It was a qualified win for the prosecution. Now the real trial could begin. It didn't take long; the three statements were very incriminating.

In one statement, read by Detective Garda Martin McCarthy, Pa Ned said that he grabbed £14 from Ms O'Sullivan's table and that both he and Baker then struck the elderly lady with their fists. The statement went on: 'I hit her all over the body. She fell on the floor. She was bleeding badly. There was a pot on the floor. We got excited and picked up the pot and hit her a few belts with it. She remained where she was lying.'

Pa Ned gave evidence. He said he had been drinking cider with Baker Walsh, and both were very drunk when they went into Ms O'Sullivan's shop. Baker claimed that they had no intention of robbing the shop at that point. They were there for biscuits. However, once they were inside, he decided to carry out the robbery. He jumped over the counter and ran into the kitchen behind and grabbed all the money from the table. Ms O'Sullivan had been counting it with her friend Maureen McMahon only a short while before. There was just £14, which Baker scooped up and put into his pocket. He then began searching for more money, but Ms O'Sullivan began shouting at him and Baker.

She yelled at Baker: 'I know you: I know you're the baker's son.'

Pa Ned went on: 'I started to run for the back door. I saw Paddy Baker pick up the pot and I ran. I did not see what he did with the pot. I saw no more of what happened.'

He was putting the blame squarely on his friend. By coincidence, Baker Walsh had done the very same thing in his trial: he had blamed Pa Ned for starting the fatal assault.

Pa Ned said that he waited outside for a few minutes until

Baker joined him, and they both left. He didn't know Lil May O'Sullivan had died until the following morning, and he didn't know she had been beaten to death until the Gardaí told him.

The jury took two and a half hours to consider their verdict. It was their unanimous decision that he was guilty of murder. Mr Justice O'Hanlon sentenced him to life imprisonment. Both friends had come together to prey on a vulnerable member of their community. Now they had several years together to contemplate the fruits of their brutish action.

8

THE KERRY BABIES CASE

Joanne Hayes and the baby on the beach

IF CHRIST HAD decided to abandon the Middle East and appear instead in Mullingar – or any town in Ireland – during the 1980s, it would have been a safe bet that Christianity would not have taken root. Ireland was not a good place to be young, pregnant and unmarried in those not-so-distant days. To produce a child out of wedlock was a huge social stigma, and a disgrace to the family of the offending girl. People went to extraordinary lengths to cover it up.

Often girls were sent to relatives in Dublin, or England, until the baby could be born and discreetly placed in an institution, or furtively adopted. Sometimes the child was kept at home and passed off as a late addition to the grandmother's brood. Often a child would grow up not knowing that its eldest sister was really its mother.

Teenage girls would go to extraordinary lengths to hide their pregnancies, often wearing baggy jumpers and coats through the summer months to hide a growing bump, rather than coming out into the open and seeking help. We all knew it was happening, but no one spoke about it. It would take a tragedy to begin to change people's perceptions.

137

Nineteen eighty-four gave us that tragedy: twice – once in Longford, and, later in the year, in Kerry. The Longford case was harrowing. Fifteen-year-old Anne Lovett managed to reach her full term without anyone realising she was pregnant. Her parents, her friends, her teachers: they all missed the clues. On a freezing day, 31 January, the labour pains hit, and no one knew she was even expecting. She was certainly not going to tell anyone and bring disgrace down on herself and her family. In desperation, she turned to aid from above. She went to the church in the village of Granard, where she lived.

She sought shelter in the grotto to the Virgin Mary, a woman who had found herself in a similar situation 2,000 years earlier. The young girl gave birth, alone and in the open. It was not a well-frequented spot, especially on a cold winter's day, so it was some time before a passer-by spotted the young girl. By the time she was discovered, the child had died and Anne had gone into shock from blood-loss. She died later that day in hospital.

There should have been an outcry, but there wasn't, at least not at first. Such tragedies were buried in Ireland. No one spoke of them. Life went on and no lessons were learned. But one local man was not happy with that situation. He phoned the *Sunday Tribune* and spilled the beans. Five days after the funeral of Anne and her little baby, the news finally broke. For the next week, the papers were full of nothing else. And attitudes slowly began to change.

Around the time that Anne was going through her secret pregnancy, at least one woman in Kerry was going through something similar. The results would be equally tragic – and far more controversial.

On the evening of Saturday, 14 April 1984, a farmer from Kimego West, Cahirciveen, decided to go out for a jog on the White Strand. He was planning to check on some cattle while he was out. The beach is a popular place for walkers and joggers. There is an extensive crescent of golden sand, bounded by low grassy dunes. Dusk was settling on the land when Jack

Griffin spotted something between two rocks on the shore. He thought it was a doll. He stopped and went for a closer look, and was shocked to find the battered body of a naked and very dead baby boy. The tiny body, with full head of black hair, was lying between the rocks, and had cut marks and bruises.

The horrified farmer ran for help. He went to the nearby house of his brother-in-law, Brendan O'Shea, and phoned the Gardaí. Then he and Brendan O'Shea went back to the beach, and stood vigil over the body until the authorities arrived. Sergeant Reidy and Garda Collins were the first officials on the scene. They confirmed the find: a naked newborn infant, with cuts to the neck and chest. The body was removed to Currnane's funeral home in Cahirciveen, about three miles away, and held there for the night. The following day, the body was removed to Killarney hospital for a post-mortem. State Pathologist Dr John Harbison travelled down from Dublin.

It was not immediately obvious that it was murder, but the State Pathologist was called in when a body was found under suspicious circumstances. There were marks on the child and no sign of a mother. His autopsy confirmed their suspicions. There was a fracture and a dislocation of the baby's neck, and four stab wounds to his chest. There was bruising to the right side of his back. With an infant so tiny, the first question to determine was whether this was a live birth, a stillborn birth or a late miscarriage. The evidence pointed to a live birth. There was the stump of an umbilical cord, and an examination of the lungs showed that the infant had drawn breath.

Following the autopsy, a full-scale murder hunt was launched. As the body had been discovered near Cahirciveen, Superintendent J.P. Sullivan was put in charge. This did not necessarily mean that the investigation would be centred on the small town; it could be that someone had dumped the body from further afield. At that stage, they did not know whether they were looking for a local person or not.

The first step was to put together a list of possible suspects. The starting point had to be pregnant women, or women who had just given birth. The Gardaí canvassed the local hospitals. It did not take long before a viable suspect emerged. And she wasn't local. Joanne Hayes was a 25-year-old woman from Abbeydorney, a small community about eight miles north of Tralee. She was a single mum and she worked at a sports centre in Tralee. What made her a suspect was the fact that she was known to be pregnant again, yet there was no new arrival at the Hayes household.

A quick investigation revealed Joanne's history. She lived at home on the farm, just outside Abbeydorney, with her parents. As a young woman she had started an affair with a co-worker of hers, Jeremiah Locke, a married father of two. Neither Jeremiah's nor Joanne's family approved of the relationship, and their disapproval peaked when she discovered she was pregnant. Their daughter, Yvonne, was born in 1983 and was being raised by Joanne at the family farm. The affair with Locke had ended a few months after the birth of the girl. However, at the age of 25 she found herself pregnant for the second time.

Gardaí enquiries established that Joanne had attended Tralee Hospital on 16 April and was examined by an obstetrician. She was not pregnant on that occasion, and the doctor asked her what had happened to the baby. He reported that she replied, 'I had no baby. Do you not think I would know the difference between a 26-week miscarriage and a full-term baby?'

The Gardaí kept digging. They interviewed Joanne's own doctor and found that on 13 April she had told him she feared she was on the verge of miscarrying. By that stage, Gardaí believe, she had already delivered the baby. She also told co-workers at the sports complex in Tralee that she had miscarried.

On Monday, 30 April – two weeks after the discovery of the dead infant – a team of Gardaí arrived at the sports complex and asked Joanne to go to Tralee Garda Station to answer some questions. She agreed and accompanied them. Jeremiah Locke, the groundsman at the complex and Joanne's lover, was also brought to the station.

Joanne's father farmed 60 acres a mile outside Abbeydorney,

six miles from Tralee. The land was reasonably good, and he had a herd of milch cows that provided a steady, if unimpressive, income for the family. Joanne had two brothers and a sister.

Joanne was interviewed by a local Garda, Detective P.J. Browne, and a detective from Dublin, Gerry O'Carroll. She was asked about her recent pregnancy, and she told the investigators she had miscarried and flushed the foetus down the toilet. About two hours into the interview, one of the detectives said that they would search the septic tank of the farmhouse to find the remains, at which point Joanne became very distressed and said that she had killed the baby.

She then made a statement:

Around midnight I felt very hot and flushed, and started getting labour pains. I went out to the back of the house and after a while I delivered my baby. The baby cried and I caught it by the throat and held it until the baby stopped crying. I laid it on the ground and covered it up with some old hay. I then went back inside the house and cleaned myself up in the bathroom.

I then changed my nightdress and put the old one in the rubbish barrel outside. I went up to bed. I got up the next morning at around 5 a.m. and went out to where I had left my baby. I carried out two bags: one was a brown paper bag, and the other was a white plastic bag. I picked up the baby and it was cold. I then put it into the brown paper bag, and then I put it in the white plastic bag, and I tied the bag at the top by the handles. I then took the body and dropped it into a pond of water near a river about 100 yards from the house. I then returned to the house and went back to bed.

I was so sick that I got my neighbours to bring me to the clinic in Tralee. I told the doctor that I had had a miscarriage, but he told me that I was still pregnant, and was gone about sixteen weeks.

A few days later she went to the hospital, where she was examined by an obstetrician. 'He told me that the scan revealed that I had just given birth to a full-term baby. He asked me what I had done with the baby, but I only told him lies,' she told the detectives.

Following this statement, the Gardaí carried out a search of the farm, but failed to locate the body of the infant where Joanne had said she had left it. However, they did find a carving knife with a wooden handle, a white bath brush and a large grey bag. When these items were shown to Joanne, she said, 'That carving knife is the one I stabbed my baby to death with. I hit my baby with that white bath brush, and that grey bag is similar to the one my family used to take the baby away.'

This was new: the first mention that anyone apart from herself might have been involved in the baby's death.

Joanne then made a second statement. She said that she had begun dating Jeremiah Locke in 1981, knowing he was married. She was in love with him. She became pregnant, but miscarried. Then she became pregnant again, and this time delivered a healthy girl. However, Locke only saw the baby twice, and did not leave his wife, as Joanne had hoped. Yet the relationship continued, and in August 1983, Joanne missed her period. She was pregnant again.

'My mother and all the lads at home were upset about the first baby, but they accepted it and decided to help me rear it. They were all very upset when I became pregnant again, and I was thoroughly and absolutely ashamed of myself, and I tried to hide it. I wore tight clothes and I tried not to let it show,' she said.

Joanne lived with her brother, Mike, and her aunt, Bridie Fuller, in one house on the farm, while her mother, her sister Kathleen and her other brother, Ned, shared a second house on the land.

Joanne said that she went into labour on the night of 13 April, and her aunt, Bridie Fuller, helped deliver the baby. What came next was harrowing.

The baby was alive and crying, and my auntie Bridie placed him at the end of the bed. She left the room to make a pot of tea, and I went to the toilet. On the way back to the bedroom, I picked up the white bath brush, and I went to the cabinet in the kitchen and picked up the carving knife. I went back to the bedroom and I hit the baby on the head with the bath brush. I had to kill him because of the shame it was going to bring on the family and because Jeremiah Locke would not run away and live with me.

The baby cried when I hit it, and I stabbed it with the carving knife on the chest and all over the body. I turned the baby over and I also stabbed him in the back. The baby stopped crying after I stabbed it. There was blood everywhere on the bed, and there was also blood on the floor. I then threw the knife on the floor. My mother, Auntie Bridie, Kathleen, and my two brothers Ned and Mike ran into the bedroom. I was crying and so were my mother, my sister Kathleen, and my auntie Bridie.

I told them that I would have to get rid of the body of the baby and then my two brothers said they would bury it. I told them to take away the baby from the farmyard and they said they would. The boys then brought in a white plastic bag, and they put the baby into it and then they put this bag into a turf bag.

She said that the boys left in a car, and she tidied up, cleaning the blood and disposing of the afterbirth.

She concluded: 'Since the night that I killed the baby, there was never any talk of it in the house. When the body of the baby was found at Cahirciveen, I knew deep down it was my baby. I was going to call him Shane. I am awful sorry for what happened. May God forgive me.'

This confession was the major breakthrough the Gardaí were seeking. With the knowledge of what Joanne had admitted to, they then interviewed the other members of the family whom she claimed were present on the night. Not one of them contradicted Joanne's basic account of the death of the baby, but they differed in some of the details. Some remembered the bath brush; others the knife. Some remembered both. There was some confusion as to the date of the birth. However, the biggest discrepancies arose when it came to the disposal of the body.

Joanne's sister Kathleen said, 'I went to the drawer under the television and got a white plastic bag, and Ned put the dead baby into it. Ned then put the white plastic bag containing the baby into a turf bag. Ned took out the bag and put it in the boot of our car. Ned, Mike and I left our house at around 3.50 a.m. We drove through Tralee and on to Dingle town for about six miles, and we stopped at a place where the road runs beside the sea, and Ned, who was driving, got out and opened the boot of the car and took out the bag containing the baby and threw it into the sea. It was about 5.30 a.m. on Friday, 13 April, when Ned threw the bag into the sea.'

Ned Hayes said, 'I saw the body of a newly born infant at the foot of the bed. The infant was lying face-downwards naked on the bed. I said to my sister: "Why in fuck's name did you do it?" My mother suggested that we would have to get rid of it. I was in favour of burying it on the land, but my mother and Auntie Bridie weren't.'

He said that they had lifted the infant by the legs and dropped him into a plastic bag. He could see the blood on his chest. Once they had the baby wrapped in two bags, they were ready to dispose of it.

I placed the bag [with the baby] on the floor of the car behind the driver's seat. I drove the car and my brother accompanied me in the front passenger seat of the car. We brought a shovel with us in case we might get a quiet place to bury it. We had fully intended when we left the house that we would go to the sea with the bag, and the further away the better. I drove the car out the Dingle Road. We went into Dingle and went out on the Ventry Road. It was then we decided to go to Slea Head. When I got to the spot that I thought was the most suitable place, I got out

Some of the victims of the Ballyseedy Massacre. Back: Tim Twomey, Michael O'Connell. Middle: James Walsh, Pat Buckley, John O'Connor. Front: Pat Hartness, George O'Shea. (Republican Sinn Fein Kerry)

Stephen Buckley, killed at Countess Bridge. (Republican Sinn Fein Kerry)

The modern monument commemorating the Ballyseedy Massacre, created by Yann Goulet.

The memorial to the state murder at Countess Bridge in Killarney.

The lonely spot on the road where the Ballyseedy Massacre was carried out.

The deep pool in the river near Knocknaloman where the body of Ellen O'Sullivan was dragged by David O'Shea.

Charlie Kerins, the GAA star
(Republican Sinn Fein Kerry)

IRA Chief of Staff Charlie Kerins
(Republican Sinn Fein Kerry)

The murder of Moss Moore by Dan Foley was turned into a powerful play called *The Field*, then a film starring Richard Harris as 'The Bull' McCabe, based on Dan Foley. (Avenue Pictures)

The deep gully along the road where Moss Moore's
body was dumped.

All that remains of the well down which farmer Pat Daly was thrown by his brother Sean.

The house where Patrick Daly lived until his death, just yards from the well where he was dumped.

The caravan park where Charlene McAuliffe's body was discovered.
(Photo courtesy of *Kerry's Eye*)

Gerard Graham being led away by Gardai. (Photo courtesy of *Kerry's Eye*)

Thomas Barrett being led into the Garda Station.
(Photo courtesy of *Kerry's Eye*)

Thomas Barrett tried to hide his face after a court appearance.
(Photo courtesy of *Kerry's Eye*)

of the car and took out the bag containing the baby.

I asked my brother to keep a watchout and I went in over a stone ditch, walked about twenty yards to the edge of the cliff, and I flung the bag from the cliff into the sea. I would say that there was a drop of about ten feet, and I watched the bag fall directly into the water.

According to Ned's account, only two people were in the car, and they had driven far further than Kathleen had said.

Mike Hayes's statement also contained discrepancies and contradictions: 'Joanne stabbed the baby on the chest three times. The bedspread was all blood. I saw Joanne catch hold of the toilet brush in her hand, and she hit the child a number of times on the face and body. My mother said we would bury the baby on the land, and the rest of us said we would throw it into the sea.'

This differed from what his mother said.

According to Mike, the body was wrapped in newspaper – a detail mentioned by none of the others – then put in a clear plastic bag and a brown shopping bag. This was then placed in a manure sack with a big stone to weigh it down. Ned and Mike set out in the car. They drove about seven or eight miles from Dingle, where Ned got out of the car and threw the body into the sea. Here both brothers were in agreement.

Slea Head is not far, as the crow flies, from Cahirciveen. A body thrown into the sea at Slea Head could quite conceivably wash ashore on the opposite side of Dingle Bay at the White Strand, a distance of about 15 miles.

'We drove home then,' Mike said. 'I had my breakfast and milked the cows and went to the creamery. We tried to keep it all quiet and it looks like we didn't succeed.'

Joanne's mother, Mary, said. 'I said to Joanne: "You will have to bury the child," and Mike or Kathleen said: "We will bury the child on the land." I said: "The child cannot be buried on the land."'

This was a complete contradiction of Ned's statement.

Bridie Fuller said, 'The baby was born and I did the best I could to help her. It was a baby boy. I saw it move. It was bubbling with mucus. I was not in the room when the baby died. I think I was making tea in the kitchen.'

She denied knowing anything about the disposal of the baby.

Bridie, Mary, Kathleen and Joanne said that the brothers were back home by 7 a.m., following the disposal of the body. But Ned said it was nearer ten. Both brothers agreed they had travelled alone and gone as far as Slea Head. Kathleen said she had been with them, and they had not gone far beyond Tralee. Those were serious contradictions. Despite this, the Gardaí felt they had enough to go on.

At a special sitting of Tralee District Court (held in the Garda station), Joanne was charged with murder. In answer to the charge she replied: 'Guilty.'

Four members of her family – brothers Ned and Mike, sister Kathleen and aunt Bridie – were charged with concealing the birth of an infant, by secretly disposing of the dead body of the child. In answer to the charge, Mike said, 'I helped conceal the child.' But Ned replied, 'No, no!' while Kathleen said, 'I didn't conceal the child.' Bridie said: 'I have nothing to say.'

It seemed like the Gardaí had done an exemplary job. They had solved the mystery in a fortnight and had statements of admission that would help secure a conviction.

On 2 May, at a sitting of Tralee District Court, Joanne Hayes was remanded in custody to Limerick Prison. Before she was taken away, she had a word with her sister. Following that, Kathleen, Ned and Mike went to a spot on their farm. Then they went to their solicitor in Tralee. The bottom had just fallen out of the Garda case. The fallout would throw a very harsh light on the Garda investigation and put a cloud over the force for years to come.

What they had found on the farm, in the spot indicated by Joanne, was the body of a dead baby boy. In her first interview, Joanne had said that she had dumped the baby on the farm. However, that did not account for how the baby ended up in

Cahirciveen, a two-hour drive away. So the Gardaí had kept up the questioning, ignoring the discrepancies in the statements, until they had a story that better fitted the facts as they knew them.

Yet now they had a second body – and this one had been recovered on the Hayes farm. It had to be the baby boy that Joanne had given birth to. That left a huge mystery: who had given birth to the baby found in Cahirciveen?

At 7 p.m. on 2 May, a team of Gardaí arrived at the Hayes farm and removed a plastic bag from a drain in the corner of a field about 200 yards from the house. On opening the bag, they found the body of a newborn baby. If they had listened to Joanne and conducted a proper search of the farm, they could have found the body days earlier and perhaps got more accurate and truthful statements from members of the Hayes family.

Now they were back to square one – but this time they were playing two games.

Dr Harbison returned to Kerry, where he conducted yet another autopsy on an infant. This is an extract from his report:

It was the body of a fully developed normal male infant. There was a length of umbilical cord still attached at the abdomen. Vernix caseosa, or cheesy material, was still present on the skin, indicating a newborn infant. There was no evidence of obvious injury on the body. There was no external injury or bone injury. Apart from the dark area on the left side of the neck, there were no signs of skin injury to suggest strangulation of the neck. The lungs showed areas of non-expansion.

No firm opinion can be expressed concerning the achievement of a separate existence. The impression, however, is that full expansion of the lungs had not taken place, and therefore breathing had not been properly established.

Dr Harbison found slight bruising on the neck, which would have been consistent with an attempt to prevent the infant from breathing, but the bruising could just as easily have been caused by gripping the neck in an attempt to help a self-delivery. The report said, 'Strangulation cannot be inferred as a cause of death. No other marks suggestive of injury were found on the body. Cause of Death – Unascertainable.'

This was a bombshell. Joanne Hayes had a child which could well have been stillborn or died of natural causes within minutes of birth. She might have been guilty of nothing more than concealing a birth.

Worse was to come. Forensic scientists did blood tests on both babies. The baby found on the Hayes farm was blood type O, as were Joanne and Jeremiah Locke, the father, so the baby on the farm could have been theirs. However, the baby found in Cahirciveen was a different blood type. His was type A, which meant he could not have been the child of Joanne and Jeremiah. He could have been the child of Joanne, but only if the father was a man of blood type A.

DNA testing was introduced in America in 1985 and took a few years to become widely accepted. In 1984, it was not something Irish investigators even dreamed of, so no DNA comparison of either baby with Joanne Hayes was ever conducted. It would have answered some questions, but not all.

The Gardaí knew that the discovery of the second body threw their case into disarray, but they were reluctant to accept defeat. On 8 May, a preliminary file was sent to the Director of Public Prosecutions. The full report followed ten weeks later. Finally, the word came back: the DPP had decided not to prosecute any member of the Hayes family.

On Wednesday, 10 October, all charges were struck out at Tralee District Court. Detective Donal Browne said, 'It would not be proper to put persons through the ordeal of a trial when there simply is not evidence to justify the charges.'

It should have been the end of the matter, but it was only the beginning.

The Kerry Babies case highlighted everything that was wrong

with Ireland in the 1980s. Single mothers were pariahs, bringing shame and disgrace on their families. Yet contraception had been illegal up to 1980, and even after that contraceptives of any sort were only obtainable with a doctor's prescription. It was not until 1985 – partly as a result of the Granard and Kerry Babies incidents – that contraception became more widely available without prescription. Infanticide was more common than people liked to admit. At a conference in 2012, an academic historian said she had found over 4,000 cases listed in an analysis of a few hundred years' of Irish judicial records. That is a staggering number of babies killed, and mothers driven to the brink of despair.

Joanne Hayes had her supporters in the media, writers and columnists who felt that she was the victim of a conservative witch hunt. The Gardaí did themselves no favours in the way they handled the investigation. They began well, by locating a woman who had had a baby but whose baby had disappeared. From there on, their investigation was a succession of bungles.

It began with their slipshod search of the Hayes farm. After Joanne said that she had dumped her baby on the farm, they should have done a thorough search to either prove her statement or catch her in a lie. But they didn't. For some reason, they never brought her to the farm and asked her where she claimed to have put her baby. If they had, they could have saved her and her family a lot of grief.

What is extraordinary is that the investigators managed to get statements from so many members of the Hayes family admitting their role in disposing of the baby, when the baby was in a ditch on their own farm. The brothers had both spoken of driving to Slea Head and flinging the body into the sea. Clearly this never happened. There were inconsistencies in their stories, but the Gardaí had managed to get what they wanted: confessions admitting complicity in an event that had never happened. It was inevitable that the investigators would come under scrutiny.

From the beginning the newspapers were all over the case. By the end of October, the Hayeses had gone to their solicitor and made a formal complaint against the investigating Gardaí. The complaints alleged that the family had been assaulted by Gardaí while they were being questioned and had been intimidated into making incriminating statements, which they were then coerced into signing.

It was not long before there was a public clamour for an inquiry. The Gardaí launched their own internal inquiry, but the Hayes family refused to cooperate with this. That inquiry got nowhere, but the careers of several of the investigators were under a cloud. Even the politicians got involved, with the Justice Minister Michael Noonan promising in the Dáil to weed out the 'bad apples' in the force.

In December, the public got what they were calling for. A Tribunal of Inquiry into the Kerry Babies case was established. It met in the Urban District Council offices in Tralee and was chaired by Mr Justice Kevin Lynch. The tribunal was to investigate both the circumstances leading to the Hayes family facing criminal charges in connection with the death of the Cahirciveen infant and also the allegations of Garda intimidation made by the family. For the purposes of the inquiry, the baby found on the Hayes farm, whose cause of death could not be established, was referred to as the Tralee baby. The original baby washed ashore at the White Strand in Cahirciveen was referred to as the Cahirciveen baby.

As the tribunal began, nine months had passed since the discovery of the Cahirciveen baby and the Gardaí still had no clue who that baby was or who the mother was. If you accept – as most people did – that the Cahirciveen baby was not Joanne Hayes's, then the original investigation had not just stalled, it had reached a complete dead end.

The Tribunal of Inquiry took several months to interview all the people involved: Joanne Hayes, her family, the investigating Gardaí, and forensic and medical experts. This is a book about murders, not public inquiries, so I will not go into it in detail.

However, it was such an important background to everyone's lives back then, and was so instrumental in forcing social change on Ireland, that it does need to be looked at.

Quite early in proceedings, a letter was read into evidence that Joanne Hayes had sent to Liam Bohan, her boss at the sports complex where she worked, some short time after her arrest. At the time, she was being detained in St Joseph's Psychiatric Hospital in Limerick. In the letter, she said, 'I had to make a false statement because they told me that if I didn't my mother would be jailed, and Yvonne [her young daughter] would be put in an orphanage. I am now in a hospital for mental cases. Am I mental, Liam? I can't think straight any more. I don't mind being punished for what I did, but I don't want to be punished for the baby at Cahirciveen.'

The tribunal was told that there was no sign of life in the Tralee baby. If that was the case, Joanne Hayes should have been charged with nothing more serious than concealing a birth. In today's world, she would have been treated with sympathy and given whatever medical and emotional help she needed, not questioned relentlessly and charged with murder. Forensic evidence was produced proving that blood found on Joanne Hayes's clothing by the investigators could not have come from stabbing a baby. Also, there were no traces of blood on the knife alleged by the Gardaí to have been used on one of the babies. The patterns were all wrong. The Garda investigation was coming under harsh scrutiny and their case was looking weaker and weaker.

Joanne Hayes was in the witness box for a number of days, and several times she broke down in tears. More than once, the proceedings had to be interrupted to allow her to compose herself. She came under a very gruelling cross-examination, but she stuck to her story: she had given birth to just one baby, the Tralee baby. Her statements to the Gardaí had been bullied out of her. She gave birth outside and disposed of the body in a ditch on the farm.

The Gardaí were quite clearly committed to the idea that

Joanne had given birth to twins. They believed that she did not know she was carrying twins. The first child was born as Joanne said, outside and on her own. She disposed of the body and then returned to the farmhouse, weak and distressed. Some few hours later, she went into labour again and delivered the second baby. This was the birth that members of the family, including her aunt, assisted in, and this was the baby her brothers took to Slea Head and consigned to a watery grave.

On the face of it, that is an unlikely theory. For a start, the babies were of different blood groups. That is not unknown; if one parent was type O and the second type A, then the babies could well have had different blood types. However, both Joanne Hayes and Jeremiah Locke were type O, so any offspring of theirs would be type O. Moreover, no doctor who had examined Joanne had suggested she was carrying twins.

However, the theory is not as far-fetched as it appears at first. Gardaí believed that Joanne had been pregnant by two different men. They said that her first child, Yvonne, was Mr Locke's. That was never disputed. Her second pregnancy, and subsequent miscarriage, may have come from a different lover. According to herself and others, she had broken off the relationship with Mr Locke shortly after the birth of Yvonne, so that is plausible. Gardaí believed that she was still seeing this second man – never identified – when she resumed her relationship with Locke. As a result, she was expecting twins by two different men.

This is a rare but not unknown occurrence. It is called heteropaternal superfecundation. In some species, such as dogs, it is almost normal. In the wild, it is quite common for bitches to give birth to litters that have pups from several different fathers. It is rarer in species such as humans that normally give birth to single infants. However it is certainly not unknown. Research has shown that in cases involving paternity lawsuits, one pregnancy in forty involving twins shows up different fathers.

Gardaí believe that Joanne Hayes was caught up in that

medical anomaly. In fairness to them, there was a 2.6 per cent chance they were correct. However, that also means that there was a 97.4 per cent chance they were not. Their inexplicable failure to search for a second woman was a serious flaw in their investigation.

Joanne suffered terribly during the tribunal. Barristers questioned her closely about her personal life, her affairs, and her sex life. The most intimate details of her existence became the fodder for the next day's newspapers. That was a feature of the Irish judicial system back then. Women could be bullied horribly by barristers. It was particularly common in rape trials. As a junior reporter, I was often very uncomfortable listening to some poor woman, who had already suffered the horror of a rape, being raped anew by the defence barrister.

The Irish public felt the same, and they, particularly women's groups and those fighting for social change, rallied around the young Kerry mother. By extension, they were anti-Gardaí. The tribunal was often picketed both by supporters of Joanne and by women's groups from all over the country. It got so bad that the judge had to issue a warning: protesters could be jailed for disrupting the legal proceedings.

The Gardaí did their best in the tribunal, and occasional bits of evidence supported their statement of events. For instance, on 4 February Mike Hayes said that Joanne's baby had been born inside, 'in the top room, above my room'. This was a flat contradiction of what everyone else in the family had said. He told the tribunal that he had not been present at the birth, but had heard from his sister Kathleen. He said that from what he understood, Joanne was alone for the birth. Later the same day, his mother, Mary Hayes, contradicted her son's testimony. She said that she was surprised when Mike said the baby had been born in Joanne's room.

'It did surprise me, because it did not happen,' she said. But she added that she was not aware of what had happened in the house that night, because she was in bed with the flu. So one person said – purely on the basis of what he had heard – that the birth had occurred indoors, while another witness said – again purely on the basis of what she had heard – that it was outdoors. The little contradiction did the Gardaí case no good. However, it did shake the unified story of the Hayes family to a degree.

On the 22nd day of the tribunal, Bridie Fuller, now in a convalescent home, testified that she had been present for the birth of the baby, a story that went completely against the evidence of Joanne, Kathleen and Ned. She described cutting the umbilical cord with a pair of scissors, and said that the baby had been weak and chesty, and had deteriorated through the night. However, she was adamant that only one baby had been born that night, and the family had nothing to do with the Cahirciveen baby.

As the Hayeses stuck to their story, so the Gardaí in turn stuck to theirs. Superintendent Donal O'Sullivan told the inquiry that he believed Joanne had given birth to the Cahirciveen baby and killed it. He did not believe they had got the wrong person. Then he muddied the waters by throwing in the possibility of a third baby.

He told the stunned tribunal that he believed Joanne had given birth to twins. The first twin was buried at the farm. The second was dumped into the water off Slea Head. But as the Cahirciveen baby was the wrong blood type to be the child of Joanne and Mr Locke, clearly the baby that had been thrown into the water off Slea Head had been washed out to sea. There was a third baby that had not been found. This was dubbed the Azores baby, in reference to a group of islands in the North Atlantic.

A clearly confused Mr Justice Lynch interrupted, saying, 'Now we have three babies. Where does this all lead to . . . where does it all leave me? I have to sort all this out at some stage and where am I left now?'

The superintendent repeated that he believed Joanne had had twins. However, he offered a glimmer of hope when he said that they could not completely rule out the idea that Joanne had given birth to the Cahirciveen baby and that some human error could account for the different blood group.

Yet Dr John C. Creedon, a gynaecologist at Tralee General Hospital, gave testimony that a woman as small as Joanne Hayes – less than five foot, and just over seven stone – would have been huge with twins. It would have been obvious to all that she was expecting on the double, yet no one at the sports complex where she worked, or any of the medical professionals who saw her, or her family, had remarked on her size. This evidence tended to throw doubt on the Garda theory.

But they stuck to their guns. Detective Sergeant Gerry O'Carroll said that there was a possibility that Joanne had had sex with a second man within 48 hours of having sex with Jeremiah Locke. 'Ireland is a promiscuous society, and there are umpteen such cases,' he said.

He admitted that there was no evidence that Joanne had been seeing anyone else. However, he said that it still remained possible that Jeremiah Locke had been the father of the Cahirciveen baby and that the blood group had changed through immersion in salt water.

Barrister Brian Curtain asked the detective whether there was any evidence as to who was the father of the Cahirciveen baby. Detective O'Carroll said, 'There is a great likelihood that the father is Jeremiah Locke.' This was an extraordinary contradiction of the medical evidence.

With the question of whether there had been twins so central, the tribunal called in an expert witness, Joseph Corr, the chief paternity tester of Northern Ireland. He said that if Joanne was the mother of the Cahirciveen baby, then he was satisfied beyond all doubt that Jeremiah Locke was not the father. But if Joanne had been faithful to her lover, then she could not have been the mother of the Cahirciveen baby.

No evidence had been presented to show, or even suggest, that Joanne had been involved with any other man. That seemed to knock the twins theory out of contention. But the initial blood testing should have ruled out twins and forced the investigation in new directions. The tribunal heard this had not happened.

Sergeant Reidy admitted that charging Joanne with murder had effectively ended the investigation into the death of the Cahirciveen baby.

'Has the investigation ever recommenced?' he was asked.

'No,' he replied. He added that the Gardaí had no definite views on where the Cahirciveen baby might have come from. 'It could have come from anywhere,' he said. But from his 37 years' experience, anything dumped on the south of the Dingle Peninsula would eventually wash up near Cahirciveen.

The tribunal lasted 82 days, which were spread over a number of months, and cost the state £1.5 million. The findings were published in October 1985. They put an end to the matter, without actually answering many questions.

The tribunal found that the Tralee baby was born inside the Hayes house (not outside, as Joanne claimed) and had died when Joanne put her hands on his neck to stop him crying. The report also found that Joanne had struck the baby with a brush in the presence of her mother and sister. The report damningly said that none of the Hayes family had attempted to stop Joanne choking or hitting her baby.

But Joanne was not the mother of the Cahirciveen baby, and had not given birth to twins.

The report criticised the Gardaí severely for the way they handled the investigation. The Gardaí 'resorted to unlikely, far-fetched and self-contradictory theories' to suggest that Joanne gave birth to twins, in order to link her to the Cahirciveen baby.

The Gardaí were criticised for not bringing Joanne to the Abbeydorney farm to search for where she said she had dumped the body of her baby, and for not searching the farm properly at the time. Their search was described as 'deplorably inadequate'. And when the forensic evidence showed that Joanne could not have been the mother of the Cahirciveen baby, the Gardaí had given little or no thought to re-evaluating their investigation and widening their net.

However, the report exonerated the Gardaí from mistreating

members of the Hayes family, rejecting their allegations of brutality, violence and intimidation. It said that the family had guilty consciences over the death of Joanne's baby and their complicity in the cover-up. This led them to make statements to the Gardaí that implicated them in the case of the Cahirciveen baby.

The report also expressed its deep sympathy to a woman wronged by the whole affair: not Joanne Hayes, but Mary, the wife of Jeremiah Locke:

Mary Locke married Jeremiah Locke on 31 August 1980, before Joanne Hayes had put her eye on him. Joanne Hayes knew perfectly well of the marriage. Yet a little over a year later, on 26 October 1981, Joanne Hayes had sexual intercourse with Jeremiah Locke and he, for his part, did not hesitate to take advantage of what was so readily available to him.

What public sympathy and support was shown to Mrs Locke for all these wrongs committed against her? None whatsoever.

What was the public attitude shown to the wrongdoer? She was heaped with bouquets of flowers, greeting cards of support, and even Mass cards! Pickets were organised to try to stop the proceedings of the tribunal because it was said she was being cross-examined too harshly on behalf of the Gardaí.

Similar public support was offered to other members of the Hayes family and especially the female members thereof. Mrs Mary Hayes got into the witness box, solemnly took the oath, and commenced patently lying through her teeth. What was the public reaction to this? A glowing write-up in one of the morning newspapers and heaps of flowers and cards of support.

Why no bouquets of flowers for Mrs Locke? Why no cards, no Mass cards, for Mrs Locke?

Is it because she married Jeremiah Locke in 1980 and thus got in the way of the foolish hopes and ambitions of Joanne Hayes? That attitude of mind emerges from some of the publicity about the case.

All the tribunal can do is express its sympathy to Mrs Locke and wish her better days in the future than she has experienced over the last few years.

It was an extraordinary addition to the report, but it did highlight one important aspect of the case. For many, particularly women's groups and the media, Joanne Hayes had become a figurehead for groups objecting to all that was wrong and backward-looking about Irish society. She was seen as a woman wronged and harassed by the judicial system. All that was true, but it was forgotten in that interpretation that her baby had died under very suspicious circumstances and that all her family had stood by and let it happen, then joined in the cover-up.

Nearly 30 years have passed since the tragedy of the Kerry Babies case. Joanne Hayes still lives locally, but leads a quiet life out of the public spotlight. She has not spoken to the media, apart from contacting journalist Nell McCafferty a number of years ago, pleading with her not to allow her book about the case, *A Woman to Blame*, to be turned into a movie.

Some things can be said for definite. Joanne Hayes gave birth to a baby boy in Abbeydorney. She may have – and probably did – contribute to the death of that baby. Her family knew all about it and helped her conceal what had happened. It was a tragic event, and today she would be treated with far more compassion than she was back then.

Joanne may have given birth to a second baby, but it is very unlikely. Far more likely is that the little infant found washed up in Cahirciveen was the child of some other mother. Because of the ineptitude of the initial Garda investigation, we will probably never know who the mother of that baby – christened John by the local undertaker – was, or who stabbed him to death.

It was not a good moment for the Gardaí. Their efforts brought no honour to the force. Some members, notably Detective Sergeant Gerry O'Carroll, have called for an exhumation of both the Tralee and the Cahirciveen babies, so that modern DNA tests can throw further light on the twins question, but there is no political will for such a move. Perhaps that is just as well: the results would in all probability heap more embarrassment on the force.

The only thing we can say for certain is that Ireland has changed. Perhaps as a result of what Joanne Hayes – and a second unknown Kerry mother – went through, social legislation has moved on. Contraception became available over the counter a year after the case, and attitudes have changed. It was a snapshot of a different era, and Ireland will never again go through a Kerry Babies saga.

9

INTO THIN AIR

The disappearance of Charles Brooke Pickard

IT IS A commonly believed fallacy that you cannot have a murder without a body. If you could magic away the body, you could magic away the prosecution. Without a body, how can the authorities prove there has been a killing?

This is a beloved device of film-makers and thriller-writers, but it has no basis in fact. If Gardaí are convinced you murdered someone, they will conduct a full-scale investigation. And if they find credible evidence that you murdered someone, then the lack of a body will not stop them prosecuting. In fact, if someone has been missing for seven years, and there is a strong reason to suspect they are no longer alive, the family can apply to the courts to have them declared legally dead. Lack of a body is no impediment.

But while the lack of a body won't stop a murder investigation, it will certainly impede it. The body gives you so many clues. It yields up forensic details that no amount of witness interviews or supposition can replace. And it gives you, often enough, the location of the killing. More clues. A body makes the Gardaí investigation so much easier.

Perhaps that is why the family of Charles Brooke Pickard

have waited almost a quarter of a century and still have no idea what happened to the man. Everyone knows he was killed within hours of his disappearance, but no one knows where, why or how. Most importantly, no one knows who killed him. His family have been left in limbo, with no closure. He just walked out of their lives one spring morning in 1991, and was then confronted by a group of armed men. He was bundled into a car and then disappeared.

Born in 1949, Charles Brooke Pickard, known as Brooke, was an Englishman who grew up in the post-war years, then hit the swinging '60s as a teenager. That is not as glamorous as it sounds; he was in Leeds, in Yorkshire, rather than cosmopolitan London. But the ideals of the '60s did filter through: make your own path and follow your own dreams. Pickard eked out a living doing odd jobs, remaining in Leeds. He had a van, and a man with a van is never without a few quid.

In the '70s, there was a decisive change in his life. He got asked to do someone a favour, move some furniture. It was a routine job. Someone was leaving Leeds and needed her stuff brought to a nearby town. Brooke showed up with his van and fell for the pretty brunette, Penny, who was two years younger than him. After the move, they stayed in touch and soon began going out. Eventually they married and decided to build a new life together in a new location.

Initially they looked at the Highlands of Scotland, because they were drawn to the rugged landscape. Penny's parents had a holiday home there and they knew the place well, but the winters were harsh. Then they thought of Kerry, which had similar mountainous terrain, but was washed by the warm winds of the Gulf Stream.

In 1983, they moved to Ireland. Their ambitions were modest. They pooled their savings and bought five acres of land with a dilapidated farmhouse. The farm was near the village of Castlecove, between Waterville and Sneem. It was on the famous Ring of Kerry, a scenic route around the Iveragh Peninsula, which draws thousands of tourists. Behind them there were mountains, before them wonderful sea views. The young family moved in that November, and Brooke immediately set to work doing home improvements.

He was a handy man around the house, and over the years their level of comfort improved as he extended and added utilities. They also worked the land, keeping ducks, geese, chickens and goats, as well as planting vegetables. Eventually they got a few cattle and sheep. It was *The Good Life*, without the neighbours.

They had four children – Lisa, James, Crohan and Dan – and life really did seem to be idyllic. The family were what are sometimes pejoratively called hippies. They were living a green lifestyle of self-sufficiency, away from the rat race. Brooke had the long hair and the beard, but he was a hard worker, not an idler. The family kept their small farm working efficiently, and they were well liked locally. Their kids went to the local school, and they were very much part of the community at Castlecove.

There were bad times. Brooke had a brush with the law in 1988 that could have had serious repercussions for the family. In a foolish attempt to retrieve money he was owed, he committed a firearms offence. The story had a strong drug-related twist, and cast a shadow over Mr Pickard's activities in Kerry. Gardaí suspected him of being involved in running a drugs ring in the county, and perhaps of heading it.

These are the facts that are known. In 1988, Stephen Terence Mead, then 27, had arrived in Castlecove and was staying with the Pickards. Mead was from Bristol. He had become a habitual drug user following a family tragedy. He was addicted to heroin.

While he was staying in Castlecove he continued to use heroin, and it is alleged that Pickard was his supplier. Gardaí believe Pickard was involved with people from the North in bringing drugs into Kerry and so had the supplies available for Mead.

That winter, Pickard was owed the sum of £4,000 by a man in Dublin. Gardaí believe the debt was the result of the drugs business. They believe that Pickard had given the man the money to purchase heroin, and the man had defaulted by not supplying the drug. Now Pickard wanted his money back and he decided to take the law into his own hands. He persuaded Mead to travel with him to Dublin. They came prepared: they brought a gun and ammunition.

When they arrived in Dublin they confronted the man, but he did not have their money. He pleaded that he was owed money from various drug users around the capital, and if he could collect that money, he could pay back Pickard. Ever resourceful, Pickard and Mead decided to go around the capital with the man to 'persuade' people to pay up. Their method was simple. They had a wooden bat and they had a gun. Pickard, tall and bearded, had the bat. Once the drug users saw the three men arriving with the weapons, they coughed up quickly enough. On at least two occasions the gun was produced to addicts. Pickard had apparently warned Mead not to fire the gun because he had had to doctor it and the chamber was 'a bit dodgy', as he explained in the subsequent trial.

The Gardaí did not approve of such methods of debt collection. They confronted Pickard and Mead in Dún Laoghaire on 4 December. They were in a car when stopped by detectives. Mead made a motion towards his pocket, where he kept the gun. The detectives immediately drew their own guns and pointed them at Mead and Pickard. Slowly Mead pulled his hand back, and then surrendered. The men were arrested. The following day, Gardaí searched Pickard's home in Kerry and found two rifles and ammunition.

Both men were charged with possessing firearms with intent to endanger life. Mead was charged that on 4 December, at Marine Avenue, Sandycove, Dublin, he was unlawfully in possession of a firearm with intent to endanger life. He was also charged with possessing a revolver and seven rounds of .22 rifle ammunition with intent to endanger life at Adelaide Street, Dún Laoghaire, on 2 December, and with falsely imprisoning Maurice Dubarry, one of the men they had tried to intimidate, on the same date.

Brooke Pickard faced a charge that on or before 5 December 1988, at his home he was unlawfully in possession of two .22 rifles and eight rounds of .22 ammunition, without firearms certificates. He was also charged with possessing the firearms and ammunition for an unlawful purpose.

Both men were released on bail, on condition that they would not contact or interfere with any of the alleged injured parties. They had to sign on twice weekly at the local Garda station and had to stay in Castlecove.

However, when the case came up for mention in May 1989, the court was told that Stephen Mead had done a runner. Detective Garda Seamus Kane told the court that he had received information that Mead had left the country and returned to England. He applied to Judge Hubert Wine to issue an international warrant to open the way for extradition proceedings.

Mead had fled Ireland because while he was in Castlecove awaiting the trial, three men called to his home and threatened his life. As Mead was living with Pickard, by extension the three men had visited Pickard's house too. It is not known if Pickard was home at the time.

In June, Pickard faced the court alone, while the slow extradition process against Mead began. Pickard was given a suspended sentence, and he then returned to Castlecove to resume his idyllic life.

It is hard not to link the debt collection and subsequent trial with what happened two years later.

Friday, 26 April 1991 began cold and wet, but as the morning progressed, the rain turned to showers, with frequent clear spells. It was a long way short of good weather, but the forecast was for it to clear from the west, bringing mixed weather with bright spells. It could have been worse. That morning, Brooke Pickard was going out to a bog near Waterville to cut turf for the coming months. It wasn't his bog, but he had been given permission to cut there, in payment for some work he had done for a neighbour. He was due to call on the neighbour that morning and then head to the bog for a day of digging. He would not be home until evening.

Around eleven o'clock, Brooke left his house and drove the short distance towards the main road. He dropped in on one neighbour along the way, who reported he was in fine form.

What happened next has been pieced together from witness accounts gathered during the subsequent Garda investigation. Apparently there was someone at the side of the main road who flagged Brooke down and asked for help. There was some speculation at the time that it was someone he knew, because he immediately took time to help out. But Brooke was a helpful man, the type who would go a bit out of his way for a stranger. If the man at the side of the road was someone Brooke knew and trusted, he would not have led him into a trap. If it was someone he knew and did not trust, Brooke would not have stopped. So the man on the side of the road was likely to have been a stranger.

He told Brooke that his car had broken down on a nearby beach, the White Strand, and that he needed petrol. Brooke, driving a long wheel-base blue Ford Transit, popped the door open and let the man in on the passenger side. They drove to Castlecove and stopped at O'Leary's shop in the village. There was a petrol pump there, and Brooke filled a big jerrycan. According to witnesses, he did not appear to be under any sort of pressure or duress. Then they got back into the van and headed towards the White Strand.

This should have raised alarm bells for Brooke. He lived to the west of Castlecove, but the White Strand was a kilometre to the east of the village. That meant that the man who stopped him had walked through the village, past the petrol pump, then on the main road west, to where he flagged down Brooke. Perhaps he had some explanation for the anomaly; perhaps it never struck Brooke.

As they pulled into the White Strand, it was almost deserted.

In the car park there was one orange car, and they headed towards it, pulling in behind it. It was now 11.20 a.m.

The orange car, a Toyota Corolla, had been seen earlier that day in the village, with three men in it. A number of witnesses spotted it during the day. Earlier, it had been spotted at the beach, with about five men nearby. Later in the morning, it had driven fast through the village. One observant witness had recorded the registration number. Gardaí were able to determine that the car had been stolen from County Kilkenny. It had been seen around Sneem (nine miles away) the day before, leading to the suggestion that a team had come down to abduct Mr Pickard, and had either put him under surveillance or had checked in with people in the locality to plan their snatch efficiently.

As Brooke got out of his van, a teenage girl on a pony was riding on the main road. He knew her well. As she passed, he waved and called hello. She recognised him and waved back. She did not know the man with him. However, she did remember having seen him in the village that morning. In a small place like Castlecove, strangers stand out.

Suddenly the girl was shocked to see a man jump out from behind a holiday home nearby and run towards Mr Pickard. He was wearing a balaclava and seemed to be beckoning to someone behind him. Then he spotted the girl on the horse and he pulled up, staring at her. They were barely 15 yards apart. Spooked, she turned the horse and rode away quickly. But as she did, she saw more men coming out from the cover of the house and running towards the blue van.

The girl rode away swiftly. Later, when she told her story, people were not inclined to believe her. They thought it was just kids play acting and that she was exaggerating. That was until they heard a man was missing . . .

Back in the car park, about five men converged on Brooke Pickard. They began to beat him, but he fought back. Gardaí believe he put up a strong fight, and was only subdued when one of his attackers struck him on the back of the head with the butt of a gun he was carrying. Brooke was probably bundled into the back of his own van, which one of his attackers then drove. The other men got into the orange car. Both vehicles then exited the car park and were certainly clear of there by 11.30 a.m. It had all taken just a few short moments.

Brooke Pickard disappeared from the face of the earth. He was never seen again.

Back in his home, there was no sense of panic. He was expected to be on the bog all day. When he didn't return in time for his dinner that night, there was still no worry for his safety. Days on the bog have a way of stretching, and he could have had problems with the van. There could be any number of reasons for the delay. It was a decade before mobile phones became ubiquitous, so there was no way of contacting him, and no feeling of worry when he didn't contact home.

The family ate their dinner, and by the time his wife, Penny, went to bed, he still had not arrived home. But when Penny woke the following morning to an empty bed, she realised something was wrong. She immediately contacted the man Mr Pickard had been due to cut turf with the previous day, and was stunned to learn that her husband had not shown up. This was not like him.

However, on at least one other occasion he had unexpectedly gone to England without telling anyone. She rang friends and family across the water, but no one had seen or heard from him. Now she was beginning to worry. She went into the village and began making enquiries. It was while she was doing this that she bumped into the father of the girl who had spotted the incident on the beach the previous day. He related his daughter's story, but now it was seen in a different light: it had been very real.

A call was put through to Cahirciveen Garda Station. Sergeant Michael Griffin and Detective Garda Dan Coughlan immediately drove to Castlecove, where they spent a number of hours interviewing people and trying to piece together the final hours before the abduction. From the beginning, they treated it very seriously. It was an armed abduction, and there were genuine fears for Mr Pickard's life. A large team of Gardaí quickly assembled under Chief Superintendent Donal O'Sullivan and Superintendent Thomas Lally. They began by conducting a major search around Castlecove and the surrounding countryside for the two vehicles involved: the blue Ford Transit of Mr Pickard and the orange Toyota Corolla of his abductors.

An army helicopter was called in to zoom over the mountainous terrain, and the coastline was also searched. Brooke Pickard's description was released to the media, and the whole of Kerry seemed to be looking for the missing man. As the hours turned into days, more evidence began to come to light. There were reports of a second attempted abduction along the same stretch of road some hours after Mr Pickard was taken. The man in that case had managed to escape his attackers. Gardaí believed the incidents could be linked.

A picture began to emerge that a couple of men with Northern accents had been seen in the area a few times in the weeks leading up to the abduction. Other names began to pop up, names of men in Cork and Kerry who were known to the Gardaí. All had to be interviewed and questioned. Experienced officers travelled from Dublin to assist the local men.

A witness was found who said that he had seen men with balaclavas and shotguns near the abduction site.

A Garda spokesperson told the media, 'We are considering the possibility that abduction was the cause of his going missing.' It was the only possibility they were considering. They had dismissed any idea that the man had deliberately disappeared or had just gone missing.

The orange Toyota Corolla was the first vehicle to be found. It had been abandoned by the abductors in the car park of Limerick Regional Hospital. Gardaí carried out a thorough forensic examination, but discovered nothing. There were no clues in the vehicle.

Twenty days after Brooke Pickard disappeared, there was another break: Mr Pickard's own vehicle was found. It had been burnt out in a mountainous area 27 miles from Castlecove. On the afternoon of 16 May, an anonymous tip-off to the Gardaí at Cahirciveen told them that there was an abandoned van near Shronaloughane Forest, in the hilly hinterland north-west of Waterville. It took Gardaí an hour to get to the place. They drove to the end of a track at the entrance to a wood in the townland of Derreennageeha, south of Shronaloughane. The van had been abandoned at the end of a dirt track that ran out from a winding hilly road. It was about 300 yards off the road and had been set on fire when it was abandoned, but the number plate was still on it and corresponded to the missing blue Transit. It was a significant find.

The area was immediately sealed off, and a team from the Garda Technical Bureau came down from Dublin to do a minute forensic examination of the wreck. They found that the van had been burnt out almost three weeks previously. The forensics team included a photographer, a fingerprints expert and a ballistics expert, among others. If the abductors had been even a little careless, these guys would find the evidence.

They did find some things, adding to the sinister aspect of Mr Pickard's disappearance. In the back of the van, they found a spent bullet. However, they were able to determine that it had not been fired; it had been lying in the van when it went on fire and had exploded under the intense heat. At least it had not been fired at the missing man, but the fact that there was a bullet in the van, and presumably there had been a gun, did not bode well.

The other objects recovered were the normal items you would expect to find in the back of the van of a busy man: tools, some odd coins and other debris. There was nothing to give a clue as to who had abducted him, and what Brooke's ultimate fate was.

The site where the van was dumped was desolate and isolated, about 27 miles from the Pickard home. It would have taken the best part of an hour to get there, and it indicated that there was at least some local involvement in the disappearance of

Mr Pickard. If his abductors were from Northern Ireland, as was suspected, they had had help from someone in Kerry. They could not have found the isolated dumping spot without that help, and it was too much of a stretch of the imagination to believe they had just stumbled on a place to burn out a van so that it would not be discovered for weeks.

Gardaí combed the 400-acre forest where the van was found, as well as the surrounding roads for miles. They searched ditches for anything thrown out and looked for disturbed earth on the forest floor. Yet a major search operation failed to uncover anything new. The search for Brooke Pickard seemed to have come to a dead end.

The most reasonable interpretation of events is that the farmer was driven in the back of his own van straight from the car park of the White Strand beach near his home to the deserted forest: an hour's journey. At that point the alarm had not been raised, and his abductors had all the time in the world. Perhaps they wanted information from him, and he was questioned. Perhaps they always knew they were going to kill him, so they wasted no time.

The most likely scenario is that when they pulled up at the end of the forest track, well away from prying eyes, they opened the back of the van and released Mr Pickard, then made him walk the final distance to where he was killed. If his body had been left in the isolated woods, and even if it had been concealed with vegetation, it would have been discovered once the van was found. However, the Gardaí searched the woods thoroughly, so if Mr Pickard was killed and left there, his body must have been buried.

Gardaí had heard from a number of sources of people with Northern accents in the vicinity in the period before the abduction. Mr Pickard's co-defendant in the firearms trial had been menaced by a gang from the North, so it was a logical conclusion that there was a northern element to the disappearance. Gardaí did not feel there was a paramilitary angle, as Mr Pickard was not known to be politically active so there would be no reason for him to be a target of the Provisional IRA, or the other side. However, the criminal gangs in the north operated side by side with the paramilitaries, and there was sometimes an overlap between them. It was not unknown for paramilitaries to kidnap a person, make them walk into the wild, dig their own shallow grave and then shoot them. Had this been the fate of Mr Pickard?

To this day, no one knows. The forest was searched using the technology of the time. Perhaps a fresh search, using more modern equipment, would be more fruitful. Or perhaps he isn't in the forest at all.

Gardaí continued their search, and the case remains an open file. During the initial weeks of the investigation, a number of people were arrested and taken in for questioning. These included people from Kerry and Cork. However, nothing came of these arrests and everyone was released without charge.

In 1993, it was reported that Gardaí were anxious to interview a number of men from Northern Ireland in connection with the disappearance. They were working on the assumption that Brooke Pickard had been murdered after becoming involved in a dispute over drugs money. This emerged when his friend Stephen Terence Mead was finally extradited to Ireland and brought before the court on the old firearms charge. Mr Pickard had been given a suspended sentence. Mead was not so lucky. He was given a two-year sentence.

The court heard that he had used a revolver to intimidate drug addicts into paying debts to his co-defendant, the missing Mr Pickard. Detective Sergeant Seamus Kane told the court that Mr Pickard had been kidnapped from his home soon afterwards, and added that the investigation was ongoing. Mr Pickard's family were hoping for a good outcome, but the assumption was that Mr Pickard had since died 'in suspicious circumstances'. Mr Pickard had been given a suspended sentence for the offence before his 'apparently drug-related disappearance'. Detective Kane said that it had been suggested that the missing man had run a drugs ring in Kerry.

Mead explained to the court that while he was on bail awaiting the firearms charges, three men had called to the Pickard house, where he was staying, and threatened his life. As a result of this, he had fled the jurisdiction. He told the court he was trying to change his past and turn his life around. He had become involved in a Christian organisation, the Baptist Church of Jesus Christ. This church worked a lot with people involved in the New Age and hippy communities, and with those who had become addicted to drugs. Mead himself had turned to drugs after a family tragedy, so he knew first-hand what addicts were going through. The court was told that Mead was using his personal experience to help others.

He had recently been ordained a Baptist minister by the World Christianship Ministry. A quick look at the World Christianship Ministry website reveals them to be an ordination-on-demand service. They make an appealing offer: 'Become an ordained minister, start a church of ministry. Receive ordination almost immediately as a minister, pastor, reverend, evangelist, bishop, chaplain, missionary, elder, deacon, preacher or other. As a minister ordained and licensed by the World Christianship Ministries you have full authority to do all standard Christian services, including marriage ceremonies, baptism ceremonies, and funeral services. We have been providing this seminary alternative way to ordain for over 30 years.'

For a basic fee of $58 you can get the basic ordination package, which includes a laminated identity card. For an extra $54 you can get your new church chartered. This was the ordination that Mr Mead – or Pastor Mead, as he was now known – had gone through.

After hearing the evidence, Judge Moriarty sentenced Mead to two years, but suspended the last year, after hearing that Mead would leave the jurisdiction on his release. In the meantime, he could continue his ministry behind bars.

The conviction of Mead revived interest in Pickard's disappearance, but no new leads were generated. Gardaí admitted they had a number of people in Northern Ireland that they would interview if they came into the jurisdiction, but they believed that there were people in Kerry and Cork who were involved and who also knew the ultimate fate of Mr Pickard.

A couple of very strong suspects were identified. In fact, the Gardaí submitted a file to the Director of Public Prosecutions for consideration. However, the DPP felt there was not enough evidence to secure a conviction, and no proceedings were issued.

That is how the situation stands after more than two decades. Charles Brooke Pickard was probably abducted by five men, some armed. They were probably made up of a few Northern Irish men, backed by Kerry colleagues who knew the terrain. Brooke was probably killed within a few hours of his abduction, and his body is probably buried in the remote Shronaloughane Forest. The Gardaí probably know who did it.

More speculative is the reason why. It would be strange if the murder had nothing to do with the firearms with which Mr Pickard's suspended sentence was connected. He might have been associated with the drugs trade in Kerry, or he might have just been involved with people who were involved in the drugs trade, but those associates almost certainly lie at the heart of his disappearance.

The Gardaí never stopped trying to get to the bottom of the mystery. In 2000, they applied for a warrant to bring a man down from Northern Ireland for questioning. He was accused of firearms offences in the republic in 1992, a year after Mr Pickard's disappearance. He, along with others, had used an imitation firearm to intimidate someone. He fled to Northern Ireland, but the authorities applied for his extradition. He fought the application. One of the grounds on which he fought the extradition was that he said that Gardaí were not just looking for him in connection with the 1992 offence; they also wanted to question him about the disappearance of Pickard.

The High Court in Belfast was told that the Gardaí confirmed this. They wrote to the man's solicitor, saying:

Mr Charles Brooke Pickard was last seen on 26 April 1991 at White Strand, Castlecove, County Kerry.

An intensive Garda investigation was conducted into his disappearance which involved the arrest and interviewing a number of persons. To date nobody has been charged with any offence connected with Mr Pickard's disappearance. Our enquiries revealed that Mr Pickard was a victim of an abduction by possibly five persons some of whom were in possession of firearms. The purpose of this abduction would appear to have been related to an attempt to steal money which it was suspected he had in his possession. There is no evidence that such abduction was carried out by an illegal organisation.

From an early stage of this investigation [a named suspect's] alleged involvement in the disappearance was established and the Gardaí were anxious from this point on to interview [a named suspect]. We are satisfied that [the named suspect] visited the South Kerry area prior to the disappearance of Mr Pickard, and was involved in a plot to steal money from him.

It is our intention that (the named suspect) will be arrested for the offence of false imprisonment of Charles Brooke Pickard, and interviewed re same.

The High Court ordered that the man be sent to Dublin and questioned. Although the Gardaí said that there was no paramilitary involvement in the disappearance of Mr Pickard, the man they wanted to interview had Irish National Liberation Army (INLA) links. Nothing came of the interviews, and no one was charged as a result.

However, more than two decades after the abduction, the suspect is still actively involved in illegal activities. In the spring of 2012, he was one of three men charged at Newry Magistrates Court on suspicion of involvement in terrorism and blackmail. The men were charged with being members of the INLA, of blackmail and of threatening to kill a man if he did not pay them £35,000 by the following day. At the time of writing, they are in custody awaiting trial on those charges.

Gardaí are fairly sure they know who abducted and killed Brooke Pickard, but they are no nearer to bringing closure to the family.

After the abduction, life went on for the Pickards, but it was a life blighted by more tragedy. Nearly three years later, in January 1994, the eldest child, Lisa, was involved in a traffic accident. The 17 year old was looking forward to college and a bright future, but all that was torn away from her. She was laid to rest in the local cemetery.

Because Brooke Pickard was missing rather than dead, it caused further problems for the family. It takes seven years to have a missing person declared dead, and dealing with the day-to-day issues thrown up by that conundrum must have been a constant headache. Eventually Penny Pickard moved back to the United Kingdom, where she now lives. Her three sons are all grown up, and the grandchildren have begun to arrive. But they are still no closer to the truth of what happened that April morning in 1991 than they were a month after the abduction. At this stage, it seems unlikely they will ever find out what really happened to Charles Brooke Pickard.

10

THE FARMER IN THE WELL

The murder of Patrick Daly by his brother and nephew

AMONGST STRANGERS, MURDER can be a casual or a cruel affair. Between people who know each other, it is always cruel. And the better they know each other, the crueller it becomes. When close family members fall out, the results can be horrendous. Sometimes rows simmer for years, before breaking to the surface in an orgy of violence that stuns a community. But it is a sad truth that the longer a row is simmering, the more violent the eventual resolution will be.

Patrick Daly and his brother Sean had been quietly resenting each other for 30 years. No good could come of it.

Patrick Daly was born on a farm in Dooneen, Kilcummin, near Killarney, in 1927. His older brother, Sean, was already two. The farm had been in the family for generations. Their father had emigrated to America, but returned home when he inherited it. The boys had what must have been an idyllic, if tough, childhood. The farm was 105 acres, which guaranteed the family a comfortable living. They had a two-storey farmhouse, and they were only five miles from a substantial town. They wanted for nothing.

The brothers reached maturity as the new nation was getting

on its feet. They lived through the depression of the 1930s, then the austerity years of the Second World War – known locally as 'The Emergency'. Rationing was in force, but as the sons of a strong farmer, they got their share of what was available.

As the war ended and the bleak '50s began, both men reached adulthood. Sean got married and eventually had two sons and two daughters. He remained on the land, working the farm. Eventually his sons, James and Eugene, joined him on the farm.

Younger brother Patrick never got married. He was a bit of a loner, and was considered a quiet man. He was about six foot, and slim but muscular. He was tremendously strong, and feats of his strength are still remembered, such as one occasion when he lifted the back of a tractor out of a ditch single-handed. Like his brother, he continued to work the land.

The death of their father left the boys in charge of the day-to-day running of the farm, but the land belonged to their mother. In the usual course of events Sean would eventually inherit, securing his future. He probably married on the strength of those expectations.

However, a rift developed between Sean and his mother. His mother and his wife, Mary, did not get on. And as the old woman neared her end, there was no resolution in sight. She died unreconciled with her daughter-in-law in the mid-1960s. When the will was read, Sean was shocked to find that he, as the eldest son, had not inherited the farm. Instead it had gone to his younger brother, Patrick.

Both men continued to run the farm together, but their relationship had changed. Now Patrick was in charge, and the land was in his name. Although they shared the work and shared the profits, one man's name was on the deeds and the other man had no legal entitlement.

Sean lived on a house on the land with his wife, sons and daughters. He continued to work the land and make a good living off it, but deep in his soul he felt a spark of resentment, and as the years became decades, that spark burned brighter with each passing year.

Things came to a head in 1995, when Sean was 71 and Patrick was 69. Tensions between the two were reaching breaking point. Perhaps the trigger was the fact that Sean's sons, who helped work the farm, were getting older and were anxious that their future would be secure. One of Sean's sons, Eugene, was an intense young man, who was regarded as a bit strange by neighbours. He tended to ramble in his conversation and was not regarded as very bright. He was not working as hard as the others on the land. There were also rows over the sale of livestock.

In the summer of 1995, three local dogs went missing. Two belonged to Patrick, while the third belonged to his neighbour Jack Finnegan. Mr Finnegan was about a decade older than Patrick, but they were good friends. Dogs are important farm animals, and Patrick's dogs were also companions for the bachelor. One of Patrick's dogs was cruelly hanged. Although he could not prove it, he suspected that it was his brother or one of his nephews who had killed the dog. In this he was right; it emerged later, during a trial, that Eugene had hanged the dog. The other two dogs were never found.

A neighbour, Tom Kelleher, later said that the disappearance of the dogs led to bad blood in the locality. The truth was that the bad blood had been there for decades; the killing of the dogs just brought it out into the open. That summer Patrick Daly developed a nervous complaint and had to be treated at the psychiatric hospital in Tralee. The strain was beginning to tell on the elderly farmer. He was suffering from periodic bouts of depression.

There were a number of issues between the brothers. Patrick felt that he was not getting as much cooperation around the farm as he wanted. He also felt that his nephew Eugene was not pulling his weight and was a slacker. Patrick considered letting out the land rather than continuing with the existing arrangement. He is believed to have contacted an auctioneer.

His brother heard about this, and his eldest son, James, called on the auctioneer. However, the auctioneer refused to discuss the matter with him.

Then Patrick Daly visited his solicitor, and two letters were sent from the solicitor to Sean, saying that the services being provided by Sean and his sons were unsatisfactory. This exacerbated the problems between the siblings. Things were coming to a head. Even though Patrick was a quiet and uncommunicative man, his friends knew something was troubling him.

Jack Finnegan, a lifelong friend of Mr Daly, said that the disappearance of the three dogs during the summer had troubled the murdered man. 'They were good dogs, but we never saw them again,' he said. 'It was deeply upsetting, and it led to bad blood in the area.' He added that in the lead-up to Christmas Mr Daly had appeared troubled, but he had not talked about what was on his mind.

Around that time, someone began daubing slogans on the walls of Mr Daly's house and on his car. There was clearly an attempt being made to intimidate and frighten the old man.

The second solicitor's letter arrived on 9 January. The letter accused Sean Daly of interfering with his brother's affairs. The letter left Sean feeling upset and annoyed.

On Thursday, 18 January, Patrick Daly was spotted around by neighbours. He was dressed in wellington boots and a green waxed jacket and was wearing a cap. He was seen in the local post office. A neighbour, Nora O'Connell, was one of the last people to see him alive. She took a walk every day and she spotted Patrick at 10.50 a.m. He was cleaning out a calf shed, and he called good morning to her. She replied and continued on her walk.

The following day no one saw him around, which was unusual. One of the neighbours, Tom Kelleher, asked Sean Daly if he had seen Patrick, but he said that he had not. When Kelleher suggested reporting the farmer missing, Sean replied, 'He's stone mad, and he's gone away.'

The following day, the Gardaí were alerted that the elderly man was missing. They were told first by two neighbours, but Sean then phoned them with the same news. He said that he had been at home sick in bed the day his brother had disappeared.

On Saturday, a small team of Gardaí carried out an examination of the farmyard and the house. There was no sign of a disturbance in the house, and no sign of Mr Daly anywhere close to the house. The farmyard was empty. They checked outhouses and ditches and came up with nothing. But one of the team, Sergeant Michael O'Donovan, spotted an old well in the farmyard. The well was obviously disused. There was a cement cap over it and a rusty barrel on top. It was probably a relic of the days before the council hooked the house up to the local water scheme.

The sergeant walked over and shifted the cap from the well. He could see that the well had been filled in; it was covered in rocks and sand. The rubble came up to the rim of the well. He replaced the cover and continued the search. During the course of his examination, he had stepped into the sand and left a deep footprint.

The following day the search was resumed, both on the farm and throughout the locality. Many of the neighbours got involved. A team from the Civil Defence joined the Gardaí in the farmyard and this time the search was extremely thorough. But again it showed nothing.

However, Sergeant O'Donovan was again drawn to the well. He walked over and shifted the concrete cap. He was surprised to see that the sand had settled, and was several inches lower than the previous day. And his bootprint was not there.

Two days later, on Tuesday, 23 January, a team of Gardaí arrived back at the farmhouse, and this time their search was very specific. They made straight for the well and removed the cap. They could see that the sand now reached the top of the well, and was both wet and swept level.

Sean Daly walked over with a long iron rod and told them they were wasting their time. He thrust the stick deep into the sand, and it struck a rock. He told the investigators that his brother had filled in the well a few weeks previously, and they would find nothing there but sand and rocks.

Undeterred, the Gardaí began to shovel the sand out of the

well. It was 3.30 p.m. and they had about two hours of daylight left. Sean Daly watched sullenly from a distance. They pulled out some of the rocks, and then spotted a line of blue baler twine. That didn't belong there. Now there was a sense of urgency to their work. Very quickly they removed the layer of sand and the rocks underneath it. Now they could see large sheets of black plastic. Every farm uses those large sheets, generally for wrapping up wet grass to make silage during the summer months. It wasn't particularly valuable, but no one would waste it on filling a well. The sheets seemed to be covering something.

The Gardaí quickly pulled out the plastic and were horrified at what they saw. The bottom of the well still contained water. Protruding from the water was a green wellington and a human leg. A hand also stuck out.

Garda Noel Browne, who was one of the team, was standing beside Eugene Daly when someone shouted out that they had found a wellington boot. Eugene turned to him and said: 'Jesus, 'tis awful. He should not have gone that way. People who do that stuff don't stay around, no way.' He then asked the Garda would he still be able to go to Killarney on Thursday to collect his dole, as neighbours might suspect the family had something to do with the body in the well – a strange thought at such a time.

Work immediately stopped, and the area was sealed off to await the arrival of State Pathologist Dr Margot Bolster. Once she had made an initial examination of the scene, the fire brigade had the task of raising the body from the well. This happened the following morning. The fire brigade attached a rope to the protruding leg and pulled the victim from the well. He was then removed to the hospital. The post-mortem, at Tralee General Hospital, revealed that Mr Daly had suffered horrific injuries.

He had suffered a broken shoulder bone, a broken arm, a perforated eardrum and a broken jaw. There were several injuries and fractures to his skull, and bones on his back and ribcage had been smashed. His brain had been beaten to a pulp, which was the immediate cause of death. His spleen was lacerated. It was apparent that he had been beaten savagely by a blunt instrument, such as an iron bar. He had also been kicked or stomped on. His injuries were so extensive that death would have been swift. He died of swelling, contusion and laceration of the brain due to blunt-force trauma.

There was some evidence of post-death injuries, but the majority of the injuries had been inflicted before he died, and he was dead before he was pushed into the well. Dr Bolster was unable to determine the time of death, as the body had been preserved to an unusual extent by the burial.

The 20-foot well had been hastily filled in after Patrick Daly's body had been flung head-first down it. Layers of plastic were dropped on the body, then stones and sand. It was an isolated spot. One of the nearest houses was 150 yards away, and it was where Patrick's brother, Sean, lived. The attackers would have been undisturbed.

The death of Patrick Daly was one of two brutal murders of elderly farmers that week. In Galway, Tom Casey, a retired farmer, had been beaten to death. He was found lying in a pool of blood in the ransacked kitchen of his home near Oranmore, a few miles outside Galway city. His hands and feet were bound, and he had been lying in his own blood for more than two days. 'The discovery of the two bodies comes against a background of increased attacks on elderly people living in isolated rural areas,' the *Irish Times* noted. Gangs were targeting old people all along the west coast, terrorising them in search of money. It was easy to assume that Patrick Daly had fallen foul of such a gang. But the Gardaí were not so sure. A great effort had been made to conceal the body, and that would have taken time – time an intruder would not have had.

Robbery was swiftly ruled out as a motive. Gardaí began extensive door-to-door interviews, gleaning information from shocked neighbours. People were genuinely shocked at the savage attack. Patrick's nephews James, 29, and Eugene, 21, spoke of their revulsion at what had happened to their uncle. Both men worked the land with their father. James was a hard worker who got on well with his uncle. There was a more troubled relationship between Eugene and Patrick.

James said that his uncle had no enemies. He then said something rather unusual: the family were not involved. At that point, no one had accused them of anything. 'He had no troubles, because if he did, he would have told us,' said James, speaking to journalists. 'The family had nothing whatsoever to do with this. We're totally out of it. We gave the Gardaí every possible assistance and in fact we were the ones who called them when he went missing.

'Paddy was in good spirits and we all got on very well together. We worked well together as a team. He had nothing on his mind and there was nothing worrying him before he disappeared. I have no idea why anybody would do it. There was no reason why anyone would want to hurt him. It's unbelievable.'

He said that his uncle had a history of depression, for which he had sought treatment the previous summer, but there was no question of suicide, because of the way the body was covered.

'We always saw eye to eye and got on very well. We were shocked when the body was discovered and we still are. Paddy would go to the pub for a drink sometimes, but he wasn't really a drinking man. I suppose you could say that he didn't have too many interests. He was very easygoing and hard-working. We all felt dreadful when we found out about this. It was a desperate shock. My mother, Mary, and my father are very upset, but they are trying to get to grips with it.'

The other nephew, Eugene, also spoke to the press. He said that the Gardaí had asked him if he had put the plastic sheeting over his uncle, and he had burst out crying at the accusation: 'I started crying and said that I wouldn't be here if I had done it. It's ridiculous. Why would we do it? It's bizarre and macabre. Nothing like this ever happened before in this area. Still, we have to try and keep going. We're bearing up as well as we can, but I hope nobody gets the idea that we had anything to do with it.'

Shocked neighbours were also interviewed, and they shared their memories of a quiet man with prodigious strength.

Jack Finnegan, 80, recalled an incident once when a tractor had got stuck in a ditch. While others went to fetch something to tow the tractor out, Patrick remained with the vehicle. When the others returned they were stunned to see that he had, single-handedly, managed to lift the rear of the tractor out and free it from the ditch. A man of that strength would not have been easy to kill.

Mr Finnegan had visited his neighbour a few days before his death and had spent an evening watching television with him. He would pass him several times a day. He said, 'I knew him all my life. I'd pass him maybe 20 times a day. It's a terrible shock. We don't expect this type of thing around here. This is a quiet place.'

Gardaí continued to search the farmyard and surrounding area for a weapon of any sort, and several items were collected and sent for forensic examination. They were not expecting an early breakthrough, but were confident that their investigation was going in the right direction. They distributed questionnaires to households in the locality, seeking information on the movements of the dead man and asking about prior incidents in the area.

Sean Daly broke his silence and said he was shocked at his brother's death, and did not know why anyone would want to harm Patrick.

On Friday, three days after the body was discovered, the funeral of Patrick Daly took place. A small crowd gathered at Kilcummin Church for the Mass. Fr John O'Sullivan, the parish priest, said that the death was tragic for the small community. 'These days our newspapers are full of news concerning violence. But when it comes so close to home we feel double the impact. It will take our community a long time to recover from this tragedy,' he said.

Sean Daly was there with his wife, Mary, and their children, James, Margaret and Eugene. About a hundred people followed the coffin to the Old Kilcummin Cemetery, where Mr Daly was laid to rest.

Meanwhile, Superintendent Mick O'Neill, leading the investigation, continued to direct the searches of the farm, as well as the interviews and questionnaires throughout the parish. He said that the Gardaí were receiving excellent cooperation from the public. 'As yet nobody has been questioned in connection with the killing, but we are satisfied with the way the investigation is going,' he said.

Gardaí were homing in on the family, and as they pieced together evidence of the tensions between the two brothers they were growing in confidence that they were on the right track. Eventually Sean Daly and his sons were taken in for questioning. Sean was interviewed in the back of a patrol car for three hours, during which he denied any involvement. He said that the well had been filled a few weeks previously by his brother, and he did not know how Patrick ended up under the rubble. He said his relationship with his brother was 'all right', and added that he would 'never lay a hand on that man'.

The questioning continued, and all three were detained for interview in Killarney Garda Station on 8 February. Eugene denied any knowledge of his uncle's death, but after repeated questioning he was the first to crack; he made a statement admitting his involvement in the concealment of his uncle's body and implicating his father in the murder.

That evening at a special court in Kenmare, Sean Daly, 71, was charged with murder. He was remanded in custody. His two sons were released, but a file was sent to the Director of Public Prosecutions for consideration.

The following day, again at Kenmare Court, Eugene Daly, 21, was charged with the murder of his uncle. He was also remanded in custody.

On Monday, 19 February, both accused applied to the High Court in Dublin for bail. Superintendent O'Neill opposed their application. He told the court that Patrick Daly had been battered to death with a steel bar, kicked and beaten, and dumped into a well. He believed that if Eugene Daly was released he would interfere with and intimidate potential witnesses in the parish. 'This is a rural area where a lot of elderly people live alone, and they are terrified,' he said. He added that Eugene was a loner who did not socialise and who only left the farm once a week to sign on for the dole in Killarney. If released, the Gardaí were confident he would not flee the jurisdiction, but he would intimidate elderly witnesses. The superintendent asked that if he was released, a condition of his release would be that he could not live at home. He could get a flat in Killarney, away from the rural parish.

John O'Sullivan, representing Eugene Daly, said that the family had lived in the area for 200 years, and there was no evidence he would interfere with any witnesses. It would be unfair if he had to leave his home. He was willing to sign on at a local Garda station daily.

There were no objections to granting bail to Sean Daly.

Mr Justice Flood granted both men bail, ordering them not to talk to anyone on the Garda list of potential witnesses. Eugene was allowed to live in the family home, but had to sign on in the Garda station in Killarney daily.

It was more than two years before the case came to trial. Both men were tried independently. Eugene Daly was the first before the court. His trial opened in the Central Criminal Court on Tuesday, 21 April 1998, before Mr Justice Carney.

The court was told that Eugene had acted in concert with another to carry out a cold-blooded, premeditated murder that involved considerable violence. Mr Daly pleaded not guilty.

Prosecuting barrister Gregory Murphy told the jury there was an element of teamwork in the killing. He outlined the family circumstances and how both brothers worked the land together, though it belonged to Patrick. He said that Eugene was not as helpful on the farm as his older brother or his father, and this had led to issues between Patrick and Sean. Eventually,

Patrick had become dissatisfied with the work being done on the farm.

Towards the end of 1995, Sean and his family became convinced that Patrick had put the land in the hands of an auctioneer to be let, but when James Daly went to the auctioneer, he refused to discuss the matter. Then Patrick Daly had his solicitor send two letters to Sean complaining that the services being provided on the farm were unsatisfactory.

Mr Murphy said, 'Eugene Daly and another [his father, Sean, not mentioned by name in the proceedings so as not to prejudice his own trial] decided they would rid themselves of this man.'

'Let's call a spade a spade,' he went on. 'The State's case is that the accused and another man murdered Patrick Daly in a dispute related to land.'

Dr Margot Bolster told the court that Patrick Daly had been beaten to death with considerable force, causing swelling and laceration to the brain, the direct cause of death. She identified an iron bar as the probable weapon.

On the second day of the trial, Garda witnesses read statements taken from Eugene Daly during the course of the investigation. In one statement he said that he had 'worked it out' with his father to kill his uncle. He said that in the weeks leading up to the murder he had painted slogans on the walls of his uncle's house and on abandoned cars nearby. He did this at the instigation of his father, to scare his uncle. After the body was discovered in the well, he tried to scrub much of the graffiti away.

He described how his father was in a towering temper on 18 January 1996 – the Thursday when Patrick disappeared. He lost control and hit Patrick with a rusty iron bar: 'He did it, and I couldn't do anything about it. I am an accessory, like.'

After his father was charged with murder, Eugene told the Gardaí that he had not been completely straight with them in his statements. 'We had discussed where we would get rid of Paddy when we were in the car on the way down from our house on the Thursday morning. We worked it out that we'd end Paddy like, and we did,' he then told the investigators.

Sean and Eugene confronted Patrick at his house and argued with him about money. The argument became heated, and Sean started to lose his temper. Patrick attempted to get into his van and drive off, but Sean hit him repeatedly with the iron bar, knocking him to the ground. Then Eugene joined in. 'I started kicking Paddy in the ribs and back to make sure he was gone,' he said. He was doing this to do his father 'a favour and to make sure he was killed'.

Once it was obvious Patrick was dead, the statements went on, Eugene dragged the body across a small road in the farm, towards the disused well. He threw the body head first down the well.

Eugene Daly gave evidence himself, but often appeared vague and rambling in his answers. He said that he had stood by a pillar and watched as his uncle was killed, but, contrary to his statements to the Gardaí, he had not participated. He admitted throwing the body into the well. During his evidence, he told the jury: 'I will walk.' Later, he said that even if he was convicted, 'I will do 20 years and still be out a young man.'

The trial was a short one, lasting just three days. On the closing day, the defence argued that Daly should not have been charged with murder but should have faced a lesser charge. However, the prosecution argued that while the accused might be odd, this hid a streak of cunning.

Barrister Adrian Hardiman, defending Daly, said, 'No one would want to convict a severely disadvantaged, poorly equipped young man, bordering on mental handicap, unless there was very clear evidence that he had participated in murder.' Saying that Daly had a tendency to ramble and give vague answers, he said that his client had 'talked himself into this charge' and should have been charged with concealing the body, not with murder. 'Eugene Daly was released from custody on 8 February 1996, while the DPP had decided to charge another man [Sean Daly] with murder. The following day Eugene rang the Gardaí, and by the end of that day, he was charged too,' said the barrister.

He put it to the jury that if the murder was premeditated and planned, why had the younger man not carried it out, instead of leaving it to his 71-year-old father? He said, 'There is no evidence of a conspiracy to murder. Instead the evidence suggests the most likely thing was that Eugene Daly was tagging along, like a little boy, doing whatever was asked of him.'

Gregory Murphy, for the prosecution, disagreed. He said that there was a temptation to feel sorry for Daly, but he knew what he was doing. 'It is only five miles from Dooneen to the centre of the tourist trade in Ireland, Killarney. Yet it was here that Paddy Daly was killed in a manner that reminds me of the film *Deliverance*, with its poor white folk living on a mountain out of the mainstream of modern life,' he said. 'But behind this behavioural abnormality there is a streak of cunning.'

Mr Murphy reminded the jury that the statements made to the Gardaí, and read to the court, were uncontested, and Eugene Daly had admitted to hanging a dog belonging to his uncle. He said, 'You could say he showed as much indifference to the killing of his uncle as he did to the death of the dog.'

Mr Murphy also highlighted the time of the murder – a Thursday, when Eugene's brother, James, would be in town collecting his dole. James would not have approved of the murder, or been a part of it. He concluded: 'If there was no intent to murder, why had Eugene, who never did any work around the farm, knocked down a wall and piled the stones into a heap to be used later to fill the well?'

The jury was discharged for the weekend, and they began their deliberations the following Monday morning, after being addressed by the judge. They spent the rest of Monday in deliberations, to no avail. At the end of the day they were sent to a hotel for the night, and then resumed their deliberations the following morning. Finally, at 5.55 p.m., they returned to the court. They had been deliberating for almost ten hours.

Mr Justice Carney asked them if they had arrived at a verdict that ten of them could agree on. He was told that they had not. He asked the jury foreman whether the jury wanted to be sent to a hotel for another night, to resume the following day. The foreman said that was not likely to result in a verdict, and the judge dismissed the jury.

However, Eugene Daly was not off the hook. He was released on bail, and a new date was set for a retrial.

Before that retrial, his father, Sean, was in the dock, facing the murder charge. His trial opened on Thursday, 16 July 1998. Like his son, he pleaded not guilty. Barrister Patrick McEntee, defending Daly, had asked that the trial proceed swiftly. 'My client is a very old man who has great difficulty coping with the strangeness of the court,' he explained. 'He is 72; he's infirm.'

The trial proceeded with more swiftness than anyone could have imagined. The jury of eight women and four men had been sworn in on Monday, but on Thursday, when the trial began, the prosecution told the judge that the trial would run into August, and several of the jurors had pre-booked holidays and would have to be discharged. There were 60 witnesses and 92 exhibits. It would be a lengthy trial. It was estimated to take two weeks, but could run longer.

There was a half-hour discussion between prosecutor Gregory Murphy, Patrick McEntee and Mr Justice Shanley. Mr McEntee said his client wanted the trial to go ahead, but the judge said he knew one of the jurors had a flight booked for 25 July, while another three had flights booked for the first week in August. Under the circumstances, an adjournment was the only option.

It was proving difficult to get justice for Patrick Daly.

Although the court reconvened after the summer, in October, it was the following June before Sean Daly was in the dock again. His trial reopened on 28 June 1999. Barrister John Edwards, prosecuting, said that tensions were running high between the brothers in the final months of Patrick's life. The brothers had not been getting on particularly well. There were rows and arguments between them, especially around the sale of animals. In early January 1996, Patrick Doyle instructed his solicitor to send a letter to his brother. The solicitor wrote that Patrick 'instructs us that you interfere in his affairs. This is causing him distress. Be good enough to know that your brother wishes to organise his own affairs.'

Patrick Daly disappeared nine days after his brother got that letter.

'He was hurt; he was annoyed about this letter,' said the barrister.

Tom Kelleher, a bachelor farmer and a long-time friend of Patrick Daly, said that they met up regularly, often several times a week. He last saw Patrick on the Wednesday before he disappeared. That night Patrick was irritated, but would not say why. The tension between himself and his brother was obviously preying on his mind. Patrick was meant to visit Mr Kelleher's house, about two and a half miles from his own, on Friday. But he never showed up. 'He was supposed to call to me on the Friday morning to load some cattle for the mart,' Mr Kelleher said. 'I thought he was sick.'

That night, as Mr Kelleher was driving cattle in from the fields, he met Sean Daly and his son Eugene. He said, 'Sean asked me if Paddy was in my house. I told him he wasn't, and he said he was gone.' Mr Kelleher said that Sean said Eugene had gone up to Patrick's house that morning and had seen that the small front gate was open, with footprints leading away to the right. 'I said he couldn't be gone too far away. Sean said he was stone mad and gone away.'

Asked what else Sean had said that evening, Mr Kelleher said: 'He told me he [Paddy] was very bad, like.' He added that Sean Daly said that himself and Eugene had cleaned up Paddy's house because it was dirty, with dog droppings all over it. 'He said the house was locked and he had to force his way in. When he forced the bedroom, he found his bed dressed and he hadn't slept in it that night.'

The following morning, Mr Kelleher joined James Daly, Sean's oldest son, and they searched along the riverbank and around a lime kiln on the farm, but they found nothing. Mr Kelleher suggested reporting Patrick missing, but Sean Daly was against the idea.

'He told me he was stone mad and gone away, and he'd left all the lights on in the house, and he might come back,' Mr Kelleher told the court. Not satisfied with that, he went into Killarney that afternoon and reported his friend missing at the Garda station.

Sergeant Margaret Nugent of Killarney Garda Station told the court that she had interviewed Sean Daly a number of days after the body of his brother was recovered. He told her that he lived with his wife on the farm owned by his brother, and that they were in partnership together 'for tax purposes'. Patrick was pleased with the work done by himself and his sons, Sean Daly had insisted. Relations were all right between them. 'I'd never lay a hand on that man, even if he was giving out to me. I tried to do my best by the man,' he had said to her.

He told her he had last seen his brother at 9 a.m. on Thursday, 18 January, at the back door of his house. At around 10.30 a.m. he had gone into Killarney with his sons and a daughter, returning home at 1.30 p.m. He was feeling a bit unwell, so he took to his bed for the afternoon. At around 5.30 p.m. he had got up, and he noticed a fire smouldering outside Patrick's house. He could see that his son Eugene was burning papers and rubbish there. Half an hour later, he spotted 'a figure of a fellow' passing inside a window in the house, and he assumed it was his brother, but he could not be sure.

At around 9 p.m. he went over to his brother's house. They lived about 150 yards apart. Eugene shone a torch into Paddy's window, but they could see nothing. The next day he searched for his brother along the river and in other areas, to no avail. After speaking to a neighbour, Tom Kelleher, he was getting worried.

The following day he checked the house and found that Patrick's bed had not been slept in. He consulted his wife about calling the Gardaí. She said that he should, and that if he delayed too long, the Gardaí would be looking into it anyway.

The statement taken by Sergeant Nugent went on to relate that when Gardaí searched the farm, Sean told them he hadn't seen Patrick filling in the well, and didn't know when he'd done it, but he was surprised to find that he had. Just before the Gardaí began searching the well, he told them that he had already looked there and 'wrote it off'.

Sean Daly also told the sergeant that he believed Patrick had sold the milk quota of the farm recently, without telling him. He believed that Patrick got around £1,100 for the quota, but he had no idea who had bought it.

Inspector Michael O'Donovan told the court that he had been a sergeant in Killarney at the time of the search for Patrick Daly. He had asked three civil defence volunteers to remove the concrete cap covering the well and saw that it was filled almost to the top with dry raked sand.

When he returned to the farm on 23 January, he questioned Sean Daly and his three sons in Patrick's house; then he went straight across the farmyard to the well. 'I was suspicious of the well,' he told the court. 'I had the cover moved back again. I noticed that the sand was different in that it had been filled to the very top, flush with the concrete, and it was wet.

'Minutes later, Sean Daly arrived down to the well and he had a bar of iron in his hand, and I had said that it was my intention to dig out the well. Sean Daly lifted the iron bar and stuck it down into the sand and said, "There's nothing down there but stones."'

He said that Sean Daly had not been there when the actual excavation was being done, 'But at one stage I looked up the farmyard. He was standing there, holding a pike. He was looking down at us and he was shaking his head.'

Inspector O'Donovan noted his impressions in the questionnaire that he had asked Sean Daly to fill in. He scribbled: 'Tough, stubborn, said very little. Everything had to be dragged out of him. Seemed to be letting on that he was confused.'

However, on the fourth day of the trial, there was a sensational development. After legal submissions, Mr Justice

Barr told the jury that new evidence had come to light, which had to be investigated. 'A difficulty has arisen in connection with this trial relating to possible additional evidence that has just come to light,' he said. Under the circumstances it would be unrealistic to try to continue with the trial, so he discharged the jury. He remanded Sean Daly on continuing bail, to await a retrial. It would be another year before justice was done for Patrick Daly.

However, unforeseen events prevented the third attempt to bring Sean Daly before the courts. The elderly farmer, at the age of 75, died at Tralee General Hospital on the night of Tuesday, 16 May 2000. His trial was scheduled to begin in less than five weeks, on 21 June.

Mr Daly had been ill for some time. His solicitor said that his death deprived him of the opportunity to have his good name vindicated. 'I was saddened to hear of his death because I would like to have had the opportunity to have had his good name vindicated before a jury,' Killarney solicitor Padraig O'Connell said. 'He had pleaded his innocence at all times.'

Sean Daly had evaded the courts, but his son Eugene still had to face the music. His retrial began on Monday, 26 February 2001. Once again he pleaded not guilty.

Dr Margot Bolster, the pathologist, once more repeated that Patrick Daly had been beaten to death. Pressed by the defence, she said that his brain had been beaten to a pulp, which had caused his death. The injuries to his ribs, back and spleen, caused by kicking, had not been what killed him. Brain tissue had been found on his shirt and jumper.

However, the trial was still young when it collapsed. It was the fifth time that the state had been forced to abandon the trial of someone accused of killing Patrick Daly. This time the reason for the trial collapsing was that someone had attempted to interfere with a juror. The juror had reported the matter to the judge, and the trial was off. Eugene was back on bail. It was becoming a way of life for him.

Finally, on 1 September 2003, Eugene Daly stood up in the

Central Criminal Court in Dublin, and pleaded not guilty to the murder of his uncle. It was the sixth attempt by the state to secure a conviction against someone for the brutal killing.

The prosecution said that Sean Daly had carried out the actual fatal assault, but Eugene assisted him and was the one who threw the body down the well. Statements were read to the court in which Eugene admitted kicking his uncle as he lay dying on the ground.

He had told Gardaí that he had gone to his uncle's house with his late father, who 'wanted to sort it out once and for all'. Asked what he wanted to sort out, he replied: 'The bad blood between Paddy and ourselves that started 30 years ago. Dad said if he did not agree with us he would finish him off – kill him, waste him, rub him out.'

But when they got to the yard, Patrick was argumentative. Sean said that he did not like the way Patrick was carrying on and that there would be trouble if he didn't stop. Patrick told his brother to get lost and leave him alone. Sean replied, 'I'll fix you.'

Sean was in a temper. He picked up a brown bar from the tool room and went up to Patrick, who was facing away from him. Eugene said, 'Dad hit Paddy on the back of the head with the bar. Paddy slumped to the ground. Dad then hit him a few times when he was on the ground. Paddy just said, "What?" Startled like, just before he got the first belt. He lay in a heap on the grass. There was blood trickling from his head.'

Eugene then kicked his uncle 'three or four times, maybe more' in the ribs and in the back. 'I went over to Paddy. I kicked him a number of times just to make sure he was dead,' he said in his statement.

Eugene was asked when he realised his uncle was dead. He said, 'I presumed when I was dragging him and there was no noise out of him.' He dragged the body by the shoulders over to the well. 'I lifted up the cover of the well and let him fall in head first.'

He then spent the rest of the day, until around six, cleaning up behind him. He cleaned up the blood with a rag and some water, and then scrubbed the yard with a brush. His father had left the iron bar lying against a wall, and Eugene brought it into the kitchen of his uncle's house, where he washed it in a sink. 'There was blood at the end of it. I was afraid the Gardaí would find it and we'd both be caught, so I put it in a barrel.'

He then burnt some items in the yard, including his uncle's hat.

Detective Superintendent John O'Mahony testified that he had interviewed Eugene during the investigation and asked how things had got to such a state. He answered, 'Just years and years of troubles over money and the land. Dad was afraid Paddy would sell and the land would be lost. It got out of hand.'

Asked if he had any remorse, he replied, 'Indeed I do, but I can't turn the clock back. I wish it would play differently.'

He had not told his brother James about what had happened, to protect himself and his father: 'I was afraid if I told Jim the truth, he would go nuts and turn us in to the police. He knows nothing about it. We never told him. We just wanted to keep Dad and myself OK, so we said nothing.'

Superintendent O'Mahony said that James had been a 'reasonably good worker', but Eugene had no interest in much apart from watching cowboy and detective films on television. He had a preoccupation with mafia and criminal gangs.

John Kelly, a retired community psychiatric nurse from Killarney, testified that Eugene Daly had received psychiatric treatment after the murder and had been admitted to the hospital for psychiatric services. 'He was initially admitted for post-traumatic stress disorder, possibly related to the stress of the whole business that was going on,' he said.

Mr Kelly also said that he had received a phone call from Sean Daly a week before Patrick's murder, in which Sean had expressed concerns about his brother's behaviour. He told the nurse that he had got a solicitor's letter telling him to keep away from the house. As a result of this, he arranged for Patrick to have an outpatient appointment for 22 January. He said that there was a history of mental problems in the Daly family. Eugene's mother had been hospitalised for schizophrenia when he was 16, and his sister Eileen also suffered from the condition.

Mr Kelly added that the murdered man, Patrick, had suffered from bipolar disorder, and had mood swings. He said, 'Sean supported Paddy over the years. He was always concerned.'

Detective Garda Browne told the court he was standing beside Eugene when the body of his uncle was first discovered: 'He asked me: "Will I still be able to collect my dole on Thursday?" When I asked him why, he replied: "The neighbours will think we did it – we did nothing." I thought the remark was odd in the circumstances.'

Eugene Daly took to the stand to give evidence on his own behalf. He said that to suggest he planned and actively participated in the murder was 'hocus pocus, fiction, like something from the world of Peter Pan'.

Daly's evidence rambled a bit. He said that he 'wanted to be a tough guy', and compared the killing to a scene from a war movie or a thriller. He said that he 'used to retreat into a fantasy world of detectives, police and cowboy movies'.

He then dropped a bit of a bombshell. He said that he had purposely implicated himself in the killing after his father's arrest: 'I was very close to my father and I couldn't leave him suffer in jail alone. So I started to implicate myself in these matters so I'd get busted with him.'

When asked why he had suggested the murder had been planned on the way over to Patrick's house, he replied: 'That was just copying the tough guys, like in *Taggart*.'

Brendan Grehan, barrister for Daly, said that his client 'walked in the shadow of his father' and was not responsible for striking the fatal blow. He told the jury it was 'hollow' to expect them to be able to put themselves in the shoes of a troubled man who lived an impoverished and isolated life. 'You could be forgiven for concluding that, for Mr Daly, the lines between reality and fiction are not entirely convincing,' he said, arguing that Mr Daly should only have been charged with being an accessory to the murder after it happened.

But Denis Vaughan Buckley, for the prosecution, argued that Eugene Daly, by his own admission, had discussed the killing beforehand, and was a willing and active participant. 'The evidence against the accused in this case – by his own statements and admissions – is overwhelming of his guilt and participation in the crime,' he said.

It was eight years since the death of Patrick Daly and the sixth attempt to try someone for the crime. It was no surprise that the jury could not reach a swift decision. They deliberated for a full three days.

At the end of their deliberations they did not convict Eugene Daly of murder, but of the lesser charge of manslaughter.

Mr Justice Henry Abbott said that he took into account a number of mitigating factors, including Daly's young age at the time of the murder, his disadvantaged social circumstances and the stress he had endured in the seven and a half years since the killing. While he accepted that there was no strong evidence of premeditation, the killing was not 'entirely spontaneous', and Daly had shown a degree of callousness in disposing of the body. 'He stood by and took no steps to assist, defend or protect Paddy Daly from the attack, which proved fatal,' he said.

Defence barrister Mr Grehan said that the irony of the guilty verdict was that Eugene would be disinherited from a farm which was worth an estimated €1 million. The farm had been left to him and his brother James by his uncle, but after the conviction, the farm would pass entirely to James.

The judge said that he had taken consideration of this. 'He was promised a share in the only asset the deceased had, and he must bear the burden of his loss,' he said.

When the verdict was announced, Eugene Daly bowed his head and smiled briefly. He remained impassive as the judge spoke. He was sentenced to ten years and eleven months. As he heard the length of his sentence he looked slightly shocked.

None of his family was with him at the end. He was on his own, surrounded by his team of lawyers.

The judge refused leave to appeal, but recommended that Daly serve his time in Cork Prison, which would be nearer his home and his relatives.

An appeal was made, however. In February 2004, Eugene's conviction was upheld, but his sentence was reduced to just six years – almost half of that imposed by the original trial judge.

Once the trials were over, the legal proceedings arising out of the death of Patrick Daly were almost concluded. All that was left was the inquest. The conclusion was simple: the farmer had been beaten to death, in accordance with the medical evidence.

Solicitor Pat O'Connor, who had represented Eugene for several years, attended. He told the inquest he was acting on behalf of Eugene, saying, 'At all times my client's position is that he is innocent of any wrongdoing. I am here on his behalf, again, to protest his innocence.' He asked that this be reflected in the record of the proceedings.

Another solicitor was also present. Padraig O'Connell was acting for the late Sean Daly, who had died before he could face a jury of his peers. Mr O'Connell said, 'My client died an innocent man, and no allegation has ever been proved against him. It is extremely important that the late Sean Daly be allowed to lie in peace and be in no way implicated in any crime.'

However, coroner Terence Casey was having none of it, saying that the determination of guilt or innocence belonged to a different court. All the inquest had to do was determine cause of death. The coroner summed up by saying, 'Now that this matter has come to its final conclusion, I hope that all involved will be allowed to be in peace without any further interference.'

TRIPLE TRAGEDY IN TRALEE

The murders of Anne Marie Duffin, Hannah O'Sullivan and James Healy

IF DINGLE CAN be considered the soul of Kerry, and Killarney the smiling public face, Tralee is the commercial heart of the county. Located in the north, at the gateway to the Dingle Peninsula, it is the largest town in the county, and one that does not depend on tourism for its existence. In some ways, stepping into Tralee is like stepping out of Kerry.

The town is large and busy. The wide streets contain shops, offices and thriving businesses. It is the administrative centre of the county, and there is even an Institute of Technology and a large student population. Tralee does not have the mountains brooding over it that make Killarney, Killorglin, Dingle and Cahirciveen so distinctive. It could be a thriving market town in any part of the country.

For one week a year, Tralee reverts to pure stage Kerry, for the Rose of Tralee festival. But once that peculiar celebration of an Ireland that thankfully never existed outside of the distorted memories of American emigrants is over, Tralee is once again a big town with all the facilities of the twenty-first century. However, the size and prosperity bring their own problems. A huge population of young people has made the town a target for drug dealers. Petty crime abounds. Tralee has become quite a rough place.

Violent crime still retains the power to shock. During one bleak ten-month period in the late '90s, three savage murders rocked the town to its core. Two mothers of young families were hacked and slashed to death, while a young man met his end in a lonely field. Adding to the horror was the fact that one of the victims was still in his teens, while one of the killers was barely out of his childhood.

It was one of the bleakest periods in Kerry's history. On Wednesday, 26 March 1997, there was an almost unprecedented situation in Tralee District Court. Three cases of murder came up before Judge Humphrey Kelleher. He remanded all three defendants in continuing custody, while the higher courts dealt with the Kerry murder spree.

ANNE MARIE DUFFIN
Killed by a schoolboy

Anne Marie Duffin was a native of Holland. A friendly, outgoing woman who enjoyed the great outdoors, she settled in Ireland as a young woman and found love there. She married Paul Duffin, and the couple had two children, sons Kevin and Timothy. The family moved to Kerry. But after more than a decade the marriage hit the rocks, and the couple split up. Paul followed his work to Dublin, but Anne Marie decided to remain in Kerry with the two children, who went to the local secondary school.

Anne Marie lived in a bungalow at Curragraigue, Blennerville. Blennerville is a little village a mile to the west of Tralee, and it has become a suburb of the town. It is on the main road to Dingle and was once the port of Tralee. Now it is best known for the windmill that dominates the flat landscape and the small canal that links it with Tralee. It was also famous for reconstructing a famine ship, the *Jeanie Johnston*. This replica wooden sailing ship was begun in 1993 and the whole community got behind the project. An interpretative centre was built in the village, and many of the locals worked on the ship. It took nine years to build, went massively over budget and was eventually sold to the Dublin Docklands Authority to defray costs, thus losing a tourist asset that would have been valuable to the area. Curragraigue is a townland off the main road, and inland a little bit, where the land begins to rise to the ubiquitous hills that seem to cover most of Kerry. It has a rural feel, but is only a walk from Blennerville.

By 1996, work on the famine ship was well underway. Anne Marie, who had now been on her own for two years, had settled into her new life as a single mother. She had worked at a health shop, but had recently started working at a local restaurant, Keanes of Curraheen, frequented by the many tourists stopping on their way to Dingle. She also worked part-time at some of the local crèches. She had a good name in the area and was well liked. Her small red camper van was parked outside her door all the time, and she loved taking the children off camping during the summer months.

On Sunday, 14 April 1996, Anne Marie finished her shift at Keanes at 10.40 p.m. and returned home. According to restaurant owner John Keane, she was in great form when she left.

She spent the rest of the evening at home with her two sons. The following morning they were up early, and both boys left the house at 8.30 a.m. to walk to the local secondary school, where they were pupils. They left their mother alone in the house.

At 4 p.m., school ended. The boys met each other. The day was cloudy and misty, but it was warm for the time of year and the rain was holding off. It wasn't a day for a quick dash home. They met with some friends – Graham Ryle and Paul Walsh, both 14 – and began their way home.

At 4.30 p.m. they arrived at the bungalow at Curragraigue. They said goodbye to Graham, who lived in the next house along. Everything seemed to be normal. Their mother's red camper van was parked outside as usual. She was in. The front door was closed. Kevin, at 16 the eldest, walked up to the door, took out his key and turned it in the lock. Calling a cheerful greeting, he pushed the door open and stepped inside. Then he screamed . . .

A few hours earlier, another student had left school early. He too had headed towards Blennerville, then turned off the main road and headed towards the shadow of the mountains, and Curragraigue. Though he was just 15, he knew exactly what he was going to do that afternoon.

Before he reached his destination, he stopped at the house next door. He checked that no one was home, then snuck into the garage and looked around. Finally he found what he was looking for: a screwdriver. He placed it in his pocket, then cautiously made his way out of the garage and onto the road. He turned in to his destination, passing the red camper van in the driveway. He paused for a moment and then knocked at the door.

Anne Marie Duffin heard the knock and opened the door. As soon as it opened, the youth sprang forward, striking her on the head and knocking her to the ground. Before she had a chance to fight back, he launched a frenzied attack on her, striking her repeatedly on the head with the screwdriver. As she struggled, he kept driving the implement into her face and head. He struck her dozens of times. Finally she stopped moving. The hallway of the house was covered in blood.

He stood up and went to the kitchen, looking for the cutlery drawer. He found a bread knife, then came back to the hall and cut Mrs Duffin's throat, just to make sure. There was no doubt: his victim was dead.

In an effort to throw off the investigation that he knew must follow, he pulled off Mrs Duffin's pants and threw them aside. He then pulled up her jumper, to make it look like a rape. But he made no attempt to interfere with the body beyond that; sex had not been any part of his motivation.

Then he took up the screwdriver and slipped out the front door, pulling it closed behind him.

Graham Ryle, speaking to reporters, remembered the moment his friend Kevin opened the door to his mother's house: 'Kevin went into his house with Tim, and I went to mine next door. I was in the house with my brother James when Kevin came running over. He was crying and very upset. He said that when he went in, he found his mother inside the front door, lying in the hallway. There was a lot of blood around her head. James and myself went back over with Kevin, but we couldn't get in, because Tim had got such a shock that he had banged the door after him and locked himself out.'

James Ryle ran home and phoned for an ambulance and the Gardaí. They arrived a few minutes later, almost simultaneously.

'It was terribly upsetting, really horrible,' Graham told reporters.

As darkness fell on north Kerry, the Gardaí swiftly swung into action, launching a full-scale murder investigation. They set up roadblocks around the surrounding roads, not knowing the man they were looking for was not old enough to even apply for a learner's licence.

The State Pathologist and the Assistant State Pathologist are based in Dublin, several hours' drive away. Gardaí could not wait for an initial report. A cursory examination led to an initial suspicion that Mrs Duffin had been shot. However, they very quickly realised this was not the case. They also began door-to-door enquiries and interviewing potential witnesses. The first few hours of an investigation can be critical.

One thing they discovered quickly was there was no sign of forcible entry at the house, which meant Mrs Duffin had opened the door to her attacker. This could indicate it was someone she knew or someone who would not have stood out if he knocked at the door.

Mrs Duffin's two sons had relatives in Tralee. Rory Duffin and his wife Gertie came and picked up the boys, and they stayed with them that night. Their father, Paul, was notified, and immediately left Dublin to come to his sons. He was there within a few hours. Meanwhile, Gardaí got onto their counterparts in Holland, to pass the devastating news on to Mrs Duffin's family there. The boys' aunt, Gertie Duffin, said that it was a very difficult time for the family, and the tragedy was hard to come to terms with.

The following morning, Assistant State Pathologist Dr Margot Bolster arrived in Tralee and carried out an examination of the body, which was then removed to Tralee Hospital for a full post-mortem. She confirmed that Mrs Duffin had been murdered, but she had not been shot. She had been stabbed a huge number of times with a sharp implement.

The bungalow was sealed off and kept under tight security as a forensics team from the Garda Technical Bureau carried out a full examination. Chief Superintendent Donal O'Sullivan of Tralee said that there was no obvious motive for the murder. He said the popularity of the victim and her unassuming manner made it all the more difficult to understand why anyone would have wanted to attack her.

The investigation initially concentrated on locating the murder weapon, which the pathologist told them was a sharp instrument. Though it would take a week for the medical report to be complete and confirm it, Gardaí were convinced from the beginning that Mrs Duffin had not been raped. Though her clothes had been disturbed, they were fairly certain that there was no sexual component to the attack.

Mrs Duffin had lost a lot of blood in the assault, and they did not know how long she had been lying on the floor before her sons came home from school and discovered her. They spoke to family members and neighbours in an effort to trace the victim's final movements, but no one had seen anything unusual.

By the end of the week, there was still no definite line of inquiry. Extensive searches of the grounds around the bungalow had failed to unearth the murder weapon.

On Monday, 22 April – a week after her death – the funeral of Mrs Duffin took place in Tralee. Her remains were then removed to Dublin for cremation. The Garda team, based in the incident room at Tralee Garda Station, was increased to 30, but no new leads were developed. Gradually, though, a picture began to emerge. A suspect was interviewed in his home on 28 April. When an arrest was made, it shocked everyone.

On Wednesday, 1 May, a 15-year-old boy was charged at Tralee District Court with the murder of Anne Marie Duffin. It was a shocking development. The boy was local and came from a good family. His father was with him in the court, and the boy appeared flanked by two prison officers. He was a friend of the Duffin boys. Judge Humphrey Kelleher remanded him in custody. The boy's legal team did not oppose that.

It took a year and a half before the case came to trial. During that time, the youth remained in custody. He made no application to be released on bail. The trial finally opened on Monday, 1 December 1997, in the Central Criminal Court before Mr Justice Fredrick Morris.

The court heard that the youth, by then 17, had stabbed Mrs Duffin 66 times in a frenzied attack, before cutting her throat with a bread knife. He pleaded guilty to murder.

Superintendent John O'Connor, of Tralee, told the court that Mrs Duffin, who was separated, lived with her two teenage sons near Blennerville. The accused – who cannot be named for legal reasons – was a friend of the elder boy, Kevin. He felt that Mrs Duffin did not approve of him and did not want him associating with her son, because of his haircut and because he smoked. He resented this.

On the day of the murder, he took a screwdriver from the garage of the house next door to Mrs Duffin and then called to her home, pretending to be looking for her son. When she answered the door, he hit her on the head, knocked her to the floor and stabbed her repeatedly with the screwdriver, before getting a bread knife from the kitchen and cutting her throat. After his arrest, the teenager had told Gardaí that he had pulled off Mrs Duffin's pants and pulled up her jumper to make it look like rape, but he did not have sex with her. He had cooperated fully with the Gardaí and appeared to be remorseful, said the superintendent.

The court heard that Mrs Duffin had suffered forty-four stab wounds to her head, twelve of which had penetrated her skull. One of the stab wounds had pierced right into her brain stem. This wound alone would have caused serious injury or death. She had also suffered twenty-two stab wounds to her neck, two of which had cut through the jugular vein. Again, either of these two wounds could have been fatal. Mrs Duffin died from haemorrhage and shock from inhalation of blood, and from stab wounds to the neck.

The court heard that the boy was from 'an excellent family background' and had not been in trouble before. The superintendent added, 'Mrs Duffin was a good, caring mother to her two children, and it is a tragedy for both families.'

Martin Giblin, barrister for the accused, said that the youth was aware that he was facing a life sentence and he accepted that this was just. He was very sorry for the hurt he had caused the Duffin family. The judge imposed the life sentence, ordering that it be backdated to the date of the youth's arrest.

Mr Justice Morris said that he would not comment on the crime because: 'Enough unhappiness has been generated to everyone concerned. A disaster has befallen everyone in this case.'

The Duffin family agreed. After the verdict, they said that they felt worse for the family of the murderer than they did for themselves, and they pledged to pray for the teenager who had caused them so much pain.

HANNAH O'SULLIVAN
Blackmail leads to death

The next murder to rock Tralee happened in the middle of the busy summer season, just a week before Tánaiste Dick Spring was due in the town to open the Rose of Tralee festival. It bore many uncanny similarities to the first murder. The victim was the mother of a young family. She was separated from her husband. Her body was discovered by her young son. And she was violently stabbed to death, the day before her 40th birthday. However, her attacker had gone even further than the teen who had attacked Anne Marie Duffin. The man who killed Hannah O'Sullivan stabbed her 99 times. It was one of the most savage murders the country would see that year – or for many a year to come.

To tell the story properly, we need to look at the victim.

Margaret, known as Hannah, grew up in Kerins Park, in the town, and lived there until her marriage to local man Daniel O'Sullivan. She married young, and had three children. The eldest, Oliver, was nineteen at the time of her death. Eric was twelve, and the youngest, Vicky, was just seven. People who knew Hannah remembered her as a lively and vivacious young woman.

Her health was never very robust. She suffered from asthma and also had epileptic fits. In later years these conditions caused her to leave her door always ajar, so that if she had an attack, help would not be impeded. Yet she didn't complain about her physical conditions and was known as a friendly, helpful and outgoing person. 'Heart of gold' was a phrase used by many to describe her.

She liked to socialise and loved dancing. She was an outgoing person. However, she began to drink heavily, as many party animals do, and the drinking became a problem. She was an alcoholic and could not handle it. Eventually the drink consumed her life and destroyed her marriage.

Hannah and Daniel split up not long after the birth of their youngest child. She walked out of the marriage and lived in various rented accommodations around Tralee. He continued to live at Spa Road, Tralee, with the three children, while she eventually settled in a flat on Castle Street. However, she maintained a good relationship with her children. They meant the world to her. She also stayed on cordial terms with her husband.

She struggled with her demons, joining Alcoholics Anonymous

and attending meetings regularly. It was at one of those meetings, in 1991, that she met a local baker, John O'Mahony. He was about five years younger than her and battling his own demons. Some time later they met in a pub. Hannah was with another woman and O'Mahony joined them. He chatted with the two women for a while, then the other woman left. He stayed on with Mrs O'Sullivan. At the end of the evening, they went back to his house. What went on in the house is unclear, but afterwards Mrs O'Sullivan went to the Gardaí and made an allegation of rape against Mr O'Mahony. Gardaí investigated the allegation and decided there was enough evidence to bring a charge.

It was a very traumatic time for Mr O'Mahony and his family. He was unmarried, but his mother was very upset at the charge. 'It was an awful event in our family life,' he later said.

A court date was set, but a week before the trial, the DPP inexplicably dropped the charge. John O'Mahony was a free man.

He rebuilt his life, returning to work at the family bakery. Although both he and his alleged victim continued to live in Tralee, their paths did not cross again – at least not for another five years. By then Hannah O'Sullivan was living in a flat complex on Castle Street. Those who knew her said she was no longer the vivacious and outgoing woman she had been. She seemed quiet and withdrawn. She also seemed to be short of money. She was approaching her 40th birthday and her life must have seemed to have reached a dead end.

On 17 August 1996, Hannah took a desperate throw of the dice. It was the end of the summer. Tralee would come alive in a week's time with the arrival of the Roses. The town would be hopping. Perhaps she wanted to be part of it. She needed money in a hurry. She picked up the phone and rang John O'Mahony. When he picked up, she told him that if he did not pay her a substantial amount in cash, she would reactivate the old rape allegation and see him hauled before the courts.

'She was shouting for money and using very bad language,' said O'Mahony, who said that so much time had passed that he would not even have recognised Mrs O'Sullivan if he passed her in the street. He didn't agree to give her the money after that phone call. She made another call later that day, still demanding money.

The following day, Saturday, she rang him again, which upset him greatly. He again refused her money, but because he was unsettled he decided not to go out that night. Instead he stopped at an off-licence and bought two two-litre bottles of cider and went home. He went to bed early and fell asleep.

Meanwhile, Hannah was out on the town with a friend. The friend drove her home around midnight. On the way home, they stopped at a 24-hour garage, and Hannah bought two lucky bags for her two youngest children. Monday was her 40th birthday, and she knew they would be over with cards. She wanted to have something in the house to give them. The friend came into the flat and remained with Hannah until about 1.30 a.m. Then Hannah was alone.

What prompted her to leave the apartment is not known, but after her friend left, Hannah went out again. She went to the home of John O'Mahony, at Boherbee. It was less than a quarter of a mile away, perhaps three or four minutes' walk. She began pounding on his door. He was asleep when he was suddenly roused by the sound of the loud banging. He jumped out of bed and went down the stairs in his boxer shorts. He opened the door to find Mrs O'Sullivan standing outside. She pushed her way in and began demanding money. O'Mahony pushed her back out the door and slammed it. She stayed outside for a few minutes, kicking at the door and shouting at him, and then walked off.

O'Mahony ran upstairs and got dressed, fast. He then came out onto the street and began to follow Mrs O'Sullivan. It was time to bring matters to an end.

He followed her as far as her flat on the junction of Castle Street and McGowan's Lane, and pushed the door in after her.

As to what happened next, we have only his word. Mrs O'Sullivan was probably frightened to have been followed and confronted in her own home. O'Mahony was an intruder, and the last time they had been alone together she had alleged he raped her. She must have been terrified. She picked up a sharp kitchen knife and jabbed at him twice. She nicked him on the hand, drawing blood.

'She came at me with the knife, very, very fast. I had to defend myself,' he said.

He wrenched the knife from her hand and struck her with it, forcibly and repeatedly. He threw her onto the bed and continued to slash and stab. By the end of the frenzied attack he had struck the unarmed and defenceless mother 99 times. His arm must have ached from the sheer exertion.

Then he ran out with the knife, pulling the door behind him, but not pulling it fully closed.

August is a family month, when the focus switches to children and holidays. Seven-year-old Vicky O'Sullivan was excited. She had got through to the national finals of a dance competition with her disco-dancing troupe. The all-Ireland disco-dancing championships were being held in the Mosney holiday camp near Drogheda: the far side of the country. All the girls, with their instructors, had gone up by train. Some of the parents, including Vicky's dad, Daniel, also went to Mosney. He got a lift with one of the other parents. He had left his two sons, Oliver and Eric, at home. Oliver was 19 and was in charge. He already had a child of his own; Daniel and Hannah were grandparents.

On Saturday afternoon Vicky's group won their competition, and Daniel had rung Hannah to give her the good news: their daughter had won a medal and two trophies. Though they had been separated for a number of years after 15 years of marriage, they still got on well and talked regularly. Hannah had seemed to be in good form and was delighted with the news. She said she would see them when they came home on Monday.

On Monday morning, it was time for the dance troupe to

return to Kerry. Daniel brought his daughter to the train station and saw her off, then joined another parent for the drive back to Tralee. They arrived in mid-afternoon.

Meanwhile, 12-year-old Eric had phoned his mother a few times, but got no answer. He decided to call on her. He would pass on Vicky's news and wish her a happy birthday. It was around lunchtime when he jumped on his bicycle and cycled the mile to his mother's flat. He started down the Spa Road, then turned onto Strand Street, which brought him into the centre of town. He pedalled down Bridge Street and on to The Mall, which connected with Lower Castle Street. Then he passed Brenner's Hotel and on to the junction with McGowan's Lane. He got off the bike and rang the apartment block. He was clutching a birthday card.

One of the occupants of the apartment block, a Mormon elder who was in the flat below Mrs O'Sullivan, answered the door and let the boy in. He ran up the stairs to his mother's door and was surprised to find it open. Calling out a greeting, he pushed it open and stepped inside. What awaited him was a scene of unimaginable horror.

His mother's blood-spattered body was lying on the bed and gouts of scarlet speckled the room. He ran from the apartment, calling for help.

The Gardaí were on the scene quickly and established that Mrs O'Sullivan had died of multiple stab wounds to her face, head and neck. The tiny apartment was sealed off, and a team of forensics experts from the Technical Bureau combed it minutely for clues. There was no sign of the murder weapon, but from the nature of the wounds, Gardaí were sure it was a knife.

There were a number of other occupants of the flat complex, and they were the first to be interviewed. It was quickly established that no one had seen anything suspicious. Mrs O'Sullivan had last been seen by occupants of the flats at 10.30 on Saturday morning. She had been dressed casually, in the same clothes she was found wearing on Monday. All the occupants of the building shared a common entrance and some had spotted the slightly open door of the apartment, but no one had been suspicious and no one had thought there was anything wrong.

When Daniel O'Sullivan arrived back in Kerry, he got the devastating news. He had to steel himself to go to the railway station to meet his daughter, who was oblivious to what had happened. The dance troupe, under instructor Joanne Barry, had won 60 medals. They were a happy bunch as they disembarked. Little did they suspect that the bearded man in the tweed jacket who got off before them was State Pathologist Dr John Harbison.

The murder investigation was led by Chief Superintendent John O'Connor and Inspector Barry O'Rourke. They said that Mrs O'Sullivan had undergone a 'severe physical assault' and as yet they had no definite lines of inquiry. They were satisfied that the killing was unconnected to the similar murder of Anne Marie Duffin some months earlier.

The vicious stabbing brought to five the number of people who had died violently in Kerry in the past eighteen months. As we saw in Chapter 10, elderly bachelor farmer Patrick Daly had been beaten to death and tossed down a well in January. His brother and nephew were charged in connection with that. Mrs Duffin had been stabbed to death in April, and a schoolboy was in custody. In April of the previous year, two young men had got involved in a row over a girl in Kerins Park in Tralee. One of the men shot the other, and then turned the gun on himself. It was a bleak period in the Kingdom.

Hannah was laid to rest on Thursday, 22 August. As her coffin lay in the church, a photograph of her five-month-old grandchild, Jesse, was placed in her arms. Fr Sean Hannafin told the mourners, 'The peace in our town has been shattered. No human words can explain or adequately console Hannah's family.'

Hannah's ex-husband and her children led the mourners in a sad procession through the town to the local graveyard.

The investigating team quickly ruled robbery out as a motive for the killing. There was no sign of forcible entry to the flat, which indicated the victim had known her killer. Gardaí began a search for witnesses to try to piece together the last hours of Hannah's life. A large number of people were interviewed. Potential witnesses who were on Castle Street on Saturday evening were asked to come forward, and many did. The Gardaí then began going back through Hannah's life, looking for any possible reason for the heinous attack on her.

Within a week the investigation was beginning to take shape, and a few possible suspects were beginning to emerge, Gardaí said. The team was working 12-hour shifts sifting through statements and analysing the forensic evidence. Fingerprints were taken from people who were known to have had contact with Mrs O'Sullivan, which enabled Gardaí to eliminate a number of people from their inquiries. Although it was only days before the start of the Rose festival and although the town was also on high alert because of a meeting of EU Foreign Ministers, the murder investigation took priority over everything.

For a while, the investigation got bogged down in looking for people who had passed through Tralee. The murder featured on *Crimeline* in mid-September, and Gardaí appealed for information on two men who had passed through the town. One was in his 50s, bald and massive. He had stayed in Killarney for a few days before moving into the Atlas Hotel in Tralee. Another man had stayed at a bar near Castle Street. However, the Gardaí had already interviewed the man they were after: John O'Mahony had been one of the hundreds of people interviewed in the early days of the investigation. He had told the Gardaí that he had not seen Mrs O'Sullivan in a couple of years and would not even know her if he passed her on the street.

At that point his interview had not sounded any alarm bells, and Mr O'Mahony was not taken into custody. But he was clearly rattled. On 2 September he had flown to Brighton, where he remained briefly before flying to Greece. He then returned to Brighton. However, it was not a well-thought-out escape plan. He returned to Ireland in late October. He had been on the run for only seven weeks.

On his return to Tralee he was arrested at his home and taken in for questioning. After a day of questioning, he was formally arrested and charged with murder. He was brought before a special sitting of Kenmare District Court late on the night of Friday, 25 October. Sergeant Mossie O'Donnell told the court that when charged, O'Mahony had replied: 'Not guilty of murder.'

The case took a year and a half to come to trial. Mr O'Mahony finally faced the Central Criminal Court in March 1998. He pleaded not guilty.

Prosecuting barrister Gregory Murphy said that O'Mahony had a strong motive to murder Hannah O'Sullivan: he wanted to prevent the old rape allegation from being reactivated. Barrister Eamon Leahy, representing O'Mahony, said that his client accepted responsibility for the killing, but the issue before the court was whether it was a case of murder.

Mr Murphy replied, 'There is no question of the accused walking out of the court a free man.' He told the jury that there was an 'unfortunate background' to the killing, then outlined in detail the final hours and days of Mrs O'Sullivan's life. 'The late Hannah O'Sullivan was afflicted with a very severe addiction to alcohol. Six or seven years before her death, unhappy differences arose with her husband,' he said. 'She walked out of her home and lived at various places in Tralee before moving into the flat at Castle Street.'

He said that she had joined AA and attended regular meetings in an attempt to control her alcoholism. It was at one of those meetings that she had met John O'Mahony and a relationship briefly developed between them. 'Because of her addiction, Mrs O'Sullivan's standards had fallen,' he added.

In July 1991, she made an allegation of rape after a meeting with John O'Mahony. The allegation was taken seriously by the Gardaí, and after an investigation, charges were laid against the man. However, a week before the trial was due to begin, the charges were mysteriously withdrawn on the order of the DPP. 'What is not clear, and what the Gardaí don't know, is why the allegations were withdrawn,' said Mr Murphy. He said that Mr O'Mahony believed that a relative of his had paid money to Mrs O'Sullivan to have the case dropped.

Mr Murphy went on to say that Mrs O'Sullivan was known to have had money problems in the days and weeks leading up to her death. She had been going around trying to borrow money for drink from a number of people. Mr O'Mahony admitted that she had come to him looking for money. She had demanded £10,000. When that was rejected, she demanded £5,000. She threatened to go to the family bakery and announce in front of his mother that he had raped her. This threat was what pushed him over the edge.

When he followed her to her flat and pushed in the door after her, she reacted by picking up a knife. 'She picked up a knife from somewhere and nicked me twice,' Mr O'Mahony had admitted in statements to Gardaí. 'I just lost it. I don't know how many times I hit her.'

After the assault, he hid the knife in a dustbin at his family home. It eventually went out with the rubbish and was never recovered. He was also meticulous in washing his blood-spattered clothes. Mr Murphy argued that the careful clean-up and the disposal of the knife pointed to a clear head. 'This was no loss of the head, but a deliberate effort to get rid of her,' he told the jury.

The court heard that Hannah's 12-year-old son had discovered her body on Monday afternoon, more than a full day after her death. He had been let into the flat complex by two members of the Mormon church who were living there. Finding his mother's door ajar – not unusual – he had gone in, and was horrified to find her body on the bed and the wall covered in blood. He ran from the room and told the two neighbours, who rang the Gardaí.

Dale Anderson, one of the two, told the court that he had

known Hannah, but only to see in passing. When he and his colleague, Erik Vernon, were told about the gruesome discovery, he went to the flat to check. He saw Mrs O'Sullivan lying in a heap on the bed with a duvet thrown over her. There was blood splattered on the walls. He ran to her phone, but the line had been cut. So he got another phone and rang the Gardaí.

Another occupant of the apartment block, Michael Brosnan, said that Mrs O'Sullivan was a 'very timid and shy' woman who kept to herself. On Sunday, 18 August, he had noticed her door was barely open, and there was a light on inside. It was very quiet all day in the block, which was a bit unusual. He went out that night, and when he came back around 1.30 a.m. he noticed the door was still ajar, with the light still on. But he passed no remark and did not investigate. 'I just kept to myself,' he said.

On the second day of the trial, State Pathologist Dr John Harbison described the horrific injuries Hannah O'Sullivan had suffered. She had received at least 99 stab wounds in her head, neck, arms and chest. There were at least 22 criss-cross head wounds and 55 knife strokes to the head. There were also defensive wounds, including slashes to her right arm. These indicated that she had tried to protect her face, covering it with her arm. But as her strength faded, her skull had acted 'like a chopping block' for the blows rained down on it. There was also a deep slash to her throat, measuring six inches. This wound was so deep it almost went through to her spine.

Statements made by Mr O'Mahony to the Gardaí were read to the court. In his first interview, he said, 'The last time I met her was about three years ago.'

He later admitted that he had met Hannah five or six years previously, at an AA meeting. One evening, he met her with another woman in a pub. They chatted, and Hannah ended up in his house. 'Arising out of this, an allegation was made to Gardaí,' he said. 'This was investigated, and nothing came of it.' This was a bit disingenuous. He had almost gone on trial for rape. In his first statement to Gardaí, he denied any recent contact with Mrs O'Sullivan and denied any involvement with her murder.

Then he went to Brighton and Greece. When he came home, he was arrested, but he stuck to his story: his first statement was correct, and he had nothing to do with the killing. However, in a later statement that day, he changed his account of what happened, admitting that Mrs O'Sullivan had phoned him a number of times in the two days leading up to her death. She had been demanding money and threatening to renew the rape allegation if he refused her.

He said that when she called to his house after midnight on the night of 17–18 August he was drunk and in a rage. He pushed her from the house and called her names, and then he followed her home. He flipped when she confronted him with a knife, and he hit her several times with the knife.

Under cross-examination he denied that he had had a relationship with Mrs O'Sullivan. 'I met the late Hannah O'Sullivan only twice,' he said. He said that the first time was when the allegation of rape had been made. His family had become aware of the allegation. 'It was an awful event in our family life,' he said. However, after the trial was abandoned he had said, 'I actually forgave Hannah O'Sullivan for what she did to me.'

The court was packed to hear the testimony, and Hannah's family was visibly upset at this point. Her son Oliver, then 21, jumped up and interrupted the accused, shouting: 'You raped her, my mother!' His father, Daniel, quickly jumped up and joined in, temporarily bringing proceedings to a halt. Mr Justice O'Higgins had to ask that the two be removed from the court. They did not reappear, but they remained in the court building for the rest of the day and the following day, the final day of the trial.

When proceedings resumed, Mr O'Mahony said that he had not seen Hannah since the rape allegation, and he would not even have recognised her. She rang him out of the blue twice on the Friday before her death, using very bad language and demanding money. The third time she rang was on the evening of Saturday, 17 August, and she was still demanding money. Rather than go out that night, he stayed in with two bottles of cider. He was quite upset, and he drank both two-litre bottles before falling asleep. He was still asleep when she came banging at his door after midnight. He ran down the stairs in his boxers and confronted her. After a loud exchange, he pushed her onto the street. After a few minutes of kicking at the door, she went away.

'I ran upstairs,' he said. After pulling on some clothes, he ran out and began walking quickly in the direction she had left towards. He caught up with her just as she was entering a house at the junction of Castle Street and McGowan's Lane, and he pushed in behind her as she entered. He followed her up the stairs and came into her apartment. At that point, Mrs O'Sullivan must have realised she was in danger. She picked up a knife from somewhere. 'She came at me with the knife, very, very fast. I had to defend myself. I just flipped and lashed out,' O'Mahony told the court. She lunged forward and caught him with the tip of the knife, nicking his hand. She did it twice as he struggled to grab her knife hand. She put up quite a struggle, holding firmly onto the knife, but eventually he wrenched it from her hand, and then he struck her with it. 'I just kept on striking her,' he said.

When challenged about the number of times he had struck Mrs O'Sullivan, he hesitated, and blamed his anger on a reaction to the accusations she had made against him. 'I had that woman hurt because of what . . . It was self-defence. I completely lost control.'

He then panicked. When the Gardaí interviewed him, he gave them a false statement; then he absconded to Brighton and thereafter got a cheap flight to Greece. He told the court that the thing that upset him most was the thought of his mother hearing all about the rape allegation again. 'I just wanted to look her [Hannah] in the eye and ask her to stop,' O'Mahony told the jury.

On the final day of the trial, O'Mahony's barrister, Eamon Leahy, offered an unusual defence, saying: 'The killing was wrong, was not justified, and she did not contribute to her own death. But my client's intent was not murderous. He feared further embarrassment from a renewed rape allegation and wanted to be rid of this turbulent woman. When he inflicted those stab wounds, he thought he was doing it to a woman who was the dregs of society, a woman who was a matter of complete indifference to him, a different class from him. He thought he'd get away with it.'

This approach failed to move the jury. They took five and a half hours to deliberate, but in the end there could only be one verdict. John O'Mahony was convicted of murder by a unanimous decision. Mr Justice O'Higgins imposed a mandatory life sentence. As O'Mahony was led, handcuffed, from the court, Hannah's relatives and friends in the public gallery cried. Yet there was some satisfaction in seeing justice done. Outside, her ex-husband and her son Oliver embraced relatives as they emerged from the court. The ordeal was over.

O'Mahony's attempt to avoid an old rape allegation in the end brought far more disgrace on him and his family.

JAMES HEALY
Teen killed by local thug

The disappearance of a teenage boy on a weekend in February 1997 was the final horror to visit Tralee in that bleak ten-month period. James Healy never came home on the evening of Friday, 21 February 1997. When his body was discovered three days later, badly beaten and lying in a field on the outskirts of the town, it brought to three the number of murders committed in less than a year.

The subsequent investigation shone an unwelcome light on the seedier side of Tralee and exposed a culture of underage drinking and teen gangs.

James Healy, 16, was born and raised in Tralee. He was the second-eldest child of Kathleen and James Healy, and they lived in the Shanakill housing estate. Not academic, James had dropped out of school and was doing a training scheme. Although he had never been in trouble, the Gardaí knew him. He was one of a gang of teens who hung around together and were often seen drinking cider in out-of-the-way places around the town. He was described by those who knew him as 'quiet', and he had come to the attention of the authorities in the past in relation to petty crime.

James worked as a trainee at a community-training workshop organised by FAS, the Irish national training and employment agency. He was at the scheme that Friday and was due to get paid. He owed one woman a fiver, which she was waiting for him to deliver. However, he never showed up. He never came home that night.

Some of his final movements are known. A friend of his, 16-year-old Timothy Ward, said that on that night a number of teens got together for an impromptu party. It happened most Fridays; someone would buy alcohol and they would meet up and drink it. They often met in a part of the town known as the Dyke, or at the basketball court on a nearby estate, where they would hang out and drink beer and cider. That Friday was no different. James Healy was among the group.

Mr Ward chatted with James Healy. They arranged to meet up the following day, to go to a boxing tournament in the town, but James never showed up. That was the last time Mr Ward saw his friend.

A number of people had spotted James on Friday, and one of the people he had been seen with was Michael O'Brien. At 25, O'Brien was nearly a decade older than James. He had a reputation around the town as a hard man. Although he was not stupid, he had limited education and poor verbal skills, and tended to take things the wrong way. He was unstable and violent, and could often fly into a temper if he thought someone was saying something about him. O'Brien was well known to the Gardaí. He had a long string of convictions, for assault, larceny and other matters, and had done time in jail. He had never worked a day in his life, and was suspected of running a gang of teenagers who carried out robberies for him. He also wheeled and dealed in chainsaws and was suspected of dealing in guns. To most people, he was just a man to be avoided, because of his reputation for violence.

James Healy was one of the teens who hung out with O'Brien, and they often shared a flagon of cider together. After work on Friday, James would have found some friends and hung out for a number of hours, despite the wet and windy weather. But when he did not arrive home that night, his parents became concerned. Over the next few days they began a desperate search for their son.

On Sunday night, James Senior called to the house of Michael O'Brien, wondering if the man had seen his son. He knew that the older man was a good friend of his son. Michael O'Brien was in the house, along with his mother. When he was asked had he seen James, O'Brien replied: 'Someone killed him with a bar in a field.'

However, O'Brien had a reputation for insensitive humour, and his mother dismissed this remark as a 'stupid remark he would normally make'.

It was Tuesday before there was any real news in the search for the missing youth. That morning, James McCarthy, a local man, went to a field off the Monavalley Road, not far from the Shanakill estate where James lived. There was a FAS centre and a factory on the road, and on the waste ground behind the factory Mr McCarthy kept some horses. He was going to check on them when he spotted what appeared to be a man lying in the field. 'I thought it was someone drunk or something, until I got close,' he said. 'I knew he was dead by the look of him. I was frightened when I saw him. I ran into the factory and rang the guards.'

It was 10.40 a.m. One of the factory workers was Gerry Maloney. He ran out to check the story and was horrified to see the dead boy lying on the grass, staring up at the clouds. 'He was lying on his back with his eyes wide open and a lot of marks on his face,' he said. There was an open gash across his head, and he looked swollen or puffy. 'He had one arm to the side of his head with his hand up over his shoulder, away from his head.' He was dressed in jeans and a black padded jacket, and was on his back. There were signs of a struggle around the body.

An ambulance was quickly on the scene. The driver, James Pembroke, knew that it was a lost cause, but he followed the protocol and looked for a pulse. There was none. It was a murder scene. The victim had obviously been beaten badly. There was a four-foot section of electrical conduit (piping designed for carrying electrical cable underground) nearby which could have been the murder weapon, and James had clearly suffered great injuries. His jawbone had become detached, such was the savagery of the attack.

When the Gardaí arrived, they took over and secured the scene. The body had to be left in place pending an initial examination by the State Pathologist. At that time, the services of the State Pathologist were under severe strain. Ireland had one pathologist, Dr John Harbison, and the Assistant State Pathologist, Dr Margot Bolster. However, Dr Bolster had recently resigned the position, as she wanted to be based in Cork. Her job had been advertised but not filled, so all the suspicious deaths in the country became the responsibility of one man, and he was based hours away. In fact, it would be the following day before Dr Harbison could make it down to Kerry, and the Gardaí did the best they could. They erected a tent over the body, but they had to leave the dead teen in the wet field overnight in a stormy February.

This caused some outrage locally and a bit of a political storm. James's parents heard about the discovery of the body. They knew instantly their son was not coming home. However, they were not allowed to view the body or confirm their worst fears for 24 hours. They had to stand at a distance with everyone else, looking at the white tent and the circle of Gardaí through the heavy mist. That night it rained heavily.

It was only the following day, Wednesday, that Dr Harbison arrived and carried out his initial examination. The body was removed to Tralee General Hospital, where the family were finally allowed to view it and confirm that it was indeed the missing James. That was at 11 a.m., a full day after he had been discovered.

As Gardaí began door-to-door interviews and placed an appeal for witnesses on the local radio station, the politicians began to jump on the bandwagon. The Progressive Democrats called for the next Deputy State Pathologist to be based in Munster. Deputy Máirín Quill, Cork North Central, said that there had been 12 murders in the province the previous year and the Justice Minister Nora Owen's insistence that the job be based in Dublin was 'inexplicable'. She mentioned the recent murder in Schull of French film director Sophie Toscan du Plantier and said, 'The State Pathologist was not in a position to examine Madame du Plantier's body for 24 hours. The Gardaí investigation may have had more success had they been able to call on the services of a Cork-based pathologist.'

South Kerry Fianna Fáil TD John O'Donoghue said that he was 'bewildered' at the refusal of the Justice Minister to locate any future Deputy State Pathologist in the south. The minister was due to face questioning in the Dáil that afternoon about the resources of the pathology service. Just a year previously, Dr Harbison, in a report to the minister, had said that his department was understaffed and overwhelmed with work and needed more resources.

Tánaiste Dick Spring, from Tralee, said he found the situation 'appalling'. 'It is not good enough in this day and age,' he said. He said that he had spoken to the Justice Minister about the possibility of locating a pathologist outside of Dublin, but added that Cork might not be the ideal location, given that murders often took place in other parts of the state. In the Dáil, Fianna Fáil TD Batt O'Keeffe was ruled out of order when he tried to raise the question of why it took Dr Harbison so long to arrive in Tralee. 'When a body is allowed to lie for so long, the temperature drops and this hinders the Garda investigation, making it difficult to establish with accuracy the probable time of death. There is a clear case to be made for appointing a pathologist in the Munster region,' he said.

Gardaí ignored the controversy and got on with the investigation. They continued interviewing people, including students at the FAS centre. Their initial view was that the killing could be related to drugs and could have been the result of a falling-out between minor drugs gangs. Yet by the end of the week they had ruled this out as a possibility. They were exploring the idea that a violent row could have broken out between rival teenagers. They needed to establish James's final movements to piece together what had happened. They were pleased with the response of the public and the progress of the investigation.

On Saturday, 1 March, James Healy was laid to rest. At the funeral Mass in St Brendan's Church, Fr Dan Canniffe said that the presence of such a large congregation spoke eloquently of the abhorrence people felt about criminal activities in the town. 'James's death is something that will never be forgotten and is a stark reminder of the sacredness of human life and the deep appreciation that people should have for it,' he said.

Colleagues from the FAS training college provided a guard of honour at the church, and again at the graveyard.

James's parents, James and Kathleen, who were well liked and respected in the neighbourhood, were the chief mourners, along with their children, Donal, seventeen, Alan, eleven, and Sarah, eight.

The Garda investigation was a matter of piecing together who had been where on the day. Bit by bit, they began to home in on a suspect: a very violent young man. Finally, on the third weekend of March, a month after the murder, Michael O'Brien, 25, of Gallowsfield, Tralee, was charged with murder at a special sitting of Kenmare District Court. Single and unemployed, he lived a little more than half a mile from his victim. The desolate spot where James's body was discovered was roughly halfway between the homes of the two men. He was refused bail while on remand.

In April, O'Brien's legal team went to the High Court to get him out on bail, but this was refused. He remained in custody. After a year in Cork Prison, O'Brien's legal team went to the High Court once more, in March 1998. Many murder suspects are allowed out on bail, but it had consistently been refused to O'Brien.

Superintendent John O'Connor told Mr Justice Budd that he believed O'Brien would interfere with witnesses if granted bail. The accused had already threatened to kill one witness. If granted bail, Superintendent O'Connor believed he would carry out that threat. He added that O'Brien dominated the community in which he lived through fear and that he had a long list of previous convictions, including ones for burglary, assault causing actual harm, assaults on a Garda and a prison officer, and carrying an offensive weapon. This weapon had been a home-made affair consisting of a pole filled with lead, with rivets sticking out of its head. Detective Sergeant John Brennan said he would be very worried for the safety of witnesses if O'Brien was released before the trial.

Michael O'Brien testified on his own behalf. He denied that he had the people of Tralee in fear, or that he had threatened witnesses, and said that his character had changed.

After hearing submissions from both sides, Mr Justice Budd said that he was gravely concerned that O'Brien had spent a year in prison already, but he accepted the evidence of the two Gardaí that prospective witnesses were terrified of the accused. It might be that he would not interfere with them, but the reality was that he was a source of fear in Tralee and had difficulty controlling his violent temper. The judge refused him bail.

The trial finally opened in November 1998, with O'Brien denying the charge of murder. It would be a lengthy affair, lasting forty-six days spread over nearly three months. It went right through Christmas and into the New Year. At one point, proceedings had to be adjourned because the wife of a juror gave birth and he had to take a day off to attend. It was a marathon legal session.

Barrister John Edwards represented the state. He told the jury that O'Brien and his victim had been drinking buddies, often taking cider together at various locations around the town.

Dr John Harbison gave evidence of the frightening litany of injuries James Healy had suffered. Thirteen of his teeth had been knocked out, and his jaw fractured. His skull had also been fractured, and he suffered 20 head injuries. He had been beaten so badly that his jawbone, with a tooth attached, had been detached from his head, and it was found near pieces of human tissue and a piece of scalp on the ground beside the body. Dr Harbison told the jury that he had found three teeth, and a broken fragment of a fourth, in the victim's windpipe and lungs during the post-mortem examination. It was obvious that Mr Healy had been struck in the mouth with an implement that tore through his lower lip and caused his teeth to be torn from his jaw. He said he believed Mr Healy had inhaled the teeth, some blood and fragments of bone. These became lodged in his windpipe and lungs, causing suffocation. The pathologist said that the injuries were caused 'by something fairly sharp, but not as sharp as a knife'.

On his initial examination, Dr Harbison was able to feel fractures in the right cheekbone area, as well as head injuries. The scalp had a crescent-shaped laceration that caused chipping of the bone and created a 'skin flap' that revealed the skull beneath. When he examined the skull internally, he found jagged bone fragments. 'The brain surface had bruising on both sides, high up and low down, and was covered in blood,' he revealed.

The cause of death was head injuries, suffocation and a loss of blood resulting in shock.

Dr Harbison was shown the four-foot length of metal pipe, the cable conduit, which had been found lying across the body. The pipe was bloodstained. He was asked if the pipe could have caused the injuries Mr Healy had suffered. He replied, 'It was a very unique object, and one would have to say this was it.'

Kathleen Healy told the court that she had become concerned when her son did not return home on Friday night. There was an anxious weekend during which the family tried to establish where he was. Then, on Tuesday morning, she heard on a local news bulletin that a body had been found nearby. 'I was very concerned because James hadn't been home. I just put on my coat and went down the road,' she said. When she got to the scene, she approached the Garda on duty. 'I explained about my son being missing and I was very concerned that there had been a body found,' she said. She added that at that time the Garda had not told her the identity of the body.

There were explosive revelations when the next witness, Darren O'Shea, took the stand. He said that he had met Michael O'Brien on St Patrick's Day, about three weeks after the murder. They were with a group of teens and young people, drinking beers at a sports centre in the town that evening. They were chatting about this and that, and in the course of the conversation, the murder came up. 'We were talking about the murder. I asked him who did he think did it. He said himself. He said, "Between me and you, deputy, I killed James,"' Mr O'Shea told the jury. Mr O'Shea elaborated, saying that there were a bunch of people drinking in a boat shed that evening, and O'Brien had got into a row with James: 'Michael and James got in an argument. James tried to go home and he followed him and James gave him cheek, and he took something out of his pocket and hit him in the head or the face with it.'

Mr O'Shea said that O'Brien told him he had lost his head and kept beating Mr Healy. He then pushed him with a bar into a field and tossed the bar on the body, before making his way home through the fields. Mr O'Brien had sworn him to secrecy about what he had revealed to him.

Cross-examined by barrister Blaise O'Carroll, Mr O'Shea said that he had broken his word to O'Brien about secrecy 'because my best friend was after getting killed'. He said he had been shocked at what O'Brien had revealed to him, but he wasn't sure whether it was true or not. He denied that he had made up the conversation to get himself in good standing with the Gardaí because he had been in trouble with them in the past. 'I'm only saying what I was told,' he concluded.

Bernadette O'Brien, an aunt of the accused, said that O'Brien had arrived in her house the weekend of the murder and his clothes were in a state. He used her facilities to wash the clothes. He also told her that James Healy had fallen from a shed and hit his head, but he told other people a different story.

Sabrina O'Brien, a cousin of his, told the court that she asked him if he knew whether James Healy had been found yet. He replied, 'He's probably in a field across from FAS with a bar across him with his face bashed in.'

After the body was found, there was some discussion of the murder in O'Brien's house. The Sunday following the discovery, his father was reading an account in one of the newspapers. He said that the Gardaí might blame Michael for the killing. Michael's sister Linda was in the room. She told the court that Michael had denied the killing. 'Michael just said he didn't do it. He just kept saying it,' she said. She said she had also been in the house the day before the body was discovered, when James's father had called looking for news. Her brother had remarked: 'Someone killed him with a bar in a field.' Her mother dismissed it as the sort of stupid remark he often made.

The next witness, James O'Dowd, said that he had met James Healy around midnight on Friday, hours before his murder. He had been with Michael O'Brien. He knew them both well. He had been in primary school with James Healy and lived in the same estate as him. He said that James called him over. As O'Dowd approached, Healy had asked him for a cigarette. He handed over a cigarette and they chatted briefly. O'Dowd could see O'Brien nearby. O'Brien had been chatting to Healy as O'Dowd approached. 'They were talking as I came over, and he [O'Brien] walked away,' O'Dowd said.

Under cross-examination, Mr O'Dowd was asked why what he said in court differed from initial statements he had made to the Gardaí, which did not put Mr O'Brien in the vicinity. He said he was frightened at the reputation of the accused. 'I know the reputation of Mr O'Brien. I've seen the damage he's done to other people and I didn't want to be involved,' he said.

O'Brien's father, John O'Brien, gave evidence. He said that the day before the body was discovered, his son had said that perhaps James had fallen off a roof and was lying in a field with head injuries. Mr O'Brien said that his son often made comments that were unreliable. 'He was always speculating in the things he said. He imagines a lot of things and you wouldn't believe them. If there was a crime in town, he'd pick out the guys who did it. You don't take much notice,' said his father.

O'Brien's mother also gave evidence. She said that her initial statement to the Gardaí was untrue. In that statement, she said that her son had remarked, 'If they are looking for James, he's over in the field with his head bashed in.' Under cross-examination, she said that she had asked her son if he had killed James. He had replied that he had not killed the boy, and he had not been up in the field. When asked about what sort of a man O'Brien was, she replied, 'He's not like my other son at all. He's got a psychiatric problem. He's a bit slow.'

Detective Garda Martin Nolan told the court that on Thursday, 27 February – two days after the body had been discovered – Michael O'Brien had presented himself at Tralee Garda Station. He made a statement about having witnessed the murder of James, but denied he had any involvement himself. Curiously, he described James as a member of his 'staff'. He clearly saw the teens that carried out petty crimes for him as his gang.

Detective Nolan said that O'Brien came into the station early that day, and said, 'One of my staff got killed, James Healy. I know who did it. He was murdered at about 2.30 to 3 a.m. on Saturday morning. I was about 60 yards away from it. I saw [here he named a man unconnected with the killing] come out of the field where he was killed, and two others who I didn't know. I was watching them. I kept a watch always.'

The detective asked O'Brien to return to the station at midday to make a proper statement. O'Brien agreed, but he never returned.

O'Brien seemed to have a psychological need to inject himself into the investigation. He had no need to go to the Gardaí. He also had no need to tell so many people he either had killed James Healy or knew who had. Paddy Coffey was another man O'Brien had confided in. He told the court that O'Brien said that James was 'killed getting a shortcut home' through waste ground near his home.

Sergeant John Murrihy said that a few weeks after the murder he had seen O'Brien in Tralee in the early hours of the morning, and he pulled over to talk to him. O'Brien appeared dishevelled and said he had not slept in 24 hours. The sergeant told the court that O'Brien said, 'They all think I killed that young fella. A few people have said it to me. The guards will question me, but I will be ready for them. People think Paddy Coffey was with me. I know who killed him.' O'Brien then mentioned a name to the sergeant and said, 'He had gloves. Where are they?'

A number of witnesses told the court of conversations they had with O'Brien around the time of the murder. Eric Leahy met him on the day the body was discovered. He said, 'O'Brien said to me that probably James is up there in the field with his face smashed in. I didn't ask him how he knew it was James.'

Patrick O'Sullivan said that he had seen a length of piping in a ditch a few days before the murder. The ditch was at the edge of the field where James was murdered a few days later. After the murder, the piping had disappeared. Mr O'Sullivan was shown the four-foot length of piping with the bloodstains that the Gardaí believed was the murder weapon. He looked at it and said that it was the same piping he had spotted in the ditch.

A key issue that had to be addressed was the question of O'Brien's mental state and his sanity. The court had heard that he was of low intelligence, but that alone was not evidence of an intellectual disability.

Dr Mary Clarke Finnegan, based at Tralee General Hospital, told the court that O'Brien was not mentally ill. She said, 'Mr O'Brien is able to lead a gang in the town, able to organise crime, to register for the dole, to collect it, able to wheel and deal chainsaws, and possibly guns.'

Senior clinical psychologist Dr Colm Downing examined O'Brien and found that he was within normal intelligence range but on the borderline. He had limited education and performed poorly in tests involving general knowledge, but his abstract reasoning was fine. 'There is no mental retardation. There is no question about that,' he said. He then added that people with O'Brien's profile – anti-social personality disorder and a low verbal IQ – were prone to impulsive and violent outbursts: 'They are prone to acting in a very exaggerated fashion, impulsively and violently to a relatively innocuous remark.'

Statements that O'Brien made to Gardaí were read to the court. In one of the statements, made on 22 March 1997, he said he had murdered Mr Healy by giving him 'a good few belts with the bar' after learning that the youth had started taking tablets. He just wanted to teach him a lesson. 'He had started associating with drugs barons, but he was a fairly good troop. I didn't mind smoking hash, but using tablets and all . . . They fuck up the brain,' he had said. 'I gave him a good few belts with the bar and left it in the field where you found him. I know I killed him, but I only wanted to teach him a lesson.'

In another statement he said that he had seen two men beating the victim. 'I saw James Healy being killed. I was passing on the main road by FAS when I heard something, maybe a fight or something. I couldn't see that well from the main road, so I cycled towards the boat yard. I heard a lot of shouting and roaring. I had a fair idea it was James Healy being beaten. I said to myself I better get out of here or I'll get the same death.

I didn't think James Healy was dead you see. That's why I said nothing.'

During the course of the trial, Michael O'Brien wrote a letter from his prison cell to the Gardaí, claiming that he was innocent. It was an extraordinary document, which was read to the jury. In the eight-page letter he claimed that his statements admitting his guilt were false. The letter read: 'I told the police lies. I have nothing to fear. I killed nobody. I would have nothing to fear. I am the wrong man.' He described James Healy as 'dependable' and a 'good operator', and said he was upset and stunned when he heard about the murder, which he claimed was 'all over a girl and a few pound'. 'I am clean innocent. I am not going to take the blame for a murder that I never done. This is incredible,' he wrote.

But it was the end of the letter that was the most extraordinary part. It was a message of friendship to the dead man, the man he was accused of killing. He wrote that he had gone to James's grave to drink cider in his honour. He had even cracked open a bottle and left it on the grave, and he placed a lit cigarette by the bottle as he drank his own.

'He is in the grave and I'm in the jail. Incredible. Life will never again be the same,' the letter concluded.

Yet another version of the killing was presented to the court when Sergeant Mossie O'Donnell, of Dingle Garda Station, read a memo of an interview he carried out with O'Brien on 22 March 1997. The memo read: 'I had planned with James Healy to do Barry's shop on Saturday. But when I met him, he was tipsy. I gave off to him for being drunk, and he gave me cheek. He was my deputy and he should not have been giving me cheek. I did not mean to kill James Healy, but I lost the head. I did not know James was dead until I heard it on the news.'

Finally Michael O'Brien entered the witness box to give evidence on his own behalf. It was his chance to convince the jury of his version of events. He admitted telling the Gardaí that one of his 'staff' had been murdered, but he denied identifying anyone as the killer of James Healy. He said that the Gardaí had got that backwards; they had named the killers to him. 'They should be in the courtroom, not me,' he told the jury. He went on to accuse the Gardaí of using him as a scapegoat. He also denied making any of the statements attributed to him by the Gardaí. He said that he had signed statements, but they had not been read out to him and he would not have signed them if he knew they contained accounts of him killing James. He also said that a number of witnesses who saw him with James Healy on the night of the murder had been mistaken.

He seemed to enjoy the whole process of being in the witness box. Between evidence and prosecution, he was three days in the stand. He was cross-examined by barrister John Edwards, who had prosecuted him before on a larceny charge. 'You and I crossed swords before,' he told the barrister. 'You came out second best on that occasion and you'll come out second best on this occasion.' He added that he had 'magnificent confidence in this case' and said he would be 'king of the country' when he was acquitted. 'This is the most interesting murder case going on at the moment,' he said. He went on to allege that there was a conspiracy between many of the witnesses and the Gardaí to put him behind bars for the killing.

Summing up after the lengthy trial, barrister Edwards described the killing as vicious and violent, and Mr O'Brien as a 'vicious and dangerous person'. He reminded the jury that O'Brien had mentioned that James would be found in a field with his face bashed in and a bar across his chest to more than one person before the body was found. 'Nobody else could have had access to that information,' he said. 'At this point in time nobody knew that. The only person who knew that was the killer.'

Barrister Blaise O'Carroll, acting for O'Brien, said that his client was being 'stitched up'. 'This is like the Birmingham Six and the Guildford Four. The guards entered into a cold, calculating conspiracy to gather evidence to build a case that could destroy an innocent human being,' he said. 'He is convinced that you are going to see that. He is convinced he is going home on Thursday.' It was a show of bravado, but it was unlikely to sway the jury.

They retired at 2.48 p.m. on Thursday, 28 January, but failed to reach a verdict after several hours of deliberation. They were sent to a hotel overnight. The following day they returned a verdict: Michael O'Brien was guilty of murder.

As the verdict was read out, O'Brien's sister burst into tears, and shouted, 'He's innocent.' O'Brien also shouted out, saying, 'This is a miscarriage of justice!'

When order was restored, Mr Justice Kinlen said that O'Brien was a man with a personality disorder, but was not mentally ill. He said that the personality disorder had caused problems for O'Brien, his family, welfare workers and the Gardaí. He sentenced him to life in prison, with a recommendation that he be detained at the Central Mental Hospital in Dundrum. He said that he was in an 'impossible position' because he could only recommend that the prisoner be detained at the hospital. He could not insist. 'It is a tragedy in this country that we do not have facilities where you might be received, and where there might be some chance you might confront yourself and come to terms with your anti-social condition,' he said. 'But you do not wish to cooperate.'

12

KILLED WITH A WOK

The murder of Charlene McAuliffe by Gerard Graham

WHEN DUBLIN FOUR decides to get in touch with its roots and rediscover its Irishness, it goes to Dingle. Dingle is the trendy face of the Gaeltacht, a place where everything quaint and rustic and Celtic comes together in one scenic package. There is the beautiful fishing village itself, and the wild and rugged peninsula with its high mountain passes. There is the music in the pubs, the plaintive wail of the tin whistle and the birdsong on the wild cliffs.

And then there are the people – a wild and rugged race, in touch with nature and the rhythms of the year, in touch with their roots and in touch with the soul of the country. They are the noble savages, simple but wise.

Rubbish. When Valentia Island was chosen for the first transatlantic telegraph cable in 1866, Kerry did not join the information superhighway: it created it. The west coast of Kerry has the same problems as the rest of the world: unemployment, poverty, drugs, teenage pregnancy – and crime.

And Dingle fishermen face the same problems as any other self-employed men in a precarious occupation. Sometimes they have to do things that are illegal to make a living. Up and down the western seaboard, there is a small minority of fishermen who have decided that smuggling drugs or guns into the country is an easier way of making a living than hauling in half-empty nets.

One of these men was Gerard Graham. He decided to get into the drugs business. And when a teenage girl from Dublin knew too much, he decided the simplest way of solving his problem was murder.

Charlene McAuliffe was from Clondalkin, Dublin. She moved down to Dingle in 1998, at age 19, where she began working in Walker's Bar. She immersed herself in the local scene – and it was a lot racier than traditional music and Guinness. Charlene soon fell into a bad crowd, which included fisherman Gerard Graham. He was from Vestry. Vestry is a small village about four miles west of Dingle. Once it was the main port of the peninsula; now it is popular with tourists, because of the long sandy beach. At 33, Graham was a lot older than Charlene. He had a child, a young daughter. Graham and Charlene became romantically involved.

Around this time, Charlene also began using drugs. Then disaster struck: she was found by Gardaí in possession of drugs. After she was caught, she went briefly to England. When she returned home, she moved into the house of a friend, in Cork. Graham joined her. The house was owned by Linda McGowan. Ms McGowan was a mother of four who was originally from The Grove, in Dingle. But she was then living in Cork, at 188 Kilnap Place, Farranree. Farranree is a working-class district on the north side of the city. Charlene stayed in Cork for about three weeks.

Ms McGowan said that there were tensions between Charlene and Graham in the days leading up to the murder of Charlene. Gerard Graham confided in her that Charlene 'knew too much' about his drug involvement. He said that if he killed her, he would have money for a drugs deal in Limerick. Limerick is the major import point for drugs along the west coast. The drugs come in through Kilrush, a fishing port in Clare, and are distributed up and down the seaboard by the rival Limerick gangs. Graham spoke of 'doing in' Charlene, and seemed serious, though Ms McGowan did not believe it would really happen.

Graham knew that Charlene had money with her: she had a sum of €3,800, which her father had given her to go to Australia. If Graham could get his hands on that money, he could put together a deal and make quite a killing. However, he knew that Charlene would not give him the money.

'He said he would do in Charlene a number of times. He always said it in a joking manner and that's why I did not take him seriously,' said Ms McGowan at the inquest. 'I felt he just wanted her out of the country.'

On Friday, 1 October, the couple were bickering and arguing as usual. The following day, McGowan was in the kitchen. Charlene was sitting on a chair by the fridge. Graham came into the kitchen from upstairs. He was smiling. But then a row from the previous evening re-erupted. Suddenly the tension in the room rose several notches.

At some point during the argument, Charlene smirked at Graham. Like many men who like to see themselves as dominant, Graham was infuriated by a smirking woman. He picked up an iron wok that was lying nearby and struck Charlene on the head with it. It was not one of the lightweight non-stick woks that are so common, but a heavy-duty commercial one.

Ms McGowan was shocked. She ran from the room.

'He grabbed the wok and the next thing I remember is Gerard striking Charlene full force with the heavy wok on the head,' said Ms McGowan. 'I panicked and ran upstairs to my bedroom and jumped on the bed. I was shocked and couldn't believe what was happening. I thought it was all a dream.'

As Charlene stumbled from her chair, Graham struck her again a number of times, driving her to the ground. Then he straddled her and began to strangle her. It takes between thirty seconds and two minutes to strangle a normal person of average health. The slender neck of a teen would have speeded up the process – that and the wound on her head.

Upstairs, Ms McGowan heard four heavy thuds from the kitchen: each thud a crushing blow to Charlene's skull from the wok. After a few minutes, Ms McGowan got up from the bed and went down a few steps. She heard Charlene trying to say something. Then the teenager went quiet, as the life was choked from her.

Immediately, Graham got into a panic. It is one thing to fantasise about killing someone and taking their savings. It is quite another to have a dead body on your hands, and an awkward witness to boot. Would Ms McGowan help him dispose of the body? More importantly, would she squeal on him?

First things first: Graham got on the phone. He needed help. The man he decided to ring was Alan Graham Clucas. Clucas was originally from the Isle of Man. He was raised in Port Erin, a village on the south side of the island. It was a picturesque spot with stunning views; from a nearby headland, you can get occasional glimpses of the Mourne Mountains. Racing driver Nigel Mansell was one of his neighbours. But Clucas was never going to reach that level of success, or any level of success. He moved to Ireland, where he settled in Waterford. He had a holiday mobile home in Ventry, where Graham was from. That was how the two men knew each other. Clucas was in his late 20s.

Clucas, a fisherman, was a bit of a loner and had difficulty making friends, so he would go to some lengths to hold on to the few friends he had. This led to what a court later termed 'insane behaviour' sparked by a 'misguided sense of friendship'. When Clucas got the call from Graham, he immediately left Waterford and drove to Cork.

Graham had said it was a 'matter of urgency', so Clucas dropped everything to help a friend. When he arrived, he agreed to help Graham dispose of the body. They wrapped Charlene in a couple of black refuse sacks and then carried the young woman out of the house in Farranree and stuffed her into the boot of Clucas's car. They then drove the two and a half hours to Ventry. They put the body in Clucas's mobile home at Cuan Pier while they debated what to do. There were a number of options they considered. One was to dump the body in Peddler's Lake near the Conor Pass. Peddler's Lake is a small lake high up on Mount Brandon. It is deep and cold, but can only be reached by a hike. The path wends its way up past a waterfall and is tough going, even for fit people. That plan was dismissed as completely impractical. They also discussed dumping Charlene at sea. It would have to be done right; if the currents brought the body back to shore, they would be undone.

The men separated after leaving the body in the mobile home. Graham collected his daughter and brought her to the annual blessing of the boats in Dingle the following day, Sunday. While the young girl enjoyed the spectacle, her father wondered what his next move would be.

Unknown to Graham and Clucas, the next move was already out of their hands. Gardaí in Cork had got a tip-off and had called on the house at Farranree where Charlene had met her death. Following that raid, they phoned their colleagues in Dingle and suggested they pay a visit to the caravan in Ventry. The body of the young woman was quickly discovered, and a full-scale murder investigation was launched.

They might have been in Dingle, but the Gardaí were not fishing. They knew exactly who they were looking for. On Sunday afternoon, both Graham and Clucas were taken in for questioning. One forensics team swooped on the caravan in Ventry, while a second began a minute examination of the murder scene in Farranree.

As the *Irish Times* reported:

Gardaí believe the young woman, who received fatal head injuries, was murdered in Cork and her body driven to the caravan site. Following information received by the Gardaí in Cork, a search was made of a house at Kilnap Place, Farranree, on the north side of Cork city. Subsequently further information was provided which prompted Gardaí to contact their counterparts in Dingle.

The information relayed to Dingle resulted in the search of the caravan park and the discovery of the woman's body. A senior Gardaí source in Cork said last night the matter was being treated as a murder inquiry.

Within hours of the discovery of the body, Gerard Graham was in custody. When he heard that Graham had been arrested, Clucas voluntarily presented himself at Dingle Garda Station. He was also held in custody.

It was an easy investigation. Sergeant Mossie O'Donnell was the man who arrested Graham at the Garda station in Bridge Street in Dingle, after several hours of close questioning. He formally arrested Graham at 5.14 a.m. on Monday, charging him with the murder. Then, as protocol dictated, he asked if Graham had anything to say in response to the charge.

'There is no point in making a response to it,' the accused had replied.

Mr Clucas, who had been questioned at Tralee, made no response at all when charged.

Gerard Graham, a fisherman of John Street, Dingle, was charged with murder at a special sitting of Kenmare District Court. Shortly afterwards, Alan Clucas, whose address was given as Cuan Pier, Ventry, was charged with being an accessory to the murder, for putting Charlene's body in a car boot with intent to impede the apprehension and prosecution of Mr Graham. Wearing a navy tracksuit and trainers, Graham showed no emotion during the brief court hearing. He sat in silence, listening to evidence relating to his arrest.

While the Gardaí had reason to be delighted with their swift work, Charlene McAuliffe's parents had the difficult job of travelling to Kerry to identify their dead daughter. Patrick and Valerie McAuliffe were accompanied by their children Keith and Lisa. Charlene was their youngest child. The family were regular visitors to west Kerry, where they used to holiday at Ventry. It was during those visits that Charlene got to know the area she eventually moved to to take up bar work. The McAuliffes were well known in the area.

A few days after his arrest, Clucas applied for bail, but was turned down because the caravan at Cuan Pier was not deemed by the Gardaí to be a specific address. Graham was also refused bail.

On Monday, 20 October, both men applied to the High Court for bail. This time their application was successful, and both men were released. They were to enjoy more than two years of freedom before the case finally came to trial.

The trial itself was a bit of an anticlimax. It opened on Monday, 14 January 2002, in the Central Criminal Court in Dublin. Gerard Graham was asked how he pleaded to the murder charge. He said not guilty, and a jury was sworn in. But before the case began, his defence team asked for an adjournment. The jury was discharged, and Graham was re-arraigned. This time when he was asked how he pleaded, he replied: 'Guilty.'

The court heard that Graham first hit Charlene with a wok and then choked her to death. Barrister for the prosecution Michael Counihan said Charlene, from Clondalkin, had been living in Dingle in 1998 and 1999. She was a drug user and had become friendly with Graham. Following a visit to England, she stayed with a mutual friend of hers and Graham's. Graham stayed in the house, and on 2 October an argument developed, after which he attacked her.

Barrister Patrick Gageby, for the defence, read a statement in which Graham expressed 'deepest remorse'. Graham extended apologies to her family and friends, and said he was sorry for the shame he had brought on his family. He was sentenced to life in prison.

The following day, Clucas pleaded guilty to knowing or believing that Gerard Graham was guilty of having murdered Charlene McAuliffe, and of having helped him evade detection.

Mr Justice Nicholas Kearns, presiding, said that this 'insane behaviour' was caused by a 'misguided sense of friendship'. The judge had heard that Clucas had told Gardaí after his arrest that he 'just wanted to help a friend' and he 'should have gone back to Waterford' instead of getting involved. But he had got involved, wrapping Charlene's body in bin bags and transporting it to Ventry.

Clucas's defence team introduced some heavy hitters as character witnesses. Miles Walker, the former prime minister of the Isle of Man, told the court he was a close friend of the Clucas family. He said the actions of Alan Clucas 'had a very deep and lasting effect' on his family, who were upset at 'the thoughts of other people suffering'.

The accused's father, also Alan, told the court it was a 'very stupid act'. He added that his son had a non-malignant growth on his brain and was scheduled for neurosurgery the following week. Mr Clucas Senior said he was 'not a medical person' but had been informed that it had to be removed within six to twelve months.

Judge Kearns said he was 'quite impressed' with the defence submissions and was aware that Clucas had 'no hand whatsoever in the perpetration of the murder'. He also acknowledged that Clucas had cooperated with the Gardaí. However, his actions could have caused the body of the victim to have gone missing for months or years, adding to the family's trauma. Charlene's mother and some of her friends were in court as the judge summed up, and were visibly upset.

Clucas was sentenced to 18 months in prison.

The tragic case hit the headlines again in 2006, when an inquest opened into Charlene's death. Gerard Graham was allowed out of jail to testify, but he spent the day handcuffed to a prison officer. He told the inquest that he was very sorry for what he had done and wished he could turn back the clock.

Graham told the inquest that he attacked Charlene after noticing she was smirking at him. They had had an argument the previous night, which resumed the following morning. 'She was smirking and I flipped,' he said. 'I hit her on the head with a wok. I hit her again and she grabbed me. I grabbed her by the neck and I choked her.'

After hearing the evidence, the jury returned a verdict of death due to asphyxia, due to compression of the neck. Coroner Helen Lucey, extending her sympathy to the McAuliffe family, noted that none of the family was in the court, 'presumably because they did not want to hear the gruesome details again'.

13

DOUBLE MURDER IN MOYVANE

Thomas Barrett and the murder of Michael and Denis Hanrahan

MOYVANE IS NOT a location typical of Kerry. When we think of the Kingdom we think of the magnificent mountains of the Dingle Peninsula, the towering peaks of the Reeks, the rugged uplands of the Stack's Mountains to the north. Moyvane feels a world away.

The little village nestles in the lowlands south of the ferry port of Tarbert, in the extreme north of the county. Tarbert is a small village that is notable for nothing except a small gas-fired power station and a ferry that links Kerry to Clare across the expanse of the Shannon Estuary. It is on the back road between Limerick and Listowel, on the main road to Ballybunion.

Moneypoint, on the other side of the estuary, is also home to a power station, but it is a massive coal-fired one, the biggest in the country. It is also a place closely associated with the most famous Kerry murder of them all, the Colleen Bawn, as described in detail in Chapter 5.

If you turn south from Tarbert towards Listowel, after about four miles you will see the signs for Moyvane. The one-street village lies a couple of hundred yards off the main road, and is about as rural as you can get and still have neighbours. The houses along the main street are old and solidly agricultural. On one side of that main street there are still gaps where fields encroach on the village.

Its name is one of the most interesting things about Moyvane. Originally the village was created in the 1800s by a landlord, George Sandes, who called the settlement Newtown Sandes. However, in 1886 there was a forceful eviction of several tenants and the Sandes name rapidly fell out of favour. The village was renamed Newtown Dillon, after John Dillon, the Home Rule politician, but the new name didn't stick. In 1916, during the early days of the struggle for independence, the village underwent another name change, this time to honour Thomas Clarke, one of the Easter Rising leaders who was executed. So now it was Newtown Clarke. But, again, the name didn't stick. Finally, in 1939, the people of the village took a vote. It was decided to call the cluster of houses Moyvane, from the old Irish name for the area, Maigh Mheain, or 'middle of the plain'. That name stuck, though the signposts indicating Newtown Sandes remained in the area until the 1990s.

Moyvane, or middle of the plain, perfectly describes the place. The land is mainly flat, with the occasional hill rolling towards the estuary. It is good land, blessed with soft rain from the Atlantic, and both drained and fertilised by the great river flowing just a few miles away. Although the farms are small, they are comfortable and provide a good living.

It is a place apart, a throwback to an idyllic Ireland where the pace of life was slower and where people moved to a rhythm dictated by the weather and the seasons. There is a sense of community and cooperation, which is why it was so shocking when the place became the centre of a horrific double murder in March 2008.

Michael Hanrahan farmed land near Moyvane. A widower, he was a popular and well-respected man. He knew everyone, and everyone knew him. He was the correspondent for two local newspapers, the *Limerick Leader* and *The Kerryman*. Although he lived in Kerry, it was not far over the border, and the Limerick paper carried local notes from there. Michael was the right man to produce the notes. He was involved in all the organisations in the area, whether they were sporting, cultural or community. Aged 54, he lived in a small farmhouse not far from the village, on top of a hill holding commanding views over the estuary. It was at the end of a cul-de-sac, about a mile from Moyvane. He shared the dwelling with his only son, Denis, and with one of his daughters. Denis, 27, helped out on the land, but he had a job as well. He worked as a plasterer, which brought in the income.

Michael's wife, Anne, had been a nurse. She had died from cancer about twelve years previously. Denis was one of only two of the couple's children who still lived at home with his father. Denis's twin brother, Shane, and two of their three sisters were all living away.

On the night of Wednesday, 26 March, Michael and his son were at home on their own. Michael's daughter was not there that night. They went to bed at their usual time. Everything seemed to be normal. They didn't know that earlier that night a man with a troubled mind had begun living out some sort of a wild Rambo fantasy.

The man had put on an army camouflage vest and loaded six shotgun cartridges into its slots. He got his pump-action shotgun from its safe and put in three cartridges: the maximum it would hold. That alone gave him far more firepower than he needed, but he also brought an army rucksack with another 50 cartridges. For good measure, he threw in a hunting knife and a crossbow. Then he drove the half hour to his destination. He turned up at Tarbert, heading towards Listowel, and then took the road to the left into the village of Moyvane. He was just a mile from his target. But as he drove up the cul-de-sac towards the house, one of the neighbours spotted him. There was something that roused the neighbour's suspicion and he came out to the road, so the stranger turned and drove away.

Later, he returned.

Much later, he left again. As he drove away, he injected himself with an anti-anxiety drug normally used to treat pigs. He knew that what he had just done had changed everything.

On the morning of Thursday, 27 March 2008, Denis Hanrahan did not show up for a job he was meant to be doing. He should have picked up a second plasterer at 7.30 a.m. to drive to the job. When he didn't appear, the man went up to the Hanrahan house and knocked on the door. There was no answer. He hung around for a while, and then knocked again. He didn't know what to do and didn't want to force his way inside. He took out his phone and rang Denis. He could hear the phone ringing from inside. He was becoming a bit concerned.

A cousin of the Hanrahans passed by and the man accosted him, explaining his fears. The cousin was the one who pushed open the door and walked through the house. He stepped into one of the bedrooms. He stepped into a scene of carnage. Michael Hanrahan was lying dead on the floor after suffering a massive gunshot wound to the leg. His son was lying nearby, having been shot in the chest. He was lying on his stomach in a pool of blood beside the bed.

The horrified young man immediately rang the emergency services. Gardaí were on the scene swiftly, and a glance told the story. It seemed to be a classic case of a murder-suicide. The younger man appeared to have shot his father and then turned the gun upon himself. But, tragic as it was, the proper procedures had to be followed. The scene was sealed, and the bodies were left in place to await the arrival of the State Pathologist from Dublin, and the forensics unit.

There was shock in the local community as news of the tragedy began to leak out. This was not a place used to murder, and it cut deeply. The papers were being coy about exactly what the Gardaí suspected, but there were hints, such as an enigmatic line in the *Irish Times*: 'Michael Hanrahan and his son Denis are believed to have suffered gunshot wounds in the bungalow where they lived alone outside Moyvane. But it is believed that Gardaí have yet to find a firearm registered to the farmhouse.'

'It has come as a complete bombshell to all of us. We are suffering from shock,' said the parish priest, Fr John Lucid.

Gabriel Fitzmaurice, a primary school teacher in the village and a poet, knew the family well. He said, 'There is a pall of despondency around the place, there's a pall of despair. You don't expect this to happen in a small, peaceful, tranquil little backwater like Moyvane.' Mr Fitzmaurice, who had recently retired, had taught all the Hanrahan children. He remembered Denis and his twin Shane well. 'They were lovely outgoing happy-go-lucky fellows, who did their bit at school and got on with their lives.'

When the pathologist arrived to conduct the post-mortem, the investigation suddenly took on a new sense of urgency. Investigators expected that when the body of Denis Hanrahan was moved, they would find the gun under his chest. But there was no gun. Both men had been shot several times, and the weapon was missing. This was a double-homicide investigation. Murder had come to Moyvane.

Gardaí knew that Michael Hanrahan, in common with many farmers, had a shotgun for controlling pests. The gun was fully licensed, but it was missing. A thorough search by the forensic team failed to find any trace of it. Was that the murder weapon?

The crime-scene examination had revealed no blood trails, which showed that the two men had fallen where they had been shot. They had not been moved by their killer. Both men had suffered a number of wounds, and there were eight spent cartridges found on the floor. Gardaí believed both men had been shot some time late on Wednesday night and hoped the detailed post-mortem by Dr Margot Bolster would give a more exact time of death. Beyond that, the Gardaí were speculating. The victims were in their pyjamas and the lights were on, so that indicated they had been killed late on Wednesday night or early Thursday morning, in the small hours.

'It remains unclear at this early stage what the sequence of events were which led to these deaths occurring. It is expected that the post-mortem will conclude that both men died from gunshot wounds,' said a Garda spokesperson. 'A firearm, licensed to the property, has yet to be located.'

The gun was eventually located the following day. It was sent for forensic tests. The local crime-scene experts from the Kerry division had been joined by a team from the Garda Technical Bureau. In all, more than 70 officers, based at nearby Listowel Garda Station, were working the case. This included a dozen experts from headquarters in Dublin. Gardaí knew they needed a break of some sort. A spokesperson admitted, 'Because of where the house is – in a relatively isolated area – I'd say that witnesses aren't going to be a great feature of this investigation.'

An early lead came when a detailed examination of the doors and windows of the bungalow showed no signs of forced entry. This indicated that the killer knew his victims: he was someone they trusted enough to let into the house. This certainly narrowed down the list of suspects. Often when people are killed in isolated rural areas, it is by burglars from out of the area, preying on the vulnerable. With nothing to connect victim and killer, those investigations are notoriously difficult to solve. However, if the victim and the killer are known to each other, a search for motives can often point investigators in the right direction.

Gardaí now had a different picture of how events unfolded. They had found blood on the bed in the room where both men died. The bedroom was Denis's. They now believed that the intruder had disturbed Denis, and as the young man, who had possibly been asleep until he was disturbed, struggled to rise, he was shot in the chest. As he fell from the bed, he was shot a number of times again. The noise woke his father, who came running. As he entered the room, the intruder turned the gun on him and shot him a number of times.

The big break would come if the Gardaí could prove that the shotgun found in the house was the one used to kill the two men. The gun had been dusted for prints, and if the killer had used it, he could be caught.

Robbery was still a possible motive, but due to the lack of a forced entry, it was becoming less likely. Superintendent Kevin Donohoe, heading the investigation, said that the Gardaí were not advising people of the need to take extra safety precautions. They did not believe anyone else in Moyvane was in danger.

The investigation stalled slightly when the forensic results came back from the single-barrel shotgun found in the Hanrahan farmhouse. The tests revealed that it was not the murder weapon. With hindsight, this was the likely outcome of the tests. At least eight shots had been fired at the two men, and a single-barrel shotgun needs to be reloaded after every shot, making it an unlikely murder weapon.

However, that setback was quickly followed by a real breakthrough. A pump-action shotgun was found in a car in the Causeway area of north Kerry late on Saturday night. Causeway is a small village about 20 miles away from Moyvane, on the far side of Ballybunion. It was about a 30-minute drive from the murder scene. The best part of the discovery was that the gun was licensed – now Gardaí had a name for their suspect.

The pump-action shotgun was an ideal fit for the murder weapon. It was capable of firing a number of rounds in quick succession, without having to be reloaded. It fitted with the finding of a number of shells in the bedroom of Denis Hanrahan. Shotguns do not have the unique rifling patterns that rifle and pistol barrels have, which allow a gun to be matched infallibly to the bullet it fires. But the pin striking the firing cap of a shotgun cartridge leaves a unique mark. If the killer had removed the spent cartridges, he could have prevented the Gardaí matching the gun to the deaths, but he left them lying on the floor and each one was as unique as a fingerprint. The forensic team would be able to – and did – match the fatal shots to the Causeway shotgun.

The Gardaí were already looking for a personal motive in the double killing. Now they had a name. The case was coming together. Thomas Barrett, from Cleandries, Causeway, was 30, and a friend of Denis Hanrahan. On Thursday, 26 March, he had been admitted to Tralee General Hospital. He was driven there by members of his family. On Saturday evening he was discharged. Gardaí were waiting to interview him. At 7.30 p.m. he was arrested on a charge of unlawful possession of a firearm and brought to Tralee. He was then transferred to Listowel for questioning. He could be held for 48 hours, and that could be extended to 72 hours. Throughout Sunday, Gardaí interviewed the man, probing his account of events.

Finally, on Monday, before a special sitting of Listowel District Court, Thomas Barrett was charged with the double murder. He appeared in court dressed in a navy jumper and jeans, and sat with his arms folded, silent throughout the proceedings. Judge Mary O'Halloran was told that Detective Sergeant John Heaslip had formally charged Barrett with both murders. In reply to both charges, the young man had replied: 'No.' He was remanded in custody to Cork Prison.

Afterwards, he was hustled from the courthouse by the Gardaí. He covered his head with a grey jacket, but there was a crowd of about 80 outside the courthouse and they jeered as he made his way to the squad car. Several of the crowd yelled abuse at him.

Meanwhile, the community were preparing for the removal of the two victims of Barrett. That evening, their bodies lay in repose at a funeral home in Listowel before being removed to the Church of the Assumption in Moyvane. Thousands of people attended the removal. There were no flowers. Instead there was a jar for donations to a cancer charity, in memory of Michael's late wife. The remaining siblings – Denis's twin Shane, and his sisters Kayrena, 26, Marion, 25, and Aine, 24 – were the chief mourners. The removal overran by an hour, such was the crowd. There were a large number of Gardaí present to control the traffic.

Finally the cortege left Listowel, but it did not follow the direct route to Moyvane. Following a local tradition, they took a longer route, and the line of cars paused briefly at the turn-up towards the Hanrahan house, as a mark of respect. As a bitter wind whipped in up the estuary, people huddled in the street awaiting the hearse. As the coffin was taken from the hearse, members of the local Fine Gael party formed a guard of honour into the church, where Fr Lucid waited for the remains.

The following morning, the funeral Mass was celebrated by 30 priests, including the chief celebrant Fr Lucid and the Bishop of Kerry, Dr Bill Murphy. The church was overflowing, with several people outside the door. An estimated crowd of 1,500 attended.

Fr Sean Horgan told the crowd that the pain and suffering – even the anger – they felt was natural. There was revulsion at the 'violent, reprehensible deed'. But both men would want their family and friends to journey out of their grief.

At the end of the Mass, Denis's twin Shane stood up and addressed the mourners. His voice trembled with emotion as he shared memories of his father and brother. He spoke of happy days in the past, afternoons on nearby Ballybunion beach and family fun. 'I know my father and Denis are now joined with Mam in the company of the saints in the holy land of heaven,' he said, moving many to tears. Both victims were laid to rest in the nearby Murhur Cemetery.

The next day, Barrett appeared in court again. This time the court directed that he be given any psychiatric support he needed while in custody. This direction came after an application by his solicitor, who said that Barrett's family were concerned about his medical condition. The solicitor handed in a letter from a consultant psychiatrist recommending treatment while in custody.

It took three years for the case to come to trial. Finally, in March 2011, Thomas Barrett faced the jury. He pleaded guilty to the double murder. The court – and the world – finally heard what had driven the young man to commit murder.

Detective Inspector Daniel Keane told the court that Barrett had attended Pallaskenry Agricultural College in the late '90s. This is a small college in County Limerick, about halfway between Tarbert and Limerick city. It provides training for farmers and mechanics, and salespeople for agricultural and farm machinery. Numbers are limited. While Barrett was there, one of the other students was Denis Hanrahan. The men became friends. When their courses finished, the friendship endured.

Over the next decade, Barrett was a regular visitor to the Hanrahan home, which was only half an hour's drive from his own place in Causeway. Barrett could be moody and was sometimes considered withdrawn and uncommunicative. Yet he felt comfortable with the Hanrahans and was always welcome there. He often had meals there and stayed over when a visit ran late.

However, about a year before the murders Barrett stopped visiting the Hanrahan house. 'He perceived some slight,' said the detective.

Whatever the slight was, the Hanrahans were not aware of it. They just knew something was troubling the young man. Michael Hanrahan rang Barrett's father to try to get to the bottom of it, but to no avail. Whatever the issue was, it festered in Barrett's mind.

Shortly after 11 p.m. on 26 March 2008, what was festering finally erupted. Barrett took his pump-action shotgun, bag of ammunition, hunting knife and crossbow, and set out for one final visit to his erstwhile friend. He drove to the cul-de-sac where the Hanrahans lived, but he was spotted and aroused the suspicions of a neighbour, so he turned and drove away. The neighbour followed him for a while, but then stopped. But

Barrett returned, this time arriving at the isolated farmhouse.

He knew the house well. The lights were out and everyone was in bed. He snuck around to the rear, where he knew there was a key to the back door, and let himself in. He knew exactly where he was going; he had stayed over often enough. He quickly found the bedroom of his friend, Denis, and fired a shot through the open door at the sleeping man. He hit him in the leg. Denis struggled up, and Barrett fired twice more, hitting him in the chest. Denis ended up on the floor.

Barrett retreated to the living room, where he took three more cartridges from his army vest and loaded them into the gun. However, the noise had woken Michael Hanrahan. Still in his pyjamas, he ran to his son's room. Barrett followed him and opened fire. The older man was hit in the leg and fell to the ground. He was then shot in the chest. Barrett loaded the gun for a third time and fired another round into each man. In all, he had fired eight times. One shot went through the door and hit the bed. Three shots hit Denis, while four hit his father.

'The pump-action shotgun had to be reloaded three times. It could hold only three cartridges,' the detective explained.

Barrett then went to the other bedroom, where he knew Denis's sister slept. He opened the door and trained the gun on the bed. He flipped the light switch and saw that the bed was empty, so he turned and left the house, driving home to Causeway.

When he got home, he was still feeling unsettled by what he had done, so before he got out of the car, he found a syringe and injected himself with an anti-anxiety drug normally used on pigs. He walked into his house, but was overcome by an attack of nausea. He shouted for his mother. As she came down the stairs, he threw up.

Barrett was taken to Tralee General Hospital and was transferred, voluntarily, from the accident and emergency section to a psychiatric ward. He was clearly in the throes of a crisis. Three days into his treatment at the psychiatric ward, he confided to a psychiatrist that he had been involved in the double homicide that had horrified the whole country. After this, he was released from the hospital and taken into Garda custody.

The detective said that Barrett had not been able to give any good reason for wanting to kill his friend Denis Hanrahan, who was his first target.

Experts from the Central Mental Hospital in Dundrum had examined Barrett, and they found no evidence of a mental disorder. However, they did find traits of pervasive resentment. Barrett was very sensitive to slights on his character. He took offence very easily.

Shane Hanrahan addressed the court on the impact of the loss of his brother. Such victim impact statements have become a feature of modern murder trials. 'Human life is sacred,' he began. 'Murder causes chaos. Dad's and Denis's murders have cast a dark shadow over our home on the hill and have done an incalculable amount of damage.' He said that occasions such as Christmas, birthdays and anniversaries were a cruel, harsh reminder of their intense pain.

Through his solicitor, Barrett expressed regret for his actions. His family also expressed their deepest sympathy towards the Hanrahan family.

After hearing all the evidence, Mr Justice Paul Carney imposed two life sentences on Barrett. A minor slight that was almost certainly unintended had festered in a fragile and over-sensitive mind, and had destroyed two families.

'The loss of these two men, Denis's life cut so short, both their lives taken in such a cruel way . . . the community can barely comprehend it all,' the parish priest, Fr Lucid, had said in the days following the discovery of the two bodies. 'People are very sad, very upset, and the sense of loss is extremely deep. A cloud has descended on Moyvane. There is just an air of unreality about the village. It all seems so far-fetched that people can't believe it's actually happened. It will be a long time before we return to normality.'

In that he was right. Murder is so final. No matter what the motives, when someone is killed, the ripples spread far. Not only is the victim's immediate family altered for ever, the killer and his family also have to live with the consequences.

14

THE MARK OF CAIN

Ailbe Lonergan and the murder of his brother on New Year's Eve

CHRISTMAS CAN BE murder. We all say that sometimes, and smile knowingly at each other. It is a time of high stress, bringing family tensions and unresolved disputes to the surface. At other times of the year, this can lead to mild bickering. At Christmas, it can lead to full-blown arguments. We have all seen turkeys dropped on the floor and dramatic storm-outs.

It is an urban legend that suicide rates peak around the holiday season. There are too many people around, which limits opportunities and distracts people. But people do come under intense stress. Combine this with huge amounts of alcohol, and it can be a lethal combination.

And the Irish are great for huge amounts of alcohol. The mythology of our few celebrities is dotted with tales of excess. Footballer George Best, snooker player Alex Higgins, singer Shane MacGowan, and actors Richard Harris and Colin Farrell all had one thing in common, aside from their talent: they were better known for their epic benders than their legitimate work. People laugh when they hear tales of Richard Harris slipping out for cigarettes on Saturday, only to resurface on Thursday on the far side of the country, missing his trousers and a good portion of his wallet. But sometimes such excesses can lead to deadlier results than a hangover and an injured bank balance. In Chapter 6 we saw how a man nearing his pension was willing to take a knife to a young man in a pub, and throw away both of their lives, as a result of drink.

However, Kerry has moved into the modern era. Combine drink with recreational drugs and the results can be explosive. The people of Tralee found that out on a bleak New Year's Eve in 2006/07, when a two-day party turned to murder.

By all accounts, the party in Michael Lonergan's house was a wild one. The family had gathered to celebrate Christmas, and it was an open house in the few days after the holiday. The party began in earnest on Saturday, 30 December 2006. They were going to ring in the New Year in style.

Michael Lonergan was 34 and lived with his wife Yvonne, nee Coffey. They had been together half their lives and had a house in the Balloonagh Estate, on the outskirts of Tralee. The estate is an old one, with well-maintained houses and mature gardens. The houses are a mix of short terraces and semi-detached dwellings, with spacious front lawns. There are plenty of green areas around the estate, making it a fine area to bring up families. The Lonergans' house, No. 58, was at the end of a short terrace, on a cul-de-sac.

Mr Lonergan had five children. They ranged in age from fifteen down to four years old. There were four girls – Tiffany, Claudia, Tori and Amber – and one boy, Michael, the baby of the family. Mr Lonergan was a habitual cannabis user and also occasionally used other drugs, such as cocaine. It is thought he had become dependent on the stronger drug.

There was also some suspicion on the part of the Gardaí that he might have been involved in dealing. Shortly before the epic Christmas bash, Lonergan had been in court on drugs-related matters. He was on remand and facing charges arising from the seizure of €9,600 worth of amphetamines. However, he had no convictions for drugs-related offences.

About ten people drifted in and out of the house during the few days of partying. Sometimes, particularly during the evenings, the numbers swelled to more than that. Sometimes there were only a few people present. Michael's younger brother Ailbe, himself a father, was one of the visitors. Yvonne's brother Emmet and his partner were also in and out. The alcohol flowed, and lines of cocaine were also available for those who wanted a snort.

On 31 December, New Year's Eve, Louise O'Brien, the partner of Emmet Coffey, called to the house at 10 a.m. She was there to pick up Emmet, who had stayed the night. He had arrived early the previous day, and had spent the day and evening drinking. She took him home with her, but later that day the two of them returned to the Bailoonagh Estate. The party was still going on when they arrived at around 5.45 p.m.

At some point in the next hour, a fight broke out between Michael and Ailbe Lonergan. It quickly got physical, with some shoving and pushing before the two brothers were separated. After the fight, Michael removed an ornamental sword from a wall mounting. Emmet Coffey spotted him and took the sword from him, putting it back on the wall.

By the early evening, both brothers were drunk and Michael had snorted a line of cocaine. The cocaine mixed with the alcohol proved an explosive mixture, lowering inhibitions and fuelling aggression. Ailbe was certainly getting aggressive. He was becoming loud and obnoxious, and he insulted and abused a number of the guests in the house. Michael was becoming increasingly annoyed with him. At one point he told Ailbe to stop being abusive to people or he would have to leave. He tried to push Ailbe towards the door. Another fight broke out between the two brothers. This time they were not inside the house. They were both outside, in the driveway. It was shortly before 7 p.m. Michael had no way of knowing that his brother had taken a knife from his kitchen and was armed.

Louise O'Brien was at the door and was the only witness to what happened next. She was also one of the few sober people in the house. She watched as the two brothers began to push and shove. It should have been an uneven fight. Ailbe had one arm in plaster, so he was in no fit state for a confrontation, but the brothers were 'throwing digs' at one another. Suddenly Ailbe lashed out at his older brother, striking him a number of times in the chest. Michael staggered backwards.

Ms O'Brien saw Ailbe throw away something that looked like a knife, and then he ran off. Michael turned towards the door and began walking towards her. He was holding his hand to his side, and she could see blood seeping through his fingers. There was a lot of blood on his T-shirt. Michael Lonergan staggered past her and fell to the floor. As he lay there, he turned to her partner, Emmet Coffey. 'Ailbe stabbed me. The bastard stabbed me. My own brother stabbed me,' he said.

An ambulance was called and was on the scene swiftly. Mr Lonergan was brought to Tralee General Hospital, where a team of doctors began emergency surgery to save his life. He had suffered three deep wounds to the upper chest. Doctors worked on him for a few hours, but at 10.30 p.m. his heart stopped pumping and he was declared dead.

His death was the last murder of the old year, and brought the death toll from violence in Ireland in 2006 up to sixty: averaging more than one murder a week. Yet the gruesome statistic garnered few headlines; the Gardaí had managed to make an arrest within an hour of the stabbing, meaning there were severe reporting restrictions on the death in Tralee.

The house was cordoned off overnight, while a forensics team made their way down to Tralee. From interviews with witnesses, Gardaí believed that the murder weapon had been a kitchen knife and they began a minute search of the estate to find it. They knew it had been disposed of almost immediately after the stabbing. They also interviewed the ten people in the house at the time, taking detailed statements.

While all this went on, Ailbe Lonergan remained in custody at Tralee Garda Station. The Assistant State Pathologist Dr Margot Bolster arrived in the Kerry town on New Year's Day to carry out the post-mortem. Her findings showed that the fatal wound had been a stab into the chest under the arm. This would have severed the artery, resulting in rapid blood loss and shock.

That same day, Ailbe Lonergan, aged 31, of Quill Street, Tralee, was charged with his brother's murder. At a special sitting before Judge James O'Connor, he was remanded in custody to Cork Prison. The judge was told that in reply to the charge, Ailbe Lonergan had replied, 'No comment.'

On Thursday, 4 January, Michael Lonergan was laid to rest in his native town. For the 300 mourners it was a sobering start to the New Year. Monsignor Dan O'Riordan, celebrating the funeral Mass, said that it was all the more poignant and tragic for the fact that it happened during the Christmas season, traditionally a time of great joy and celebration. He told mourners at St John's Church that it was particularly sad to be holding Mr Lonergan's funeral at a time when the Christmas crib was still on display in the church. 'Little did I think when I heard the sirens go by on New Year's Eve that a few hours later we would be gathered in the hospital praying for Michael. It isn't how any of us would have planned it,' he said. He added that it was particularly difficult for Yvonne and the five children, but the local community were rallying round and showing support. He prayed that people would find forgiveness in their hearts as Jesus had done. 'Michael's family will remember him more for his successes than his failings, and that is how it should be with all people,' he said.

It took just a year for the case to come to court: quick in this age. On Wednesday, 5 December 2007, Ailbe Lonergan's trial opened in the Central Criminal Court, which sat in Tralee on the occasion. The case was heard before a jury of nine men and three women. He pleaded not guilty.

The court was told that Michael Lonergan received three stab wounds in a fight with his brother, and died shortly afterwards. There was only one witness to the incident, Louise O'Brien. The Gardaí were called at 6.47 p.m. and arrested

Ailbe Lonergan at his home, where he had gone after the stabbing, at 7.39 p.m. Garda Willie O'Neill was the man who made the arrest.

Garda Karen O'Flynn, of the Divisional Scenes of Crime Unit, told the court that she had searched the area around the murder and found a knife with a black handle behind a wheelie bin in the front yard of one of the nearby houses.

The medical evidence was that Mr Lonergan had suffered three stab wounds to the chest. The fatal one was to the right side of his upper chest. It extended through the lung and into the ventricle of the heart. Death was caused by blood loss and shock due mainly to this wound.

The jury heard that Michael Lonergan was facing serious drugs charges at the time of his death and that there was a heavy drinking session going on in the house. This had already extended through two days and a night by the time the stabbing brought it to an abrupt end.

Yvonne, his widow, said that Michael did smoke cannabis joints, but she had never seen him taking cocaine. Despite this, the forensic evidence showed that he had cocaine in his system at the time of his death, as well as a large quantity of alcohol.

Louise O'Brien told the court that she had visited the Lonergan house on a number of occasions on the day of the stabbing. Her partner Emmet Coffey had stayed overnight on 30 December, as he had been drinking there. She went in the morning to pick him up and bring him home for a few hours. Later they both went back to the house, where he began drinking again, but she didn't. Many of the people in the house were drunk, but she was sober. There was an aggressive atmosphere, and she overheard a few fights and verbal spats. The mother of three said that it was 5.45 p.m. when they went back to the house on Balloonagh Estate, an hour before the fatal incident. She described standing at the door of the house as the two brothers began to fight. Ailbe had his right arm in a cast, but that didn't stop him. She said she saw the brothers throwing 'three or four digs' at each other. After Ailbe swung at his brother, she saw him turn and throw a knife away. She then saw Michael holding his hand to his side. His hand was covered in blood, and his T-shirt was red with it. She told the court, 'He said to Emmet: "Ailbe stabbed me. The bastard stabbed me. My own brother stabbed me."'

Emmet Coffey told the court that he had seen Michael Lonergan confronting Ailbe about his behaviour that afternoon. Ailbe was aggressive with the drink, and Michael had asked him to stop being abusive to people or else leave. This led to an argument between the brothers, during the course of which Michael took an ornamental sword off the wall. However, Mr Coffey took the sword back from him and replaced it on the wall. Things cooled off for a few minutes.

But around 6.45 p.m., in response to the clamour he could hear, Emmet went into the hallway. He saw Michael lying on the floor and he knew instantly he was badly hurt. The colour had drained from Michael's face and his lips were white. Towels were fetched to try to stem the bleeding. 'He said to me Ailbe had stabbed him,' Mr Coffey told the court.

Yvonne Lonergan said that she had asked her husband what had happened as he lay on the floor. He told her things were all right, and not to be upset: 'He told me: "We'll get that cunt when I get out."' She assumed he was referring to Ailbe. She then told the jury that the black-handled kitchen knife recovered from behind a neighbour's wheelie bin was from her kitchen.

Assistant State Pathologist Dr Margot Bolster told the court that she had carried out a toxicology test on samples removed during the autopsy on Michael Lonergan. The results showed that the victim had taken roughly one line of cocaine before his death. He had also consumed enough alcohol to be twice over the legal driving limit. She had examined the contents of his stomach and found no white powder, so she concluded that he had snorted the cocaine rather than consumed it.

Dr Bolster explained to the jury that a combination of cocaine and alcohol could be a potent mix. When they were together in the body, they formed another substance called cocaethylene. 'When both cocaine and alcohol are taken, it's more dangerous from the point of view of causing death. The combination also affects behaviour in terms of aggression,' she explained. 'The important thing in the case of cocaine is dosage, and how it is administered.'

The lethal brew was found in Michael's blood. If his brother Ailbe was also mixing cocaine and alcohol, it would explain why he was behaving in such an aggressive manner on the evening of 31 December and why a row so quickly escalated to extreme violence.

Dr Bolster said that the three main wounds she had found during the post-mortem were the two deep stab wounds to Michael's chest and one to his arm. However there were around 20 fresh bruises to his body, as well as wounds to his hands. The wounds to the hands were small cuts and were consistent with self-defence as he tried to fight off his brother's attack. The bruises to his body could have come from the earlier scuffle, or from the one preceding the fatal stabbing.

The fatal wound was the one that penetrated the lung and pierced the heart and damaged the heart valve. It had gone 9 cm into his chest. Michael Lonergan had lost between six and seven pints of blood: more than half the total amount in the body.

Barrister Anthony Sammon, for the defence, asked Dr Bolster whether the three wounds could have been made by different knives. The doctor agreed this was possible. However, no second knife had been entered into evidence.

A number of witnesses gave evidence of the events leading up to the fatal row. All denied that they had seen Mr Lonergan taking cocaine. Some of the witnesses were under age (and included one of his children) and the press were removed from the court for those witnesses.

At the end of the trial, the jury took two hours and seven minutes to consider their verdict. They returned to announce that they had found Ailbe Lonergan guilty of the murder of his brother. Mr Justice Patrick McCarthy imposed a sentence of imprisonment for life.

Yvonne Lonergan said that no words could explain the loss she and her children felt over Michael's 'unfair and cruel death'. 'It devastated me, and it has left a huge hole in all his children's lives, whom he loved greatly,' she said. 'He was a devoted husband and father and to those who truly knew him he was a friend second to none. He would go out of his way to help those less fortunate than himself.'

Michael Lonergan's cousin Susan Curran spoke on behalf of his parents and siblings, telling the court their grief could not be put into words. As the court case was ending, the family were facing the first anniversary of Michael's death, in which they would have to relive the nightmare and pain of losing him, and face their first Christmas without him. 'As a family we are still trying to come to terms with this tragedy, but no amount of anger, hate or bitterness can bring Michael back to us. To see our brother Ailbe in this unfortunate position breaks our hearts also. And, remember, his daughter Shania is deprived of her father's presence,' she told the court in her victim impact statement. She said that the family hoped that time would foster forgiveness, so that they could all move forward with their lives.

Ailbe Lonergan was removed to Limerick Prison to begin his life sentence. He did appeal his conviction in March 2009. His barrister, Paul Burns, said that the judge had erred on a number of points in the original trial. He argued that the evidence of what Mr Lonergan had said as he lay dying should not have been put to the jury.

He also brought up an incident that had happened at the original trial. One of the jurors had been approached in a pub one evening by a man who had said, 'Hope you make the right decision next week.' This had been brought to the judge's attention, but he had not discharged the juror, or the jury.

Denis Vaughan Buckley, barrister for the state, countered by saying that the judge was correct in allowing the words spoken by the dying man to be heard by the jury. He also said that the judge had been right not to halt the trial after the juror was approached. 'The evidence against Ailbe Lonergan was overwhelming,' he concluded. The three-strong panel of judges at the Court of Criminal Appeal agreed. The appeal was dismissed.

No one really knows what forces were brewing in the mind of Ailbe Lonergan on that New Year's Eve day. There may have been childhood slights that festered over the years, or it might have been something far more recent. Perhaps it was nothing but the combination of drink and drugs, a mix that can turn someone aggressive very quickly. There is no doubt that drink and drugs played a large part in the case, and the evidence is clear that Ailbe had been acting out and causing problems in the time leading up to the fatal encounter.

However, there is also little doubt he had an aggressive nature, and was not averse to causing trouble. This was proved while he was in prison. On 23 February 2011, Ailbe Lonergan hit the headlines for a vicious assault on two prison officers.

He was being held on D Wing in Limerick Prison, and he managed to get hold of some shards of glass. It is believed they came from a damaged television screen. From them he fashioned a rough knife and then set fire to the mattress in his cell. He crouched down, hidden from anyone who would come to help.

Four prison wardens responded to the fire immediately and rushed to the cell. They opened the door to rescue Ailbe and bring the smouldering blaze under control. But as they opened the cell, he lunged forward, slashing with his improvised knife. He managed to get at two of the wardens, inflicting slash and cut wounds to their faces and upper bodies. He attacked a third, but this man was wearing protective clothing. He and his colleague were able to subdue Ailbe, who was then placed in isolation. The two wardens were taken to hospital for treatment, but none of their wounds were life-threatening.

Ailbe is serving a life sentence, so there is little extra

punishment that can be added to that. It is clear that he still has anger issues to work through. If he continues to behave as he has been, it will be quite a time before he returns to the bosom of his family in Tralee.